The Color of Asylum

The Color of Asylum

THE RACIAL POLITICS OF
SAFE HAVEN IN BRAZIL

Katherine Jensen

The University of Chicago Press CHICAGO AND LONDON

The University of Chicago Press, Chicago 60637
The University of Chicago Press, Ltd., London
© 2023 by The University of Chicago
Published 2023
Printed in the United States of America

32 31 30 29 28 27 26 25 24 23   1 2 3 4 5

ISBN-13: 978-0-226-82842-8 (cloth)
ISBN-13: 978-0-226-82844-2 (paper)
ISBN-13: 978-0-226-82843-5 (e-book)
DOI: https://doi.org/10.7208/chicago/9780226828435.001.0001

Library of Congress Cataloging-in-Publication Data

Names: Jensen, Katherine (Ethnologist), author.
Title: The color of asylum : the racial politics of safe haven in Brazil /
    Katherine Jensen.
Description: Chicago : The University of Chicago Press, 2023. |
    Includes bibliographical references and index.
Identifiers: LCCN 2023000326 | ISBN 9780226828428 (cloth) |
    ISBN 9780226828442 (paperback) | ISBN 9780226828435 (ebook)
Subjects: LCSH: Syrians—Brazil. | Congolese (Democratic Republic)—
    Brazil. | Racism—Brazil. | Assimilation (Sociology)—Brazil.
Classification: LCC F2659.S97 J46 2023 | DDC 305.800981—
    dc23/eng/20230120
LC record available at https://lccn.loc.gov/2023000326

Contents

Quanto mais branco melhor,
quanto mais claro superior.

The whiter, the better;
the lighter, even better.

BRAZILIAN SAYING

Color is not a human or a personal reality;
it is a political reality.

JAMES BALDWIN, *The Fire Next Time*

Introduction

Wael fled Syria for many reasons. He fled from the conflict, from the government, from the fear of the consequences of protesting the Assad regime. He had felt pulled to participate, to fight for his rights, liberty, and a more egalitarian country. In Syria, his life was comfortable. He was able to focus on his studies, but he knew Syria wasn't like that for everyone. Most acutely, he worried about being called up for obligatory military service. Usually, people of his class were able to get out of serving. But, as the conflict escalated, he feared that was no longer the case.

His younger brother, Mahdi, wanted to go to Europe. He got to Lebanon, but his contact was jailed before he could take him. Mahdi didn't make it, and he ended up returning to Syria.

After much deliberation, they decided to come to Brazil. Their father had been to Brazil before, and thought it was a better choice—a better place to be a refugee. As Wael later reflects, his father said Brazil was "better than Europe at accepting immigrants."

Brazil has been regarded as the best place in the world to be a refugee. It is lauded as an exemplar of refugee protection—a model for the region and beyond.[1] Its policies are infused with human rights, and the UN Refugee Agency has deemed its asylum-screening process "one of the fairest and most democratic in the world."[2] Brazil, different from what many may imagine possible, does not detain migrants, and there is no widespread threat of deportation. On average, it recognizes over 90 percent of asylum seekers as refugees. While many countries denied access to Syrians, Brazil instituted an open-door policy in 2013. Within the year, Syrians went from a nonexistent refugee community in Brazil to its largest. In the words of Wael, Brazil is like "no other place in the world."

While such policies and grant rates present Brazil as visionary, they belie how racism shapes how the asylum process unfolds. *The Color of Asylum* exposes asylum as a racial project—and the racial logics and lessons it entails. In its everyday practices and encounters, asylum makes racialized subjects and reproduces racial hierarchies. The experience of asylum looks very different for refugees racialized as black and white in that country. *The Color of Asylum* uncovers the racial workings of the refugee regime in Brazil, with important consequences for how we understand the meanings and consequences of refugee protection.

Asylum is often imagined as a holy grail. While we debate who should have access to it and strive to make sure those who deserve it do, rarely do we interrogate refuge itself. Questioning the efficacy and necessity of asylum—what it fundamentally can and does not do—does not arise. Yet asylum can be cruel. Rather than attenuate suffering, asylum also produces and legitimates it. It normalizes the suffering of those excluded, and mystifies that to which those included are subject.[3] The liberal premise of inclusion as an antidote for inequality rings hollow. Racial and refugee justice requires unraveling immigrant selection and differentiation itself, as racial political domination is forged in those processes.

The Color of Asylum questions what legal inclusion gets forced migrants and what that process accomplishes. It reveals the limits of refugee status and its racial ramifications for refugees. Taking readers on a journey through asylum, this book follows asylum seekers as they navigate the refugee regime—from how they arrive in Brazil, through the steps of applying for asylum and seeking assistance, to their lives after obtaining refugee status. As officials work to determine who is a refugee, they produce and ascribe a range of racial meanings to asylum seekers. Those meanings organize interactions and refugee experiences, while guiding how rights and resources are unequally distributed. Through the asylum process, the state imparts vital racial lessons as it incorporates refugees into the national racial order. In their encounters with the refugee regime, refugees learn what it means to be black—or not—in Brazil.

Asylum is a refracted expression of the racial political order in which it manifests. While legislation formally promotes human rights and racial egalitarianism, racism structures daily life and the social order in Brazil. The state has a long commitment to presenting itself as a humanitarian vanguard at home and abroad, and political elites have been invested in Brazil's international reputation as a leader in welcoming refugees.[4] But Brazil is also one of the most unequal countries in the world, one marked by discrimination and socioeconomic stratification that fall largely along racial and color lines. While Brazil maintains its celebrated image as "a country receptive to people of all origins," in practice, the refugee regime produces racial domination.[5] In a thin, overextended bureaucracy with limited capacity and resources, as officials and policymakers strive to do their best—by the institution of asylum and for asylum seekers themselves—racialized hierarchies of worth and deservingness shape how they do so, broadly pervading the practical operations of refugee governance and assistance.

Before the Syrian conflict arose, I had been embedded inside the refugee regime in Brazil. I wanted to understand the racial politics of immigration in a place so seemingly different from what I knew elsewhere. I worked alongside officials as they interacted with forced migrants and evaluated their claims for refugee status, and I assisted asylum seekers as they navigated that process. I processed files and reviewed applications, oriented asylum seekers, conducted asylum interviews, wrote up case recommendations, and discussed claims with officials as we worked together in cramped offices. I saw up close how the everyday operations of the refugee regime fundamentally changed for Syrians, a mass forced migrant community racialized as white in that country.

The arrival of Syrians marked a dramatic shift in the demographics of those seeking asylum in Brazil. Prior, most asylum seekers and refugees were African—predominantly from the Democratic Republic of the Congo. The treatment of black African refugees before, during, and after applying for asylum varied considerably from what I saw with Syrians.

Arab racialization in contemporary Brazil diverges from that seen elsewhere. Whiteness is dynamic, mutable, and contextual.[6] While Arabs are sociopolitically marginalized and denigrated in the United States—as foreign racial others, terrorists, and threats to the nation—such racial discourses do not resonate in Brazil. Instead, Arabness is celebrated. Those of Middle Eastern descent have trended into whiteness in that majority black and brown country, and they have obtained a privileged economic, political, and cultural presence in the nation in Brazil.[7] They enjoy "significant social power," as anthropologist John Tofik Karam writes, and have experienced staunch upward mobility, made possible by and productive of their inclusion in whiteness.[8] While Arab whiteness was historically fraught, and Syrian-Lebanese immigrants were variably derided as commercial peddlers in the early and mid-twentieth century, today they are associated with economic acuity and entrepreneurship.[9] Descendants of this exalted immigrant group appear prominently among Brazil's political and economic elites, including recent president Michel Temer—himself the proud son of Lebanese immigrants.[10] Presidents from across the political spectrum have emphasized Arabness as a venerated, formative contribution to the nation and its racial mixture.[11]

In the face of mass Syrian forced displacement, asylum was radically reconfigured in their favor. The emergence of a Syrian refugee community in Brazil was not a ground-up consequence driven by refugees alone, but actively crafted by the state. They have been provided multiple concessions that facilitated their immigration. For Syrians like Wael, Brazil offered humanitarian travel visas, extended *prima facie* refugee status, and fast-tracked their asylum claims.[12] The government has offered asylum to practically any Syrian willing to come. While Wael's asylum interview was short and amicable, other Syrians were not interviewed at all. Officials view and treat Syrians as credible, legitimate refugees who belong in Brazil. As Hamid, a Palestinian Syrian refugee, tells me, "I like Brazil" because "they support us, they like us, they like Arab people more. They said for us, 'Always welcome.'" Syrians are not made to wait, not interrogated, nor marginalized by the state in the ways Congolese and other black Africans are.

The asylum process looks very different for Congolese, even though the vast majority—nine out of ten—receive refugee status. Officials treat Congolese asylum claims with suspicion. They are subject to both increased scrutiny and disregard. While Syrian cases are sped up, Congolese are slowed down. Anti-black racism shapes the experiences of Congolese and other African refugees and entrenches racial inequalities—even among those the state deems worthy of legal protection. This leads them to feel very differently about Brazil and their place in it. Before fleeing, Congolese refugee Lionel reflects: "I just thought I was a man, like everyone else. I didn't know that skin color, a piece of paper, a country made such a difference." In Brazil, "I feel totally without identity . . . I don't have a voice."

Syrians and Congolese have been among the primary recipients of refugee status in Brazil over the past decade. Making sense of their experiences obtaining asylum troubles the relationship between race, asylum, and political domination. While the state response to Syrians elucidates how inclusion in whiteness can lead refugees to be welcomed rather than excluded, the experiences of Congolese refugees expose how legal inclusion can also be underwritten by racial subordination. In capturing that disparate treatment, this book underscores how examining the everyday workings of the state can show a racial political order otherwise obscured.

The racialized dynamics of asylum extend beyond Syrians and Congolese. The refugee regime in Brazil makes the search for safe haven uniquely tumultuous for black African refugees. Despite acute and protracted forced displacement on that continent, Brazil has never extended humanitarian travel visas to any African nationality. When Brazil granted such visas following Russia's invasion of Ukraine in 2022, it delimited them to Ukrainian nationals and stateless persons—excluding thousands of Africans likewise fleeing that country.[13] During fieldwork, Afghan claims based on persecution by the Taliban were not subject to the incisive doubt that Nigerians persecuted by Boko Haram experienced. While policy-makers questioned whether Mali qualified as a context of grave and generalized human rights violations, no such debates ensued with Palestine. Syrians are not made to wait years for asylum decisions like black Africans are, but neither are Lebanese, Iraqis, Palestinians, or Venezuelans.[14] Juxtaposing the experiences of Syrians and Congolese reveals the racial politics of asylum not otherwise readily apparent, and what that juxtaposition illuminates extends beyond it.[15]

Addressing how refugee treatment and experiences differ from what inclusive policies would suggest lies at the heart of this book. Grappling with those policies in their everyday processual manifestation reveals how racial ideologies imbue refugee governance in practice, while being elided from afar. By investigating how the state makes racial sense of those seeking its protection and with what consequences, *The Color of Asylum* provokes readers to take seriously how the racial order matters for what legal inclusion looks like.

Understanding how states adjudicate asylum and determine the meanings of mobility is paramount in our contemporary world. Forced displacement worldwide has reached 100 million. Roughly one in seventy-eight people on the planet is an asylum seeker, a refugee, or internally displaced.[16] This demands our critical attention to forced migration in general, but also to asylum in particular, when a person claims refugee status after migrating. Given not only grave contemporary experiences of conflict and persecution, but also limited migratory alternatives, people increasingly struggle to be included on these terms. In 2021, there were 4.6 million pending asylum claims globally. Though places like Europe, North America, and the UK predominate in how we think about refugees, 83 percent of the world's forcibly displaced are in the Global South.[17] In 2018, Brazil was the sixth largest recipient of asylum claims worldwide.[18]

Capturing the racial project of asylum in Brazil, *The Color of Asylum* shows how racialized hierarchies manifest through legal inclusion and lead asylum to take manifold forms. In doing so, it builds upon and complicates approaches that universalize the refugee condition and homogenize the political domination rendered by the state. Exposing how asylum reproduces the racialized nation-state, in the highly lauded context of Brazil, underscores the importance of addressing the racial state and asylum policies in their everyday workings, where racialized subjects and hierarchies are made. Bringing historical work on race and immigration in Brazil into the present, *The Color of Asylum* shows how refugees are understood through racial ideologies of sociopolitical worth and belonging in Brazil, shaping the meanings of nation and membership in that country today.

Localizing and Racializing the Refugee Condition

Refugees—their very existence and experiences—expose the limits of state sovereignty, the intertwining of rights with membership in a nation-state, and the workings of state domination. Political philosopher Hannah Arendt, herself a refugee, grappled with the refugee condition in *The Origins of Totalitarianism*, first published in 1951.[19] In it, Arendt identifies the binding together of the state, rights, and national community in the modern political system—and the tragic consequences for those forced from it.

For Arendt, the refugee category laid bare the limits of the political ordering of the world that produced it. Under the Westphalian system of sovereign states, the refugee—forced from their own community—ceased to bear the rights and entitlements of sociopolitical belonging anywhere. Burgeoning a field of study, Arendt exposed how refugees' exclusion from the nation-state left them not only without rights, but without political recourse to claim them. To be a refugee, Arendt reasoned, is to lack "the right to have rights." As refugees are forced from their homes, Arendt observed, they are also forced out of the "protective boundaries" of the world in which they are made to have no place. Such displacement meant not only involuntary migration, but statelessness and an attendant rightlessness.

Italian political philosopher Giorgio Agamben later built upon Arendt's classic rendering in *Homo Sacer*. Agamben theorized the refugee as exemplifying the state's ability to diminish people from political subjects with full, social existence to what he termed "bare life"—whereby state sovereign power reduces the refugee to the mere physical fact of being alive, stripped away of social presence and political personhood, with a loss of all rights and protections entailed, as they exist outside the realm of law.[20] This reduction of the refugee to bare life, Agamben contends, "represents the original but hidden core of the sovereign power."[21]

In these foundational takes, refugee status is taken as a monolith. Presented against citizenship, the refugee condition—whether to be without the right to have rights, or reduced to bare life—is treated as a universal form of political subjectivity.[22] As anthropologist Liisa Malkki writes, audiences tend to universalize "the refugee" as a singular, generic figure.[23] The refugee appears as an immutable political category encapsulating the ultimate form of state domination. Such accounts leave little room for capturing the production of political multiplicities and relations of difference among refugees.

The tendency to see political domination as rendered uniformly through legal exclusion is seen in immigration studies broadly. Legal status is taken as a master status of inequality. We often ask: What does it mean to be undocumented, a citizen, or a refugee? Scholars investigate legal status as a crucial line of social stratification—a vital category by which rights, resources, and meanings are distributed.[24] In the acclaimed *The Land of Open Graves*, on migrant death and suffering at the US-Mexico border, anthropologist Jason De León, himself influenced by Agamben, writes that "sovereign power produces migrants as excluded subjects," as they are controlled and deterred by the state.[25] "Critical studies of borders and migration tend to emphasize," as Mezzadra and Neilson attest, "the moment and technologies of *exclusion* as the decisive elements of differentiation and power relations."[26] Prevalent perspectives on sovereign power elide how migrants can be variably filtered, welcomed, and dominated through legal inclusion.

Moreover, migrant exclusion and racial subordination are seen as going hand in hand. In the draconian contexts to which we often attend, asylum seekers are presumed racially othered outsiders, threats, criminals, bogus claimants, and beyond, subject to social and political exclusion through detention, rejection, and expulsion.[27] Racism is located in how the state turns asylum seekers into "someone without rights, someone to be excluded."[28] Perspectives focused on migrant legal exclusion, and that ascribe legal status as racializing in and of itself, miss the multifarious modalities of state action and overlook how racism variably structures migrant sociopolitical belonging.[29]

The Color of Asylum offers a different view of how race and power manifest in state responses to migration and displacement. Looking beyond the racial politics of exclusion, it turns to the production of differential *inclusion* as the state variably incorporates refugees into the racial order.[30] Asylum takes on disparate political forms and meanings, as the process makes foreign newcomers into racialized subjects. Capturing the pervasiveness of racism in formally progressive contexts calls us to dynamic manifestations beyond those encapsulated by walls and borders.[31] Refugees are disciplined and dominated by the state—but not through exclusion alone. Political processes of inclusion also offer apt space for inscribing racial difference. Within a broader racialized social system, legal inclusion can likewise be tiered and produce racial divides. Rather than take inclusion as an unalloyed social good that reduces inequalities, I interrogate how it reproduces divisions and creates new ones.[32]

By grounding the conditions and experiences entailed, this book troubles broad-swath visions of the refugee as a universal political category, even in a single moment and locality. It is neither a uniform political subjecthood nor form of domination, as Arendt and Agamben attend respectively, but localized and racialized.[33] *The Color of Asylum* clarifies how the refugee regime produces varied racialized forms of political subjecthood, state-subject relations, and domination among those who navigate it. Its relational production is structured by racial ideologies and hierarchies of sociopolitical worth and belonging in Brazil—regardless of the status bestowed.

The Everyday Workings of the Racial State

The state is fundamental in the production of race and racism, crucial to both making and making sense of racial hierarchies.[34] Through the formation and enactment of laws and policies, states produce and extend racial meanings to citizens and foreigners alike, constructing racialized barriers to full personhood and political membership.[35] Racism and the state are forged together—mutually constitutive, imbricated, and interlocking.[36] And racial states—those engaged in the constitution, maintenance, and management of race—can take many forms.[37] As the state regulates immigration—defining the implications and boundaries of citizenship and national belonging—it can also engage in racial projects, constructing the symbolic meanings and political consequences of race.[38]

In the now classic *Racial Formation in the United States*, Michael Omi and Howard Winant underscore the role of racial projects in the formation, contestation, and consolidation of race-making and the racial order. Racial projects bridge signification and social structure, reciprocally connecting ideas about race to how society is organized.[39] Such projects, as Omi and Winant write, "connect what race *means* in a particular discursive practice and the ways in which both social structures and everyday experiences are racially *organized*, based upon that meaning."[40]

While work on the role of the state in manufacturing race often takes a top-down approach, state racial projects are encoded in organizations and institutions, the sites where—through administrative practices and procedures, and the organizing principles and techniques guiding decision-making—racial meanings are linked with the disparate allocation of rights, resources, and experiences.[41] While formal policy helps structure what happens on the ground, policies are lived in their enactment. As officials implement policies, they *make* them.[42] And, as they do so, they order and shape our social worlds. In racialized social systems, racism is attributable not to those who people bureaucracies or their intent, but located in the "habituated patterns of codified cultural norms and resource distribution" through which institutions shape and reproduce racial inequalities.[43] Such processes are not just the expression of racial formations, but fundamental sites where racial subjectivities are produced and racial relations constituted.[44]

The refugee regime in Brazil underscores the importance of investigating racial states in the everyday practices of bureaucratic institutions, as it is through them that race and racial inequalities manifest. While Brazil's policies present it as a vanguard in refugee welcome, turning to the process of enacting such policies tells a different story. Its everyday operations teach forced migrants the meanings of race in Brazil and their place in its racial order. This is crucial for understanding how racial projects work and their consequences. Disparate racialized notions of worth and belonging can be produced through institutional logics and processes, without formal legal stratification or settled racial categorization.[45] Turning to the everyday workings of the state shows how racialization and racial hierarchies manifest through legal inclusion, rather than exclusion.

Bureaucratic sites where policies are enacted are opportune spaces to examine the production of state-subject relations. Through encounters with such spaces, the state is given concrete form in the lives of those who must confront and navigate such policies.[46] In their seemingly mundane encounters, people learn crucial racial political lessons as they come to understand what the state is, what it does, and for whom.[47] Bureaucratic sites are fundamental places of racial political socialization—where political subjectivities are forged; rights are constituted and contested; and state practices of racial ordering and othering are negotiated and enacted.[48] As people interact with bureaucracies, they receive "daily crash courses on the workings of [racial] power."[49] These racial lessons are embodied, as refugees variably wait in heat and hunger at bureaucratic offices, and must recount the somatic details of traumatic experiences in asylum interviews.

Though crucial for understanding the production of power and domination before those seeking inclusion in the nation-state, we rarely see the inner workings of immigration bureaucracies and how officials implement such policies.[50] When immigration scholars turn their gaze to the state, research generally focuses on policymaking.[51] This is due in great extent to the difficulty of gaining entrée inside such sites usually concealed from view.[52] Yet, as sociologists David FitzGerald and David Cook-Martín note, administrative discretion is a common praxis for racial and ethnic discrimination in immigration policies.[53]

Through its hard-won, on-the-ground insider ethnographic account, *The Color of Asylum* captures the state's everyday production of racial domination in the face of those seeking protection. The political production of race and racial inequality happens not only from above—through constructing census categories, and making laws and policies—but in the quotidian operations of the state. Because the state is not a singular, cohesive unit, top-down or policy-centered approaches can fail to contend with the nuances of how racial states work in practice—and why.[54]

As officials interact with asylum seekers and determine the meanings of their mobility, they not only reflect a racial social world, but construct its forms and consequences. It is through these practices and encounters that refugees are made racialized subjects. How the state governs and racializes forced migrants on the ground exposes mechanisms and dynamics of the racial political order otherwise elided.[55]

Race, the Nation-State, and Immigration in Brazil

Race and immigration were central in the emergence of the Brazilian nation-state. After the abolition of slavery in 1888, prior to which Brazil forcibly imported more enslaved Africans than anywhere else in the world, Brazilian elites sought to whiten and thus "civilize" the nation through immigration and miscegenation.[56] Legislation prioritized white immigrants, while banning African and Asian immigration. Blackness was marginalized at the founding of the nation and excluded from the premises of citizenship forged.

Migration has been decisive in and intrinsic to Brazilian racism, though later obfuscated through a discourse of racial democracy. In the 1930s and 1940s, the notion of Brazil as a racial paradise—marked by cordiality and intimate proximity—became a popularized lens among elites to affirm a supposed lack of racial tensions in Brazil.[57] Brazilian racial exceptionalism presumed that racism could not exist in a racially mixed society that has neither firm racial categories nor instituted formal segregation.

Throughout the twentieth century, the state presented Brazil as an exemplar of racial harmony and egalitarianism at home and abroad, while perpetuating racial stratification among both nationals and foreigners.[58] Tenets of racial equality and anti-discrimination were replete in Brazilian legislation yet largely symbolic, failing to reach their articulated aspirations while providing cover for persisting racial inequality.[59] Though discourses of racial mixture (*mestiçagem*) sought to negate the salience of race, racism foundationally constitutes Brazil.[60] Conceptions of race and color overlap, and the color continuum is imbued with and underwritten by racial hierarchy.[61] A popular refrain in Brazil signals the commonplace clarity regarding racial power: "if you want to know who's black, just ask a doorman or the police."[62]

With democratization in the 1980s, and acutely since the turn of the twenty-first century, the racial democracy myth has been unseated by political sea changes, black activists, and scholarly research. The existence of racial inequality and discrimination in Brazil has obtained wide public and state recognition.[63] There is broad public acknowledgment of the structural advantages of whiteness and burdens of blackness.[64] Due to domestic demands and to preserve its reputation internationally, the state has instituted laws, policies, and programs to redress black exclusion and marginalization.[65] Governments have pursued race-based affirmative action policies, including racial quotas in public universities, since the 2000s. Yet white privilege and anti-black racism are not easily dislodged.[66] Racial inequalities are pervasive in the daily social, economic, and political life of Brazil.[67] Economic exclusion, political marginalization, police violence, and social suffering persist in the everyday lives of black Brazilians.[68]

While racial democracy has lost its ideological footing in the national landscape, it echoes in asylum today. Conservative and progressive presidents alike have touted Brazil's generosity toward refugees at the UN and elsewhere. In the National Committee for Refugees meetings, representatives emphasize Brazil's place "as a country of reference in refugee protection, a country of reference for the world."[69] Despite Brazil's lauded asylum policies, racial inequalities manifest through legal inclusion because they occur within a deeply unequal racialized social system where racial domination has rarely been given formal legal backing. For much of Brazil's history, white preference and black antipathy have played out through administrative discretion, internal directives, and everyday discrimination—rather than overt policy.

Examining immigration provides a powerful lens for understanding projects of race and nation in Brazil. Race and the nation-state were mutually constituted historically through immigration, in ways that have crucial afterlives for the nation and how Brazilians see themselves and others today. Yet, scholarship on race, immigration, and the nation-state has been historically truncated.[70] Though Brazil has reemerged as an important host country of refugees and immigrants, we know relatively little about how immigration and racialized hierarchies interplay today.[71] Bringing research on race and immigration to bear on the contemporary moment, *The Color of Asylum* makes visible how national racial projects continue to transcend state-citizen relations in Brazil. *The Color of Asylum* captures how the racial order impacts what legal inclusion means for refugees today, as racialized notions of worth delimit the national belonging purportedly offered by safe haven.

Moreover, by attending to whiteness, this book provides a more wholistic account of the racial order in Brazil. While most Brazilians identify as black or mixed, almost half—48 percent—self-identify as white.[72] Given the racialized nature of socioeconomic stratification in Brazil, those who work and volunteer in the refugee regime are predominantly white. Whiteness is prevalent and capacious in Brazil, not circumscribed to notions of racial purity or Europeanness.[73] And whiteness—its manifold meanings and consequences—is also forged as national membership is produced in the face of those seeking refuge.[74]

Looking Beyond the Global North

While international standards define the principles of refugee law, individual states are responsible for their implementation and vary greatly in how they do so.[75] Though the majority of stories we tell about asylum are European and North American ones, as Bohmer and Shuman write, "the West is not the only, or even the primary, destination of asylum seekers."[76] Given this, our inquiries should not be confined to those who migrate from South to North.[77] This "geographic bias," as Freier and colleagues explain, "impedes a broader historic[al], global, and thus theoretical understanding of the triangular relationship between racism, citizenship, and displacement." Existing research, they continue, is "ill-equipped to understand how issues of race . . . shape the integration of displaced people" in Latin America today.[78]

Brazil warrants attention for two reasons. First, our understanding of asylum—and how racism configures it—has been largely limited to contexts where draconian policies proliferate. Literature across fields has emphasized how policies and discourses affect and frame asylum seekers in hostile contexts.[79] Detention and deportation have been seen as constitutive, essential instruments of contemporary asylum and immigration regimes, as Global North states increasingly deploy these practices to control and manage migrants.[80] Yet restrictive practices of exclusion and expulsion have not become normalized responses to migration everywhere. Not all states are using these tactics or moving toward increasingly repressive immigration control.

Because scholarship has focused on selective and restrictive immigration regimes, it provides limited analytical leverage for making sense of race and forced migration in countries like Brazil that defy this trend. We know little about racial politics of immigration in the absence of such policies. Not only does Brazil not detain or deport immigrants, it has instead made its asylum and immigration policies more humane in recent decades. Brazil, and much of Latin America, contrasts sharply with the restrictive trends seen in other places.[81]

Turning from cases of hyper-security, to a highly lauded, progressive policy regime, and examining the practices and conditions of asylum as enacted and lived, makes visible how racial ideologies shape migrant legal inclusion—even in what we imagine as best-case scenarios. Building from sociologist Javier Auyero, "chronicl[ing] the ways in which these dispossessed denizens interact with a state that presumably cares for their plight" exposes how racial political domination in the face of forced displacement is not limited to contexts of legal exclusion.[82] Attending to the venerated case of Brazil illuminates how the forms of state power embedded in asylum—as migrants have the right to seek safe haven but not receive it, subjecting themselves to the will and evaluation of the state—provides for racial domination *in process*, even while extending a formal pathway to citizenship.

Second, Brazil speaks to new trends in asylum seeker destinations. As places like the European Union and the United States harden their borders and make their policies more restrictive, forced migrants seek out new destinations.[83] Within these shifting migratory patterns, Brazil has emerged as a major global player and rapidly increasing receiver of asylum seekers from Latin America and beyond.[84] In 2017, Brazil received 47 percent of all asylum claims made in Latin America and was its third largest refugee host. While Brazil saw only 872 asylum claims in 2010, this number reached over 200,000 by 2019—a roughly 23,000 percent increase in under a decade (see fig. 6).

An Ethnographic Approach

This study traces the political production of racial meanings, inequalities, and domination in asylum. *The Color of Asylum* is based on a relational ethnography conducted inside the asylum process in Brazil.[85] Ethnography entails becoming embedded as close as possible to the social phenomena under investigation, observing and participating in—in real time and space—a particular social world in order to capture how and why people think, feel, and act the way they do.[86] Turning to how officials make sense of asylum seekers, interact with them, and evaluate their claims brings us to the racial ideologies embedded in why they do so.[87] To understand how asylum works in practice and what it accomplishes, I carried out 15 months of fieldwork at sites of the refugee regime between 2012 and 2016, based principally at the Refugee Center in Rio de Janeiro. I supplemented that fieldwork with observations at Rio's Federal Police Office and at the asylum offices and refugee centers in São Paulo and Brasília. At the time, these were the only cities where officials evaluated asylum claims in Brazil.

The Rio Refugee Center proved a strategic research site for several reasons. First, it is a fundamental site where asylum seekers and refugees encounter the asylum process in Rio. There asylum seekers initiate their claims, and navigate the procedures entailed in refugee governance and assistance. Second, the organization that runs the Refugee Center is a participating member in Brazil's governing body, the National Committee for Refugees (CONARE), and thus provided entrée into the national asylum landscape. This helped to both capture discourses and practices at the top level of governance and situate and compare what I saw in Rio with the broader refugee regime. Third, Rio de Janeiro has been a major hub for asylum seekers and refugees nationally.[88] When I began field-work, the state of Rio de Janeiro was home to more than half the country's refugees. Fourth, in contrast to other hubs in Brazil, which often have a preponderance of a single nationality, the forced migrant demographics in Rio largely reflected the diversity of the national profile. Rio receives a broad range of asylum seekers in terms of nationality, region of origin, age, gender, language, type of persecution, and beyond.

During fieldwork, I traced the series of perceptions, actions, and inter-actions—of and between state, civil society, and asylum-seeking actors—that led to case decisions and constitute the refugee regime.[89] The pages that follow are peopled by various actors, organizations, and institutions—from asylum seekers, federal police officers, and state representatives to NGO lawyers, legal volunteers, and social workers—that participate in the assemblages of refugee governance and assistance in Brazil. I worked alongside officials, participated in asylum interviews, reviewed case files, and prepared case opinions. I also assisted asylum seekers and refugees in all aspects of the asylum process and as they navigated a range of legal and social procedures. I oriented asylum seekers as they filled out their asylum applications, and updated them on the statuses of their claims. In total, I participated in and observed hundreds of asylum claims from over 45 countries of origin from five continents (see fig. 7). Alongside, I attended related events in Rio—including refugee art exhibit openings, academic symposiums, and World Refugee Day events—to reflect on dis-courses circulating in the broader public sphere.

I first obtained entrée into the Refugee Center through an African Di-aspora in the Americas study program at the State University of Rio de Janeiro (UERJ). As a white woman graduate student from the United States, my trilingual skills eased access to the site. At the time, there was little local interest in volunteering with refugees. No one spoke Spanish, and my native English was taken as an asset. Coming back year after year helped build rapport with officials and lawyers, as did that I had much in common with those I worked alongside. Most likewise identified as white, often women in their mid-twenties. Many were also pursuing graduate school on refugee issues, and had studied and traveled abroad, including to the United States and Europe. In many ways, we were peers.

Research also involved interviews, and document and dataset analy-sis. I interviewed people who applied and who processed their claims. I conducted 42 interviews in total. I interviewed 26 participating officials,

lawyers, and volunteers in Rio, São Paulo, and Brasília about their everyday work practices and experiences. At some sites, I interviewed every
asylum official or participating civil society actor. All officials interviewed
were responsible for evaluating asylum claims. I also interviewed 16 asylum seekers and refugees in Rio about how they experienced the process.

I situated ethnographic and interview data in the national landscape
by analyzing asylum case files, government archives, and application statistics. I reviewed asylum files, including interview summaries and case
opinions, for claims from states across Brazil for which the Center was
responsible. I also analyzed policy resolutions and over 600 pages of
CONARE plenary meeting minutes from 2009 to 2021, examining how
racialized discourses imbued the goals and possibilities of policymaking.
I assembled an individual-level national dataset with case characteristics
and outcomes for all claims decided in Brazil between September 2015
and April 2016. I also analyzed aggregate asylum data publicly available
from the UNHCR (1996–2020) and Brazilian government (2013–2021).
Appendix A provides a more in-depth account of the data and methods
used for this book, as well as a reflexive discussion of my own positionality, as the vantage point from which I perceived and was perceived during
field research.

Syrians and Congolese

To detail the racial project of the refugee regime in Brazil, I examine the
experiences of Syrian and Congolese refugees, along with other nationalities that claim that status in Brazil. An immigrant's country or region
of origin often serves as the modality through which race-making and
hierarchies manifest.[90] Juxtaposing the disparate treatment of Syrians and
Congolese brings the racial politics of asylum into stark relief. They are the
primary refugee groups racialized as white and black in that country, and
the vast majority of Syrian and Congolese refugees in Brazil self-identify
as white and black, respectively.[91]

During fieldwork, Syrians and Congolese were the two largest groups
recognized for refugee status. They were the top recipients of asylum over
the last decade, until Brazil began extending *prima facie* recognition to
Venezuelans in 2019.[92] Over half of Syria's population has been forcibly
displaced since democracy protests in Syria escalated into a multi-sided
war in 2011. With the Democratic Republic of the Congo, war, armed
conflict, and political repression have made forced displacement a protracted reality. Ongoing conflict in the Congo has been called the bloodi-
est since World War II, with a death toll estimated in the millions. In

Brazil, their cases generally reach the same legal conclusion: recognition of refugee status. Almost all Syrians obtain refugee status, as do nine out of ten Congolese.

Syrian and Congolese refugees in Brazil otherwise share similar demographic profiles. They come from analogous socioeconomic backgrounds, in terms of both education and occupational experience.[93] Like Syrians, most Congolese have college or at least high school degrees. As with the refugee profile broadly in Brazil, men predominate among both groups, and the vast majority are between the ages of 18 and 45.[94] Regarding application profiles, grave and generalized human rights violations have preponderated as the basis for recognizing Syrian and Congolese claims alike.[95]

Yet, their similar recognition rates entail very different processes. Though Syrians and Congolese generally find the same legal outcome, their process of obtaining asylum—their treatment before, during, and after that decision—is quite different. Syrians are not subject to racial domination in the ways Congolese are. Congolese wait years longer in liminal legality.[96] They are entangled in a bureaucracy that disempowers them as they return again and again to wait at different offices seeking rights and redress, as their cases are doubted and delayed. Even after obtaining asylum, their formal rights are deferred in practice. Congolese experience emotional turmoil, confusion, and humiliation. On the other hand, Syrians experience the asylum process with ease. But they are disenchanted by a lack of state support. Race-making can likewise be detrimental to those socially venerated, as stereotypes of Syrian gumption mystify Syrian refugees' continued struggles in Brazil.

Diverse migrant groups can experience disparate racisms and significations, and juxtaposing those experiences exposes racial discourses and hierarchies otherwise missed. Attending to race-making across nationalities pulls us to the relationality of migrant racialization, as racial notions are constructed through and against other groups.[97] Congolese are not mere comparative foil to Syrians, nor vice versa. Presenting together varied refugee experiences captures the dynamism of racial projects—as racial understandings form relationally, constitutively linked and mutually imbricated, affecting and reinforcing.

The racial order enacted and reproduced in the refugee regime in Brazil expands beyond Syrians and Congolese. While I focus on Syrians and Congolese, I situate them within broader patterns of racialization I documented among forced migrants from around the globe. At the time of research, the vast majority of refugees self-identified as either black or white in Brazil.[98] In the pages that follow, I focus on refugees racialized at or near the poles of Brazil's color continuum. This places in clearest view how refugees are variably incorporated into the national racial order, and how racialized hierarchies manifest through legal inclusion and the practical operations of formally progressive policies. At the same time, blackness and whiteness are multidimensional, internally variegated categories. Race, color, nationality, and other axes of social difference interplay as officials evaluate claims and forced migrants encounter the asylum process, producing similar and different racialized experiences of asylum.

What Follows

The following chapters proceed chronologically along the steps of the asylum process. Chapter one explores how the racial order shapes how refugees come to Brazil, as well as who works as an asylum official. It situates disparities in how refugees like Syrians and Congolese arrive in the racial history of asylum and immigration policies. Examining the forced migration of African enslavement and subsequent denial of African immigration, in contrast with concurrent possibilities of European and Middle Eastern immigration, reveals how racialized hierarchies have imbued immigration in Brazil from past to present. Almost all asylum officials and volunteers self-identify as white, often themselves descendants of European immigration to Brazil when nonwhite immigration was curtailed. After tracing the modern emergence of the refugee category and its international dissemination, this chapter discusses the history of refugee protection in Brazil, its asylum process today, and how racialized hierarchies manifest through its humanitarian travel visa programs.

Chapter two turns to what happens after arriving and claiming refugee status in Brazil. It captures the racial politics of waiting and the bodily domination entailed. The circumstances of waiting differentially condition the black refugee body. As black asylum seekers and refugees wait, they experience physical indignities that communicate their racial place in Brazil. They endure heat, hunger, and discomfort. Such conditions look very different from those experienced by the officials who assist them. Moreover, the racial project that orders and gives meaning to those conditions manifests not only between officials and refugees, but also among those in search of safe haven. Syrians and other asylum seekers seen as white are rarely made to wait and are less likely to experience conditions of indignity when they do. To wait is to suffer, and such forms of political suffering are attenuated for those not racialized as black.

Chapters three and four explore how the state determines whether someone qualifies for refugee status, turning to how officials process and evaluate asylum claims. Chapter three considers the everyday cognitive operations of the refugee regime. It captures the racialized ways of seeing in how officials perceive asylum seekers and their claims. I detail the racialization of credibility and gravity, key cognitive prisms through which officials understand those they confront in their daily work.

Chapter four uncovers how epistemic privileges of whiteness shape the practices of knowing in asylum: how officials produce and evaluate knowledge to determine asylum claims. The state delimits who can know what in asylum, and that demarcation reproduces racialized hierarchies. This chapter focuses on the relationship between race, knowledge, and the body. Officials erase themselves from case files, deleting their own words from interview transcripts. They allow themselves a boundless epistemic authority; they make definitive, authoritative evaluations about matters on which they have limited expertise. In contrast, they constrain what asylum seekers can know to their bodies. Officials seek out the asylum seeker's embodied experience, while denying them broader, abstract knowledge claims. These epistemic practices, however, can be bent for asylum seekers racialized as white. The epistemic logic of asylum produces racial political domination in the face of those seeking protection—regardless of whether refugee status is ultimately granted.

Chapter five addresses the asylum decision itself. It shows the racial project in determining who is a refugee and who is a priority, detailing racialized patterns in recognition rates and decision wait times. Nearly all Syrians receive refugee status, and they wait less time to get that decision. On the other hand, though most Congolese receive refugee status, their cases are delayed. While racial subordination happens insidiously through inclusion for Congolese, for less prominent African nationalities it can manifest through rejection—despite such applicants making legitimate claims to asylum—without impacting Brazil's celebrated overall tendency toward recognition. The racialized nature of such outcomes and practices of adjudication produces racial domination through both legal inclusion and exclusion for black African forced migrants—in ways not seen with others.

While prior chapters focus on the legal process, chapter six attends to the racial project underlying the allocation and distribution of care, charity, and social assistance. By capturing both the legal and social spheres of the refugee regime, *The Color of Asylum* shows the unexpected consequences when the racial logics at work in the legal realm meet the racial logics of hospitality and social vulnerability in the public and social sphere. While Syrians are favored by the legal apparatus, and the highly visible Syrian refugee situation catalyzed a wave of donations and volunteers, they find little socioeconomic support at the Refugee Center because they are imagined as self-starters. As they unsuccessfully seek aid, they learn they must become what they are already imagined to be: self-sufficient.

On the other hand, while Congolese find many barriers on the way to obtaining refugee status, they are the main beneficiaries of the meager assistance available because social workers perceive black Africans as in dire need. This disproportionately exposes Congolese and other Africans to the subordinating relations embedded in humanitarian aid.

Chapter seven turns to the period after recognition, examining what refugee status does and does not do in Brazil. Though refugee status is often imagined as the "holy grail" of immigration statuses—saved for only the few deemed most worthy of exceptional protection—refugees can fail to see that status as transformative. After recognition, black African refugees continue to experience roadblocks in accessing their rights. On the other hand, Syrians experience disenchantment born of the divergence between the ease of their arrival and a lack of support once in Brazil. Moreover, asylum does not markedly rupture what refugees' material lives look like. While refugee status may not reconfigure how refugees understand themselves, their daily lives, or their future prospects, it is far from politically vacuous. Through asylum, refugees learn the political meanings and ramifications of race in Brazil, and their position in the racial political order where they have sought safe haven.

In the conclusion, I take stock of what the previous chapters—viewed as a whole—contribute to our understanding of asylum, the racial state, and politics of domination. I reflect on refugee status broadly, what it is and what it does. Rather than attenuate suffering, as commonly imagined, asylum also creates it. And it makes open borders unthinkable.

It was a Dantesque dream . . . the deck
With lanterns reddening the glow,
Washing with blood.
Clink of iron . . . snap of a whip . . .
Legions of men so black as the night
Hideous dancing . . .

Today miserable slaves,
With no light, no air, no reason . . .

Gold-green flag of my land,
That the breeze from Brazil kisses and sways,
Flag that in the sunlight captures
The divine promises of hope . . .
You, who in the liberty after the war,
Were raised on the hero's lance
Rather had you been torn in the battle,
Then to serve as shroud to the people!

CASTRO ALVES, "The Slave Ship [*O Navio Negreiro*]" (1869)

FIGURE 1 Art by Ninibe Forero and Leonardo Ruge. Photo by author.

1

Arrival

In Rio de Janeiro, Olivier was on the street for two days. He approached the black people he encountered, until he came across someone who spoke his language. His compatriots brought him to the Refugee Center so he could apply for asylum.

Olivier is from an eastern province in the Democratic Republic of the Congo, where he was violently conscripted by a Rwandan rebel group. He was forced to train, beaten, and tortured for three weeks. They made him wake at 4 a.m. There were no showers, and he wasn't allowed to relieve himself. He witnessed great atrocities. "For no reason," he says, "so many inhumane things." He escaped to Burundi, but he didn't feel safe there. After a week, he continued to Kenya, where he worked as he could at the port.

He made friends with a Brazilian crew member who helped him stow away on a ship set to round the tip of Africa and cross the Atlantic. After a long, harrowing journey at sea, Olivier arrived in what he would learn to be São Paulo, Brazil. A local brought him to the bus station, where he boarded a bus destined for Rio—they told him there he would find his people. When I met Olivier, he had no news of his wife, child, or two brothers who were still back home. Given protracted violent armed conflict, Congolese like Olivier have been among the largest asylum-seeking and refugee nationalities in Brazil over the past few decades.

On the other hand, the arrival of Syrian refugees is new. In 2011, a democracy movement emerged in Syria, part of the broader wave of mobilization against authoritarianism in the Middle East and North Africa often called the Arab Spring. It was violently repressed and escalated into a full-scale war. By 2013, 2.5 million people had fled Syria.[1] Adnan was one of them. After a bomb went off in his home, he escaped to Turkey, where his sister was living. In Turkey, Adnan searched Google, sent emails, and contacted researchers to try to find where he could go as a Syrian refugee. He contacted "the countries of the whole world." He kept searching, without any luck, until he got a response from the Brazilian consulate in Istanbul. The consulate gave Adnan a visa so he could come to Brazil to seek asylum. He got a plane ticket and came to Rio. The following year, Brazil formalized a humanitarian travel visa program for Syrians.

"So, the only reason you ended up in Brazil," I ask Adnan, "was it just happened to be the first country that responded positively?" He laughs. "To be honest with you," he says, and he nods yes. Violence catalyzed both Olivier and Adnan to flee their homelands, and neither planned to seek safe haven in Brazil. Yet how they each arrived to do so was very different.

Brazil has connected histories with Syria and the Congo alike, through immigration and the Atlantic Slave Trade. While political elites invoked ethnic ties to explain the Syrian visa program, such visas have not been extended to Congolese. Syrians travel by plane with visas furnished by the government to any willing to come, but some Congolese arrive like Olivier: as stowaways on ships crossing the Atlantic. Half of Congolese refugees arrive in Brazil without authorization, and a third arrive by boat.[2] Their disparate paths to Brazil are shaped by racialized imaginaries of affinity and desirability, as some histories are conjured and others marginalized.

This chapter examines racial projects of immigration and the nation-state from past to present in Brazil. By moving across time and space, and addressing together modalities of human movement often siloed—from enslavement and immigration to contemporary asylum—it captures how the Brazilian racial state structures and is structured by human mobility. After abolition, Brazil pursued a whitening project through immigration, in which European and Syrian-Lebanese immigrants were included. Almost all asylum officials and volunteers self-identify as white, often descended from twentieth-century European immigration when black immigration was barred. Tracing "the inter-coursing connectivities of the ethno-racial across their geographies and temporalities," as David Theo Goldberg writes, illuminates how the past has "shaped the contemporary, [and] planted racisms' roots in place."[3]

Through the twentieth century, the image of Brazilian racial democracy served a wide political spectrum, both to quell recognition of racial inequality domestically and to present Brazil as a leader in racial tolerance and egalitarianism abroad. While national racial disparities are now broadly acknowledged, the ideological legacies of racial democracy and whitening reverberate in its contemporary refugee regime. Brazil frames itself as a champion in refugee protection, uniquely welcoming and receptive, while racialized inequalities manifest in how asylum seekers arrive today.

Whitening the Nation

In the words of Brazilian anthropologist Lilia Moritz Schwarcz, "the whiter the better" is "a well-worn saying that sees in the white person not just a color but also a social quality."[4] At the turn of the twentieth century, "the whiter the better" emerged as a common maxim in Brazil. In 1888, Brazil became the last country in the Western hemisphere to abolish slavery. After abolition, Brazilian elites were confronted with the racial consequences of 200 years of slavery in which Brazil imported more enslaved Africans than any other country in the world.[5] Almost half of those forcibly brought from Africa to the Americas during the Atlantic Slave Trade were destined for Brazil. At nearly five million, more than 12 times as many Africans were estimated to have been taken to Brazil than to North America.[6]

The desire for a whiter Brazil did not suddenly emerge after abolition. Throughout the nineteenth century, elites dreamed of transforming the country's racial demographics.[7] With the formation of the First Republic in 1889, whitening, or *branqueamento*, became national policy.[8] Racial ideologies and hierarchies were constituted through immigration, and whitening immigration policies were central in elite projects of nation-building. Brazilian elites sought racial improvement through immigration and miscegenation. Political elites embraced scientific racism in their pursuit to transform Brazil into a modern republic—a shift they understood to be not only political but racial.[9] Whiteness signaled modernity and progress, while blackness, ascribed racial and cultural inferiority, was seen as incompatible with civilization and economic development.[10] The appeal for European immigration to improve the nation's racial makeup was explicit.[11]

Some of Brazil's initial decrees after the establishment of the First Republic pursued Brazil's whitening through immigration and naturalization. While Brazil is often considered a country lacking *de jure* racial discrimination, racism was institutionalized in the nation-state's founding. Restricting or eliciting immigration based on region of origin was the foundational praxis through which political elites pursued this whitening project.[12] In immigration policies throughout the hemisphere, race was expressed in geographic terms, as spaces were constructed as racial terrains and their populations attributed a host of unequal racial and economic meanings.[13]

In 1889, Congress granted automatic naturalization for European immigrants, and an 1890 decree declared Brazil open to all those who were healthy, able to work, not criminals—and not from Africa or Asia. State funds were invested in European settlers, providing them subsidized transportation, housing, and land, while denying such concessions to Brazilians, particularly those formerly enslaved and their descendants.[14] More Europeans would come to Brazil than any other country in Latin America except Argentina. Roughly 2.7 million white immigrants arrived between 1884 and 1913, predominantly from Portugal, Italy, and Spain.[15] Forcibly trafficked to and enslaved in Brazil for over 200 years, Africans were denied the right to immigrate. While a discourse of Brazilian hospitality later came to infuse local perceptions of immigration, it most acutely served "desirable immigrants."[16]

For immigrants from outside these regions, however, there were no barriers to entry. All non-African and non-Asian immigrants, then, could serve in whitening the nation. Prior to 1930, as historian Jeffrey Lesser writes, to the question "are all non-African and non-Asian immigrants white?" Brazil's intellectual and political elites "almost always answered in the affirmative."[17] Racialization is dynamic and contextual. Whiteness was constructed in relation to blackness, with those judged as nonblack often taken as white, or at least able to improve the nation's racial makeup and development. Immigrant whiteness was contested and flexible, linked to skin color as well as imagined productivity and labor needs. For example, Brazil made an exception for Japanese immigration beginning in 1907. In the words of a federal deputy in 1935, "Japanese colonists are even whiter than the Portuguese."[18] Japanese immigration was substantial, particularly in the 1920s and 1930s, with over 140,000 arriving between 1924 and 1935.[19]

During the late nineteenth to mid-twentieth century, immigration to Brazil included significant numbers of Arab immigrants, largely equivalent to those seen in the United States.[20] Between 1884 and 1939, 107,000 Middle Eastern immigrants entered Brazil, mostly from present-day Syria and Lebanon.[21] The classification of Arabs as white meant naturalization was fairly easy to obtain.[22] Syrian-Lebanese racialization entailed the ascription of economic qualities, and such populations were read as commercially shrewd.[23] The myth of Syrian-Lebanese economic prowess, which attributed socioeconomic prosperity to internalized qualities of hard work and unique capacities for entrepreneurship, relied on and reproduced the racial construction of Syrian-Lebanese whiteness.[24] Middle Eastern inclusion in the whitening project was tacitly apparent in government publications.[25] Syrian-Lebanese immigration was largely allowed in elite hopes that they would racially and economically displace those previously enslaved and their descendants.[26]

This whiteness was tenuous. The classification of Syrian-Lebanese as white unsettled the relationship between whiteness and Europeanness, and the white ascription of non-Europeans was fraught and contested.[27] As historian José D. Najar writes, "the public debate over the suitability of Syrian-Lebanese immigrants to Brazil exposed the instability of whiteness as a racial category because the Syrian-Lebanese simultaneously complicated and reinforced Brazil's white racial paradigm."[28] Syrian-Lebanese commercial successes were taken ambivalently, and they were disparaged as economic pariahs. A changing economic and political context— "growing nationalism, economic dislocations, and heavy doses of racial scientific theory imported from Europe"—led to rising concern "that while Syrians and Lebanese were adapting profitably to Brazil's economic climate," they were far from the Europeans the Brazilian elite desired and were failing to mix with and whiten the population.[29] There was a shrinking view of what groups classified as white, coupled with a sense that the whitening project had fallen short of its goal; Brazil's immigration policies had not led to the levels of whitening seen with neighbors Argentina and Uruguay.[30] Anti-Arab sentiment began to flourish, and found strong policy backing with populist Getúlio Vargas's entry to power in 1930.[31] Shifting economic conditions and rising nativism had ramifications for European immigration as well; São Paulo, for example, terminated subsidies for Europeans in the 1920s.[32] European immigration precipitously declined.

Racism in the Land of Racial Harmony

Marking the end of the planter-dominated Old Republic, the Vargas era (1930–1945) rearticulated the meanings of race and nation. Reconciling internal and external political agendas led to, as sociologists David FitzGerald and David Cook-Martín observe, "a curious 'racist anti-racism' that simultaneously sought to integrate indigenous and African-origin Brazilians while restricting the entry of foreign groups that supposedly threatened the national mix that had been achieved with such great effort."[33] An anti-immigrant, nationalist politics emerged that—while still holding up whiteness—constructed and celebrated a national identity of racial mixture and legitimated Afro-Brazilian culture.[34] Extolling racial mixture, as black activist and intellectual Abdias do Nascimento later asserted, marked its own form of black erasure.[35]

Vargas continued to support whitening policies of immigration meant to diminish the Afro-Brazilian population. While the Constitution of 1934 declared there would be no distinctions made on the basis of race, it simultaneously established a selective and highly restrictionist immigration policy.[36] Rather than ban particular groups as seen prior, it included proportional national origins quotas to maintain the racial balance achieved during the height of Brazil's whitening project.[37] Racial restrictions became increasingly presented in terms of ethnicity and religion, or economic, physical, and moral character.[38] This marked a new era in immigration policy in Brazil. Instead of allowing entry for all those not explicitly prohibited, as under the republican period, the federal government forbade immigrants unless specifically allowed entry.[39] Through the variable enforcement of requirements driven by eugenicist criteria, the state demonstrated a continued preference for Europeans.[40] During the Vargas era, white preference through immigration control was retained and reconfigured in line with prevailing eugenicist ideals under the guise of national security and integrity.[41]

While xenophobia and scientific racism reigned, and Brazil continued to privilege and pursue whiteness, it presented itself at home and abroad as a land of racial harmony. Miscegenation had been central to the whitening project, and during the 1930s racial mixture was transformed into a positive, fundamentally Brazilian trait. Racial democracy became a defining national ideology, with sociologist Gilberto Freyre as its most noted and influential proponent.[42] In *The Masters and the Slaves* (*Casa Grande e Senzala*, 1933), Freyre affirmed that Brazil was free of the racial antagonism that plagued other countries due to its Portuguese colonization, which had greater tolerance for racial mixing than other European countries. Euphemizing the violences of colonization and slavery, he asserted that Brazil had dimmed racial differences by blending European, native, and African "stocks" into a unified Brazilian people. Under its mythical weight, realities of racial discrimination became unrecognizable as such.[43] Recourse to administrative discretion, and the cover of racial democracy, allowed for continued practices of racist immigration exclusions while Brazil maintained its image as "a bastion against racial discrimination."[44] By the 1950s, the propagandizing of racial democracy successfully solidified Brazil's international reputation as a racially harmonious state, despite scholarship showing the realities of racial inequality.[45] While restrictive immigration practices continued, they drew little concern or interest at either the domestic or international level. The notion of Brazil as a cordial, raceless society without racism would serve government agendas through the twentieth century, while racial inequalities endured for nationals and immigrants alike.

The Face of the State Hails from Europe

It is from Europeans who immigrated to Brazil in the twentieth century that many who work and volunteer in asylum trace a heritage. Given racialized socioeconomic disparities and low education levels broadly in the country, white Brazilians are much more likely to have had the educational opportunities, including college degrees and foreign language fluency, to become a lawyer or civil servant in this area.[46]

Chatting over lunch at the Refugee Center, Adriana, the coordinator, tells us that her family came from Germany—"though they said they were Swiss"—and settled in a territory in the state of Rio de Janeiro that had previously been a maroon community, settled by Africans and their descendants escaping the violences of enslavement. As she shares the story, she forgets the word for such places. "*Quilombos*," another at the table clarifies. Adriana continues, recounting her father's words: "You know you are the product of refugees? But then we called them migrants." In descending from those who fled Europe last century, Adriana is not alone. Guilherme, a lawyer with both historical and recent familial ties to Western Europe, responds, "Yeah, I am too." After World War II, Brazil saw an uptick in European immigration.

The ease of arrival for Europeans fleeing war and devastation during the mid-twentieth century—in contrast to the experience of Africans today—was vividly present for Frederic, a Congolese refugee long established in Rio. Though he obtained refugee status, the experience was tumultuous. Later, as an interpreter and liaison for Congolese and other Francophone African asylum seekers, he witnessed the belittlement, disbelief, and delays to which the state subjected them. During a conversation at the Center, Frederic laments this disparity. "Why not us? We are the same," Frederic says. "Why don't they let us have a place, like what happened with . . . the Italians in Brazil?"

Lucas, a white lawyer, responds, "My family came because of the war."

"From Italy?"

"Yes."

"Exactly this!" Frederic retorts, the experiences of Lucas's family further affirming the gap Frederic felt. Frederic knows the path of Africans like him differs from the experiences of Europeans who came to Brazil prior.

Before I arrived at the Refugee Center in Rio de Janeiro, I did not expect what I found: almost all who worked and volunteered in the refugee regime identified as white.[47] I had imagined the Refugee Center as a site of encounter between black Brazilians and African migrants. Rio de Janeiro is coded in the global imaginary as a black city. I had imagined the Center as that image writ small.

When I first visited the Refugee Center, the staff wore uniforms: faded black cotton T-shirts, emblazoned with the organizational logo in white on the front. Such formalization to distinguish staff seemed unnecessary. A racially divided space, it appeared obvious who worked there and who came for assistance, as groups of Africans waited outside in the courtyard. For the first few years, the only black person continuously employed at the Center was the cook.

This whiteness extended beyond the Center. The racial demographics of representatives of the National Committee for Refugees (CONARE), the body that decides all asylum cases in Brazil, were analogous. When Frederic was invited to give a talk at a CONARE plenary, it was the first time a refugee had been invited. It was also, Lucas notes, "the first time a black person ever went in that room."

In interviews, I asked respondents to complete a basic demographic survey, including an open-ended question on race. Of the 26 officials and volunteers interviewed in Rio, São Paulo, and Brasília, 21 wrote "white" without pause. All but three ultimately identified their race as white. Only one self-identified as *negra*—black. To my knowledge, she had been the only black official to work in asylum. Ana, a lawyer, identified as *parda*, a complex racial category referring to ethnoracial mixture, often used in Brazil to signal being a lighter-skinned person of African descent. Yet Ana's skin is almost translucent. Aware her phenotype reads as white, Ana explains her response: "I have some indigenous in me." She continues, "But when I tell my mom this, that I identify as *parda*, she freaks out." An official in São Paulo saw himself as white but didn't know how he would be read in my country. "Here I am white, but there [in the United States]? I don't know—*pardo*?" He leaves the question blank.

Rather than a racial category imported and imposed, most lawyers and officials were aware of their whiteness and self-identified as such. During a legal meeting at the Center, we touch on this lack of racial representation. One of the volunteers, a young white Brazilian woman, slightly chuckles and looks around the table. "Well, look at us!" Through her offhanded comment, she points to the homogeneity of those gathered, highlighting the whiteness of those who assist and evaluate refugees. Another day, as Guilherme and I review asylum files slotted for adjudication that month, I ask if he thinks he's white. He looks at me, noting the absurdity of my question in his eyes: "*Obviously.*"

Many also came from privileged backgrounds. One day during lunch at the Center, Guilherme tells us we're all eating wrong. He shows us the proper etiquette for cutting food with a knife. When I ask him how he knows this stuff, he laughs and answers: "My dad's rich. I took etiquette classes as a kid." White Brazilians are also more likely to have the financial position to volunteer their time freely. Most volunteers were white and also elite—with brand-new MacBook Pros; cars; experiences traveling, living, and studying abroad in Europe and North America; and residences in the poshest neighborhoods of Rio de Janeiro. One volunteer had a vacation apartment in Miami, Florida.

Of the asylum officials I interviewed, most were women in their mid-twenties who self-identified as white and middle class. All had bachelor's degrees, frequently in International Relations, and roughly half were in some stage of graduate school. Almost all spoke three languages. The majority had previous experience working with refugees, mainly as volunteers with NGOs. They were not civil servants assigned to the sector, but rather individuals who sought out that field. In the words of one official: "The people working today in asylum, they love it." Isabela, an official in Brasília, underscores the dedication of the officials she works with. "They're people who are extremely committed, they're people who breathe this." Mobilized by intellectual curiosity and goodwill, many did so because of an interest in international human rights and concern for refugees.

The International Refugee Regime Emerges

While the ancestors of asylum officials were fleeing Europe and charting a new path in Brazil, the international refugee regime was emerging. In the aftermath of the Holocaust and World War II, with mass forced displacement in Europe, the United Nations began to formulate an international instrument for refugee protection, organizing a conference that brought together representatives from 26 countries, including Brazil.[48] From it emerged the 1951 UN Convention Relating to the Status of Refugees. While there were historical antecedents, the 1951 Refugee Convention concretized the modern definition of the refugee, declared the rights to which refugees were entitled and the legal obligations of signatory states, and enshrined the international operative role of the UN High Commissioner for Refugees (UNHCR).[49] It defined a refugee as: "Any person who owing to a well-founded fear of being persecuted for reasons of race, religion, nationality, membership of a particular social group or political opinion, is outside the country of his nationality and is unable, or owing to such fear, is unwilling to avail himself of the protection of that country; or who, not having a nationality and being outside the country of his former habitual residence, is unable, or owing to such fear, is unwilling to return to it."

The international refugee regime, however, was a product of its times. Though genocide and the violent consequences of World War II provided the impetus for the Convention, it was fashioned during the geopolitical tensions of the Cold War and as the boundaries of empire were being redrawn in much of the world.[50] The final form the Refugee Convention would take, including who counted as a refugee, was fundamentally shaped by political interests and colonial racial notions of who had human rights—and thus who was human—rather than allegiance to lofty humanitarian concerns.

Though asylum is formally rooted in legal principles of nondiscrimination, including on the basis of race and nationality, access to refugee status was racially demarcated at its inception.[51] This exclusion was produced through temporal and geographic restrictions on who qualified. The Refugee Convention applied only to those made refugees "as a result of events occurring before 1 January 1951," and provided signatory states the option to limit its reach to displacement "owing to events in Europe." The United States was keen to exclude refugee crises in India, Korea, and Palestine from purview.[52] The United Kingdom, France, and Belgium were similarly invested in restricting who counted.[53] In committee meetings, representatives from former colonies, notably India, Pakistan, and Lebanon, but also Brazil, expressed concern about the proposed limits and their implications.[54] At the same time, Brazil saw support of Western interests as a tactic to simultaneously express its dedication to humanitarian principles, recruit European immigrants, draw attention away from its policies of national quotas and immigration restrictions at home, and maintain its reputation as a racial democracy abroad.[55] Ultimately, Brazil signed the Refugee Convention in 1952 and ratified it in 1961, declaring its obligations limited to Europe.[56]

The apprehensions of representatives from former colonies went unheeded. The racial boundaries of refugee status—who had access to the protections of asylum as a human right—were incorporated at the founding of the modern refugee regime. As such, temporal and geographic exclusions were mobilized for racial ends in a range of legal doctrines in the mid-twentieth century—including both the 1951 UN Refugee Convention and 1934 Brazilian Constitution—while asserting liberal universality and humanitarianism. Claims that international forced displacement has reached unprecedented levels in our contemporary moment obscure how the world beyond Europe was excluded in early years from refugee protection.[57]

It was only with the 1967 Protocol Relating to the Status of Refugees that these limits were lifted, legally recognizing the existence of refugees beyond Europe and thus expanding the purview of the Refugee Convention to the rest of the world. This geographic expansion was motivated not by international benevolence or solidarity, but by the shifting geopolitics of the Cold War.[58] Countries like the United States feared that changing political dynamics in the Global South, including decolonization and national liberation, would produce the conditions for Soviet alignment. Nonetheless, the removal of geographic limits did not lead to an even playing field for all in search of safe haven. As Benjamin N. Lawrance and Gayla Ruffer detail: "Until the era of decolonization, Africans—as colonial subjects—did not have the option of applying for political asylum abroad. Indeed, until the 1980s, political asylum seekers originated from all continents . . . but rarely from Africa. It is perhaps no coincidence that the rise of a 'climate of suspicion' in asylum procedures in the Global North parallels the emergence of Africans as political asylum seekers . . ."[59] And, while the 1967 Protocol lifted previous temporal and geographic restrictions, it left intact the constrained refugee definition focused on individual persecution. Its global extension, then, provided for the continuation and production of other exclusions.

There were important regional reconfigurations of refugee doctrine in Africa and Latin America in the second half of the twentieth century. The Latin American 1984 Cartagena Declaration on Refugees, influenced by the 1969 Refugee Convention of the Organization of African Unity, expanded the UN definition to include as refugees those threatened by "generalized violence, foreign aggression, internal conflicts, massive violations of human rights or other circumstances which have seriously disturbed public order." Such shifts stretched, rather than reimagined, the refugee definition inscribed by the United Nations.[60] The 1951 Refugee Convention established an international system of refugee governance that remains in place, largely intact, around the world today. The refugee regime constructed in and for Europe was thus diffused globally. Though Brazil's national refugee definition includes expansions outlined in the Cartagena Declaration, as Lucas asserts, "How we do asylum . . . is from how they do it in Europe, the refugee definition is from Europe." Never imagined to be what it is today, the 1951 Refugee Convention remains an enduring vision worldwide.

Refugee status—its meanings and boundaries—has shifted in relation to the geopolitical contexts in which it manifests. "You can't have the idea that 'the refugee' is a clean, rounded category," Lucas notes, during an orientation for new volunteers at the Refugee Center. "We need to understand that we work in a field in which that is not defined justly." And that has been underwritten by a racial order, globally and nationally.

Dictatorship and Exile in Brazil

In 1964, a coup by Brazilian Armed Forces overthrew President João Goulart and established a military dictatorship that would last 21 years. Racial democracy continued as a powerful political tool. The dictatorship deployed the notion of a racially harmonious Brazil as it established a fascist, repressive order. Mobilizing the myth of a raceless nation, the military removed race from the census and banned race-based organizations and anti-racist expression, declaring them fundamentally anti-Brazilian, and "accusing activists and academics studying race of being 'racist' themselves."[61] Prominent race scholars were arrested and exiled. While the dictatorship affirmed Brazil was free of racism, it instituted the draconian 1980 Foreigners Statute, which severely curtailed immigrant rights. It expunged explicit references to regulating the nation's ethnic and racial makeup, speaking instead in racially coded ways of immigrants' productive potentiality to advance economic growth and development.[62]

Abroad, political elites affirmed that Brazil was a multiracial country without racial prejudice to provide cover for the dictatorship's human rights abuses. As historian Jerry Dávila examines in *Hotel Trópico*, the military regime's international diplomacy was contradictorily pragmatic. In early years, it affirmed ties to colonial authoritarian Portugal and aligned with the United States. That geopolitical strategy shifted in the 1970s, as the Portuguese revolution and African decolonization produced massive political upheaval and devastated Portugal's economy. Tens of thousands of Portuguese exiles and former colonists fled to Brazil, though the military regime tried to stem the exodus, trepidatious of its local and international implications.[63] Military president Ernesto Geisel (1974–1979) sought to expand Brazil's influence in the Global South, distance itself from Portuguese colonialism, and find autonomy from the United States. Africa was a mirror upon which Brazil projected itself, and diplomats marshaled racial and cultural ties to Africa as they built political and economic connections there.[64] But, with national and global economic crises in the 1980s, Brazil-Africa relations dissipated abruptly.

Despite its formal accession to refugee protection, during the military dictatorship Brazil was not a country that welcomed refugees. Instead, it produced them, with 10,000 estimated to have fled into exile. In the dictatorial period, refugee assistance was a virtually clandestine operation, focused on the resettlement of those fleeing other South American dictatorships, namely from Chile and Argentina, to a third country.[65] At that time, military dictatorships marked by mass human rights violations—including torture, killing, and forced disappearance—were seen throughout South America. Brazil was a site of refugee transit for those from within the region to countries beyond, and the operations of refugee protection and assistance fell to national and global civil society. Legal and social assistance was organized not by the government, but by domestic nongovernmental organizations, namely local Catholic charities in São Paulo and Rio de Janeiro. In 1976, Caritas of Rio de Janeiro (*Cáritas Arquidocesana do Rio de Janeiro*, CARJ) began organizing a clandestine circuit for those flee-ing dictatorships in the Southern Cone. The UNHCR established head-quarters in Brazil in 1977 and signed an accord with CARJ the following year.[66] "It's good to remember," pronounced João Guilherme Granja, Im-migration Department director in the Justice Ministry, "40 years ago, the government was *far from helpful*."

Return to Democracy

Economic recession and debt crisis, growing political pressures, and redemocratization in other Latin American countries precipitated the military dictatorship's end and sparked chasmic societal transformations in Brazil. Political elites sought to distance Brazil from its authoritarian past through legislation rooted in human rights. "In the early 1990s," as historian Brodwyn Fischer writes, "after decades of dictatorship and eco-nomic chaos, leaders and thinkers across the political spectrum seemed to agree that Brazil could aspire to be a nation defined not just by cordial-ity, but also by equality and inclusion."[67] The new Constitution of 1988 criminalized racism, affirmed universal healthcare as a human right, and enfranchised the illiterate for the first time. It "represented a victory for causes long favored by progressives," while conservative elites felt such "guarantees of human rights were politically harmless."[68]

The inclusionary ethos undergirding such visionary transformations, like racial democracy before it, formally gilded racial inequality.[69] Leg--islative shifts after democratization did not unravel racialized notions of worth and belonging in Brazil, nor upend the racial hierarchies that struc-ture its sociopolitical and economic order. Brazil has long been a country where—absent formal discrimination and segregation, and in the face of anti-racist, inclusive policies—anti-black racism imbues daily life.

At the same time, while the nation's political identity reconfigured, so too did its racial self-image. Democratization opened new space for ques-tioning whether Brazil was a racial paradise. Starting in the 1980s, racial inequalities became more visible and debated in ways not seen prior.[70] Most Brazilians recognized the existence of racial discrimination. And, while the role of Syrian-Lebanese immigrants in whitening Brazil was peripheral and disputed historically, notions of whiteness and Brazilian identity expanded and reorganized to affirm their celebrated place in the nation after democratization and the economic transformations that ac-companied it.[71]

The turn toward human rights filtered into refugee legislation. While Brazil had long officially committed to refugee protection, those commit-ments did not manifest until the dictatorship's end.[72] In 1990, five years after the return to democracy, Brazil extended its obligations under the Convention to those outside of Europe—decades after the 1967 protocol provided for such possibilities.[73] It was only then that Brazil began to accept refugees without regard for geographic origin.

In 1997, Brazil passed the Refugee Act—the first comprehensive national refugee law in South America—still in force today.[74] Then-president Fernando Henrique Cardoso (1995–2002) had a broad social agenda, himself a sociologist in political exile during the dictatorship. He was also the first president to name the existence of racial inequality in Brazil. Legal transformations in refugee protection fell within a broader political campaign to move away from dictatorship legacies and restore a favorable, democratic image of the nation at home and globally.[75] With the Refugee Act, Brazil became regarded as a regional leader by the UNHCR, and the Act has been lauded as an exemplar model for refugee protection.[76]

. The Refugee Act was a principally symbolic, minor political ask. It served Brazil's jockeying for ideological leadership regionally and branding as a guarantor of human rights internationally, while having little drawback domestically. Immigration was not a flashpoint political issue in Brazil and, given the small numbers of asylum seekers at the time, roughly a few hundred per year, affirming refugee rights was seen to come with few logistical, infrastructural, or fiscal costs. Broad immigration reform, on the other hand, was neither a topic of national interest nor central to fostering a vision of Brazilian humanitarianism abroad.[77] The Foreigners Statute would not be overhauled until 20 years later.

While the Refugee Act established a refugee definition largely following the 1951 Refugee Convention, it also, in the spirit of the 1984 Cartagena Declaration, provides refugee status for those fleeing grave and generalized human rights violations. It was on that basis that Brazil extended *prima facie* refugee status to Syrians, and has recognized more Venezuelans than any other country in Latin America, heralded as an international milestone in protection.[78] Moreover, different from the United States, Peru, and Colombia, Brazil does not set a time limit on applying for asylum. In striking contrast to restrictive asylum regimes, the Refugee Act provides, for both asylum seekers and refugees, the right to reside and work in Brazil, freedom of movement within the national territory, and equal access to public health, education, and social assistance programs. "We have the freedom to work, to study, really to do what we want," Syrian refugee Wael tells me, "because we have rights to everything."

The Refugee Act also established the broadly composed National Committee for Refugees (CONARE), which votes on all applications for asylum in Brazil. CONARE is a unique "tripartite enterprise" in which not only representatives from government ministries participate, but also members of Brazilian civil society and the UNHCR.[79] This has made CONARE the most inclusive of any such body in South America.[80] CONARE is headed by the Ministries of Justice and Foreign Relations, with representatives from the Ministries of Education, Health, and Work and Employment; the Federal Police; the UNHCR, Caritas, and the Migration and Human Rights Institute (IMDH); and, as of 2012, the Federal Public Defender's Office (DPU). Caritas obtained its unique position within CONARE in recognition of its historic role in refugee support in the country.[81] As João Guilherme Granja noted at the 2013 World Refugee Day: "these social actors made refuge matter before the state did." As such, a broad range of state and civil society actors participate in processing and determining asylum cases in Brazil. Along with formalizing asylum decisions, CONARE elaborates the policies and procedures of refugee governance.

Asylum claim decisions are made by democratic vote in CONARE's monthly plenaries. Brazil has had one of the highest asylum grant rates in Latin America, averaging 92 percent.[82] Brazil has also been a leader in refugee resettlement—when refugees are relocated from the initial asylum country to an agreeing third country—resettling more than any other country in the region, primarily Colombians and to a lesser extent Palestinians.[83]

Asylum today is an outgrowth of Brazil's long desire to be seen as the national model of tolerance. Its image as a front-runner in refugee protection has served a range of governments as they sought to affirm Brazil as a world leader. In the twenty-first century, Brazil's humanitarian policies on forced migration dovetailed neatly with broader domestic and international sociopolitical agendas. Disseminating a vision of Brazil as socially minded was central to the leftist Workers' Party (*Partido dos Trabalhadores*, or PT) government (2003–2016). Brazil's refugee policies during this time were informed by a desire to increase its international visibility and attempts to secure a permanent seat on the UN Security Council.[84]

Conservative political elites have likewise projected the laudability of Brazil's dedication to refugee protection for geopolitical ends. President Michel Temer, who came to power through a constitutional coup that overthrew the PT government in 2016, also wanted the world to see Brazil as welcoming to refugees. That year, Temer gave his first speech at the United Nations at a General Assembly meeting on migrants and refugees. Temer extolled Brazil for its openness to refugees, not its closures, and called on other countries to be as accommodating as Brazil. In a gross exaggeration, he lauded that Brazil had welcomed 95,000 refugees. The actual figure was 8,800. He celebrated that Brazil received the first refugee delegation to compete in the Olympics, and that both asylum seekers and refugees have universal access to employment, public education, and healthcare. If we give up our advocacy of these rights, Temer declared, "we will be giving up our own humanity." While Michel Temer dissolved the Human Rights Ministry at home, he marshaled Brazil's refugee policies to boast of his country's generosity on the international stage.

Its asylum policies present Brazil as an exemplar of immigrant welcome and humanitarianism, while racial notions of worth and belonging imbue their everyday operations. How those policies are implemented, in practice, racializes refugees and perpetuates racial hierarchies among them in the face of formal universality. Who is allowed in and has access to legal footing is not all that matters for understanding racial political domination.

Asylum Seekers and Refugees

Those seeking asylum in Brazil have varied over time, given both shifting conflicts and the role of the state in shaping the migratory possibilities for those forcibly displaced. While Brazil previously served as a transit country for refugees fleeing dictatorships in South America, with the lifting of geographic restrictions, the refugee profile began to change. Africans predominated by the turn of the century, particularly Angolan refugees fleeing civil war in the 1990s, whom police and media disparagingly associated with drugs, gangs, and guerrilla warfare.[85] By 2010, Africans represented 72 percent of refugees in Brazil, followed by Latin Americans at 17 percent.[86] Given prolonged conflict in the Democratic Republic of the Congo, Congolese claims have been frequent since the late 1990s and consistently appeared among those recognized.[87]

In the last decade, asylum demographics transformed again in size and composition. By 2015, the number of recognized refugees in Brazil had doubled in just four years, and the following year it hosted refugees from 81 countries.[88] The exponential growth in Syrian refugees, in particular, marked a significant shift at the time. Brazil is the third largest recipient of Syrian refugees in the Americas, after the United States and Canada. In 2014, the number of Syrian claims in Brazil were 290 times those seen in 2011.[89] That year, Syrians became the largest refugee community in Brazil; as of 2014, recognized refugees were predominantly from the Middle East (44%) and Africa (42%)—specifically, Syrians (31%), Angolans (14%), and Congolese (12%).[90] As Guilherme noted in 2016, "The majority are Syrians and Congolese in recent years."

Since then, the numbers seeking asylum in Brazil have continued to grow rapidly, most acutely with forced displacement from neighboring

Venezuela. Over five million people have left Venezuela in the last six years, almost 20 percent of the country. An estimated 260,000 Venezuelans were in Brazil as of 2021, 50,000 of them recognized as refugees.[91]

While Syrians and Congolese were the two primary populations obtaining asylum at the time of research, how they arrived was markedly different. When a large-scale possibility emerged to favor a refugee population locally racialized as white, the state reconfigured its practices to facilitate their arrival—in ways it had not done otherwise. Making sense of the racialized nature of refugee arrival requires attending to not just the objectives of forced migrants themselves, but how the state structures immigration; not only who it denies, but who it permits and who it invites.[92]

Modes of Arrival

"To Brazil I arrived with great ease," Hamid, a Palestinian refugee from Syria, says. "From when I came to Brazil until now," he shares, "everything is easy for me about the process." In 2013, CONARE passed Resolution 17 to extend humanitarian visas to Syrians so they could travel to Brazil and seek asylum. It removed usual visa requirements like a return ticket. The only requirement became basic identity documentation. In doing so, Brazil became the first country in the Americas to offer humanitarian visas to Syrian refugees.[93]

This was the second time Brazil had extended humanitarian travel visas. The first was with Haitians in 2012. That program, however, was a seeming last resort to quell irregular Haitian migration precipitated by the 2010 earthquake.[94] In CONARE meetings, policymakers first discussed deportation and increasing border control. They declared Haitians were not refugees, and they associated them with criminality and illegality. After the Haitian visa policy was implemented, the CONARE president celebrated "the expressed reduction in number of those arriving."[95] Representatives did not want Haitians to come, nor to stay. In the words of the Labor and Employment Ministry representative: "Haitians are working . . . with professional backgrounds and qualifications needed in the region. Nonetheless . . . that situation is not sustainable," because Haitians should be involved in "the reconstruction of Haiti."[96]

With Syrians, CONARE instead sought to elicit their immigration. After the visa extension, representatives focused on how to build up and streamline consular operations in Turkey and the Middle East to facilitate and expand access. By 2015, some 7,752 visas had been granted.[97] In contrast with Haitians, CONARE never established a visa limit, and thousands more have been emitted than used, suggesting the ease of their dispensation.

CONARE rooted Resolution 17 first and foremost in an imagined ethnic affinity between Brazil and Syria. The Resolution begins: "Considering the historical ties that unite the Syrian Arab Republic with the Federal Republic of Brazil, where a large population of Syrian descent resides." Mention of the conflict in Syria follows, rather than precedes, the ethnic ties used as justification for the exceptional policy shift. Resolution 17 mobilized the purported Syrian heritage of a large segment of Brazil to legitimize the decision to streamline Syrian immigration.

This was echoed by the presidency. In 2015, President Dilma Rousseff published an opinion piece called "Refugees and Hope" in the national newspaper *Folha de São Paulo*. "Brazil has its arms open to welcome refugees," she declared. "I reiterate the willingness of the Brazilian government to welcome those who, driven from their homelands, want to come to Brazil." She addresses refugee crises in the Middle East and North Africa. She references Alan Kurdi. Reflecting on the humanitarian visas for Syrian refugees, she mirrors the sentiments found in Resolution 17. "I determined that this effort should be broadened, because," Rousseff writes, "as a country with more than 10 million of Syrian-Lebanese descent, we could not do otherwise."[98]

These ethnic appeals harken back to when Brazil sought to whiten the nation, a racial project in which Syrian-Lebanese were included. Historical immigration—and how it is interpreted by political elites—configured Syrian refugee hospitality. Rather than demographic fact, such exaggerated numbers of the Arab presence in Brazil are part of an ethnoracial myth that privileges whiteness in the forging of national identity. The valorized recognition of Arabness, particularly since democratization, has led to vastly overestimating their ethnic presence in Brazil. While less than 200,000 Middle Easterners immigrated, it is broadly claimed— including by the government—that there are several million Brazilians of Arab descent today.[99] Rather than speak to demographic truths, as anthropologist John Tofik Karm affirms, such numbers underscore their venerated status. The social fact of overrepresentation, and the shifting role of Arabness in the nation, is an ethnoracial fabrication made possible by the contemporary configuration of whiteness in Brazil. This racialized veneration likewise shaped the possibility of Syrian refugee welcome. Rousseff frames Resolution 17 as a continuation of Brazil's history of welcoming immigrants and refugees, without naming how racialized hierarchies have shaped that welcome.

While Syrians come by plane with visas, many Congolese refugees arrive irregularly. Some, like Olivier, come as stowaways and find themselves, by design or by accident, on the southeastern coast of Brazil.[100] Congolese couple Luta and Joel recount the harrowing nature of that journey: "45 days in the dark hull of a ship without a hatch. With just water, crackers, and a flashlight. Never knowing the day or the hour, all notion of time is lost. Coming out of hiding upon hearing a siren: the ship had arrived at the port of Rio, the last hope among destinations."[101] Most refugees who arrive to Brazil as an unknown destination via maritime routes come from Africa, primarily from the DRC and Sierra Leone; as Brazilian commercial ships stop in Congolese and Sierra Leonian ports, refugees furtively stow away sometimes without knowing their destination.[102] In the words of Eduarda, a fair, olive-skinned social worker at the Center with thick, straight black hair, "Many who come here don't even know they're in Brazil until they arrive."

Emiliano, a white volunteer at the Refugee Center in Rio, taught a Portuguese class for English speakers. He remembers it as a diverse group, with a few from Syria and Nigeria as well as others from Ghana, Afghanistan, Pakistan, and Ukraine. During one class, his students practice the past tense. They ask and respond to questions: Have you done this? Have you done that? One student asks another: "Have you traveled by plane?" "Of course!" the student responds. "If I am here in Brazil, I came by plane, right?"

From the other side of the room, Jainaba, from Gambia, interjects. "No, I have never traveled by plane." The room fills with a general dismay. "What? How are you here?"

"I came by boat," Jainaba replies. "I came hidden in the boat."

Emiliano is just as surprised as his students. After class, back at the Refugee Center, he is still perplexed. "She said she came by boat. How can that be?"

Emiliano discovers this is not uncommon. Eduarda explains, "Ah, Emiliano. This is very normal. People sometimes come hidden." She continues: "The people that come by boat and are not discovered, they are lucky."

Such clandestine passages eerily recall the routes and journeys of the Atlantic Slave Trade. Echoing the trajectory of those forcibly enslaved, such migrants cross the Atlantic in the bottoms of ships, "with no light, no air," as Castro Alves writes in the poem that opens this chapter. "What does it mean to think of the route such refugees take from Africa to Brazil," Lucas asks, "given the histories of the slave trade?"

To that violent history of forced migration, most Brazilians can trace a lineage. Brazil is said to be the country with the largest population of African descent in the world after Nigeria. This heritage is largely traced back to Brazil's importation of forcibly enslaved peoples during the Atlantic Slave Trade, mostly from what are now Angola and the Congo.[103] As Marcia, the only black lawyer I met at the Center, noted, most refugees in Southeastern Brazil at the time were from Angola and the Congo, and "the slave trade in Brazil pulled from these same places."

While Brazil shares strong historical and ethnic ties to the Congo, CONARE has never mobilized these linkages to institute a resolution for Congolese analogous to that for Syrians. Rousseff recognized Brazil's ties to Africa but similarly failed to call for contemporary solidarity across the black Atlantic. In her opinion piece, Rousseff lauds Brazil as a welcoming country (*"terra do acolhimento"*) and conjures the trope of Brazilian racial mixture.

> Respectful of human rights, Brazil is a land of welcome. Along with the indigenous populations, the Brazilian people are made up of many immigrants. Millions of African brothers came here forced when the shameful slave trade reigned. The presence of indigenous people, Europeans, Africans, and Asians formed the Brazilian nation.

> When major crises hit Europe and the East, the doors of Brazil were open to all. We are conscious of the importance of these contributions for our historical and cultural formation. We pride ourselves on being a people formed by diversity. That is why tolerance and respect for differences are hallmarks of our identity.

While Rousseff rhetorically asserts the role of African forced migration and enslavement in forming the Brazilian nation, in the contemporary moment, she called for welcoming refugees from the Middle East alone. Despite the consistent arrival of Congolese and other African refugees over the three decades prior, ties to Africa are located historically, conjured up but relegated to a national past. This racial myopia means she makes no recognition of current political turmoil in Africa beyond *North* Africa. Contemporary forced displacement outside of the Middle East and North Africa goes unmentioned. While an open-arms policy is extended to Syrians because "we cannot do otherwise," she does not extend this welcome to black Africans. As throughout the twentieth century, while Brazil galvanizes cultural and ethnic roots in Africa, as Dávila writes, "Africa" is an abstraction, "a stage upon which questions about Brazilian race relations and national identity [are] interpreted."[104]

Some may argue that, as the Atlantic Slave Trade predated current national borders, no ethnic tie neatly maps on to the Democratic Republic of the Congo. Others may argue that the atrocities of erasure in enslavement mean Afrodescendants in Brazil cannot trace their lineage to any particular country. Yet, neither are such links, though presented as such by multiple levels of government, so obvious with Syria. As part of the Ottoman Empire prior to World War I, Syria was divided into sub-provinces whose borders varied over time, and included parts of modern-day Lebanon, Jordan, Turkey, and Palestine. Because of this, during that period, immigrants to Brazil from that region were loosely called Syrian-Lebanese, and variably called Turks, Syrians, or Lebanese.[105] The borders of the Ottoman Empire were never contiguous with Syria's current borders, a portion of southeastern Syria falling outside Ottoman control. After World War I, Syria came under the French Mandate for Syria and Lebanon. It was only with independence in 1946, after the principal immigration to Brazil, that Syria's modern borders emerged. While ties between Brazil and the Congo may appear amorphous, neither can links to Syria be clearly delineated.

Ethnic ties are not a given, they are constructed.[106] They are not the assertion of a social fact but its fabrication. Brazil's declared affinities with Syria are built on a molded history of remembrance that amplifies whiteness in the nation. As anthropologist Liisa Malkki writes, "the construction of a national past is a construction of history of a particular kind."[107] Which ethnic affinities are held up and how they are imagined in political discourse in Brazil serves a racial project, furthering its international mission to be seen as socially progressive while disparately favoring Syrian refugees.

Though Resolution 17 was discursively rooted in historical ethnic ties between Brazil and Syria, Palestinian refugees from Syria have entered through these channels and been processed as if they were Syrian. As with others from the Levant region, Palestinians are racialized as white in contemporary Brazil. While many (re)inscribe their Palestinian nationality before the state in a range of ways—writing Palestinian in their asylum applications, having their nationality changed from Syrian to Palestinian in their Brazilian identity documents—no filtering mechanism had been instituted by the state to distinguish them from Syrians. Reclassifying Palestinians as Syrians extended, in practice, legal privileges to Palestinians that were geared toward Syrians in formal policy and discourse. Obtaining these privileges incorporated Palestinians alongside Syrians, reaffirming Arab racialization as inside whiteness and the exceptions it can afford.

Ahmad is but one of many Palestinians the state willfully misclassified. In 2015, Ahmad came to Brazil with a visa from the consulate in Lebanon. I meet him the following year when he comes to the Refugee Center. Ahmad looks in his mid-twenties, with short hair and a well-maintained beard. He comes with a friend who speaks Portuguese and communicates on his behalf. His interlocutor signals to Ahmad beside him. "He is Palestinian," but, his friend tells me, "when he arrived they marked him as Syrian." Ahmad wants his documents to declare he is Palestinian, not Syrian.

I review Ahmad's case files and find that in his application he had written his nationality as Palestinian and that he is from Yarmouk, a Palestinian refugee camp in Damascus, Syria. He has consistently affirmed his nationality before the state. I discuss the case with Guilherme, who messages an asylum official on Ahmad's behalf and sets to work to have his identity document changed. Guilherme makes a copy of Ahmad's document and adds it to a larger report he is compiling for CONARE on cases of "supposed Syrian citizens." The experience of Ahmad and other Palestinians being miscategorized signals the lack of state interest in assuring only Syrians benefit from the resolution meant for them. And it belies the notion that that policy was driven fundamentally by ethnic ties, rather than a racial project. Being about Syrianness but also whiteness meant there was little interest in distinguishing Palestinians from Syrians.

Since then, CONARE has extended humanitarian travel visas to Afghanistan in 2021 and Ukrainians in 2022, despite the absence of historical migratory ties and without discursive recourse to ethnic affinity at all.[108] Such legislative shifts, for countries where conflicts have received international attention, usefully serve the government's self-image. No Africans, on the other hand, have been provided such pathways. With Ukraine visas, Brazil, for the first time, restricted them to only Ukrainian nationals and stateless persons. Thousands of African migrants in Ukraine were disqualified. Altogether, anti-blackness structures the possibilities for arrival that the state extends refugees.

By excavating how racialized hierarchies have shaped migrant inclusion and exclusion in the past and present, this chapter has addressed why the arrivals of refugees like Olivier and Adnan to Brazil look so different today. Throughout Brazil's history, asylum and immigration policies have figured in its mission to present itself as socially progressive internationally. Since the ideological emergence of racial democracy, Brazilian exceptionalism in racial harmony and hospitality has served a range of political agendas, leaving informal mechanisms of racial inequality for both nationals and immigrants, while making them difficult to interrogate. With this background as a frame for understanding the racial project of the contemporary refugee regime in Brazil, I now turn to what happens after asylum seekers arrive and claim refugee status. Chapter two addresses the racial politics of waiting at the Refugee Center in Rio de Janeiro—how refugees begin to learn through their bodies the meanings and perils of their racial place before the state from which they seek safe haven.

What is an office and what crops can you grow in it?

CHRIS CLEAVE, *Little Bee*

Just look at this waiting room.

FRANZ KAFKA, *The Trial*

FIGURES 2 AND 3 Asylum seekers and refugees wait outside at the Refugee Center in Rio de Janeiro, where they navigate their asylum claims and seek social assistance. Images altered for anonymity by author. Photos by Diogo Felix.

2

Waiting

RACIAL CONDITIONING AND THE BODY

Michele, a Congolese refugee in her late forties, waits outside at the Refugee Center. The heat is stifling. She chugs a cold cup of water, gulping it down before pouring herself another. She finishes her second cup. Holding it in her left hand, she looks down disappointedly at its empty bottom. Her long fingernails, painted opaque baby blue, match her eyeshadow. A clothing designer before she fled, Michele meticulously coordinates her ensembles. In her two years since arriving in Brazil, Michele has frequented the Refugee Center, both before and after obtaining asylum, through legal procedures, employment struggles, and persistent health problems.

For those who seek safe haven in Rio de Janeiro, the Refugee Center is an essential site. It is where they initiate an asylum claim, navigate that process and its various procedures, and seek social assistance. To go there is to wait. At the Refugee Center, "you have to wait your time," Michele tells me, resigned. "A long time." She continues, "You can come here in the morning, 10, 11 a.m., and leave here at 5 p.m." As Eduarda, a social worker at the Refugee Center, acknowledges, "They're waiting for hours, to do something that is very short."

Not all refugees, however, are compelled to frequent the Refugee Center. Though Syrians were the largest refugee community in Brazil at the time, they rarely appeared among those waiting. As Priscila, a staff member, notes, "Syrians do not have such a close relationship" to the Center. Amira, a 25-year-old Syrian asylum seeker and teacher with a warm deep voice and loose shoulder-length curls, notes how seldom she goes. "I think my process was easier than others'," she says. "And that's why I don't really go." "Why would I come! Really!" she adds, with an exasperated chuckle in her voice. "I don't like waiting." Amira does not frequent the Center because she does not have to.

When refugees like Michele come to the Center in hopes of resolving dire problems, they are exposed to protracted discomfort. As they wait, they endure heat, hunger, and unease. Such conditions look very different from those experienced by the officials who assist them. Officials work in temperature-controlled offices, while those seeking assistance must wait outside—for hours, exposed to Rio's subtropical climate, without proper seating. Though staff enjoy a bounty of sustenance, including a freshly prepared lunch buffet, asylum seekers and refugees sporadically receive store-brand cookies. Those who wait feel the pangs of hunger. "Are there no cookies?" an African woman asks me, echoing others. She pleads: "I've been here for four hours. I am hungry."

The racial logic that orders those conditions manifests between officials and refugees, but also among refugees, structuring the form and degree of waiting. Such circumstances must be endured by many—but not all—in search of safe haven. The preponderance of those who come to the Refugee Center are Congolese like Michele, and primarily Africans experience these physical indignities. "Lingala is the most spoken language at the Center," Frederic incisively notes, referencing a Central African language.

In contrast, those racialized as white, like Amira, rarely find themselves so inconvenienced at the behest of the state. They are largely provided escape from such bodily unease and its attending political domination. While they do not have to habituate the Center, when they go, they can experience respite from these conditions. Officials do not chide them that their rightful place is outside in heat and discomfort. Social barriers are softened as lighter-skinned migrants and officials share food, and they fraternize in ways otherwise off-limits. They receive different racial lessons about their position vis-à-vis the state.

This chapter is about who waits, what happens as they do, and why. Waiting is replete with racial political meaning. As refugees variably endure the embodied experience of waiting, they learn what it means to be black—or not—in Brazil. The Refugee Center is a staging ground for the racial project of asylum. The unequal conditions of climate and sustenance, character of interactions, manipulation of time, and demarcation of space and contact differentially condition the black refugee body— building a sociopolitical chasm between the predominantly black refugees who wait and the white officials who assist them. Disregarding the former, while caring for the latter, reflects and reinforces racial ideologies regarding who, and by extension which bodies, matter. In the search to construct their lives anew in Brazil, black African asylum seekers and refugees are incorporated into the bottom of the racial order.

Refugees do not learn their racial place only through waiting at the Refugee Center. I documented similar dynamics at other sites of the asylum process, including the Federal Police Office, where applicants file their claims and obtain their identity documents. Mamadou is an 18-year-old Guinean refugee who plays midfielder for a local soccer club. He sports a box fade and jokes effortlessly in Portuguese. When Mamadou goes to the Federal Police Office, he "wake[s] up at 4, 5 a.m. to get in line." Even if there's "just five foreigners" waiting, Mamadou exasperatedly notes, they make you wait and "take a number." Racialized patterns of bodily subjugation, temporal uncertainty, and spatial demarcation appear throughout the process. The Center is but one site in a pattern of racial conditioning that asylum seekers encounter as they traverse the refugee regime.

This racial domination is not the product of ill intent of those working at the Refugee Center. They dedicatedly strive and struggle to amend the chronic wrongs that refugees experience in asylum and beyond.[1] Yet, preoccupied with counteracting injustices born from beyond the walls of the Center, the inequalities in officials' immediate surrounds elude them. The prolonged strains of stress, overburden, and precarity stifle concerns among officials regarding how long and in what conditions refugees must wait. Nonetheless, such organizational constraints cannot explain why refugee experiences of waiting vary. Earnest intentions to assist and support refugees are underwritten by unthought racialized norms of political worth and belonging. Subject to conditions structured by their position in the social racial universe, refugees learn what sociologist Erving Goffman calls a "sense of one's place."[2] Such racial lessons about who matters are lived and felt at the level of the body.

Enduring Discomfort

Through the outer gate of the Refugee Center lies a large patio, partially covered by the building's overhang. This is where asylum seekers and refugees must wait. They are not allowed in the building unless called. While inside officials sit on sturdy chairs with cushioned seats and backs, outside there are no such comforts. Those who wait, in contrast, do so on wooden benches, plastic patio chairs, or along the low sidewall that borders the patio. Outside, there are only hard surfaces, without cushions and most without back support. When busy, this seating is insufficient.

As they wait, applicants endure the harsh climatic realities of Rio. While those inside have air-conditioning units—except notably the cook, who was, in years prior, a dark-skinned black woman and the only one on staff—asylum seekers and refugees are subject to the weather. With its subtropical climate, Rio is characterized by heat, humidity, and frequent downpours. During days of incessant pounding rain, those outside cluster under the overhang to wait out the downpour. On a balmy day in April, after I spend a few minutes outside on the patio, my linen shirt becomes marked by the beads of sweat pooling on my stomach. Even though it is fall, the heat is insufferable, and the temperature regularly reaches 90 degrees. While there is a misting fan out on the patio, staff rarely remember to turn it on.

In coming to the Refugee Center, asylum seekers and refugees seek to resolve manifold troubles—to claim the protections of asylum; to renew the legal documents that make possible their lives and livelihoods; to seek out food, shelter, and employment assistance; and to apply for family reunification to bring loved ones to Brazil; among others. But seeking support and claiming formal rights can come at the price of embodied unease. As they strive to enact their political subjecthood, it is debased. The "mortification of the self," as Goffman notes, also comes "by way of the body."[3]

Subjecting the black refugee body to such situations entails racial political conditioning. Conditions *condition*, imparting lessons through the body and to the mind. These circumstances of indignity viscerally confront and assault the black self, diminishing claims of worth and autonomy.[4] This politicized habituation to certain bodily conditions and attendant cognitive understandings occurs in a social field of racial power. As the state makes refugees like Michele wait, but not those like Amira, it racially conditions subjects. To the extent that those who occupy similar racial positions experience similar conditions, providing for the development of similar dispositions—it entails *racial conditioning*.[5] As black African asylum seekers and refugees wait outside, suffer the heat, and go without food—experiencing a lack of concern for their time, needs, and bodies—they see and feel that the state does not truly care about black people like them.

As refugees wait they not only endure time, but particular somatic conditions.[6] Bureaucratic sites of waiting, and the bodily comforts found or lacking in them, communicate one's worth. "The body has always been a privileged site," Fassin and d'Halluin note, "on which to demonstrate the evidence of power."[7] A sense of political belonging can bud from or be extinguished by the embodied aspects of such encounters. The body, as sociologist Hana Brown has shown, is a central axis by which refugees are incorporated into a new sociopolitical order.[8] We often forget that those who wait inhabit bodies as they do so. While state power manifests, *par excellence*, through the biopolitical management of the refugee body, such power is not exercised uniformly in Brazil.[9]

A racial logic shapes not only the different experiences of officials and those seeking their assistance, but also lies at the heart of who must habitually endure the racial conditioning of bodily discomfort. Syrians do not frequent that space because they do not have to. They do not experience the bureaucratic hassles and hurdles commonly seen with black applicants. Nor are they alone in finding such relief. Other prominent groups from the Middle East, like Iranians and Iraqis, and Afghans are also notably absent at the Center. Their presence is so uncommon that, even after Matilde worked for months as a volunteer at the Center, she is surprised to hear Lucas and me discuss Syrian cases. She asks, shocked: "There are people from the Middle East??" Such asylum seekers are not subject to political domination through the physical indignities of waiting in the ways Africans are.

There are many reasons Syrian and other Middle Eastern refugees appear less at the Refugee Center. Those at the Center are less likely to make them come. On the one hand, lawyers choose not to interview them because they do not worry officials will doubt their claims. Lawyers at the Center schedule intake interviews with asylum seekers after they submit their applications at the Federal Police Office. However, they rarely scheduled Middle Eastern and Afghan intake interviews. Of the 452 legal interviews scheduled between September 2015 and May 2017, a full 381—84 percent—were from Africa. Only 10 were from the Middle East or Afghanistan.[10] Not scheduled for those interviews, they also didn't come and wait only to have them rescheduled. Overwhelmed by other work, lawyers would regularly reschedule—"I'm not doing it today," Guilherme would say—making principally Africans come yet again. On the other hand, as social workers rarely provide Middle Easterners with aid or monthly subsidies, as discussed in chapter six, they do not come and wait to receive it.

These racial disparities are also shaped by actions outside the Center addressed in the chapters that follow. Because officials are less likely to delay their cases, as seen in chapter five, non-African applicants less often come to check the status of their claims or renew their documents. Unlikely to be denied, they do not have to come to the Center to navigate the appeal process. Because Syrians have access to humanitarian visas, they do not have to file for family reunification to bring their family to Brazil, nor return to see the status of those requests. Moreover, as they do not suffer the same employment struggles Africans do, discussed in chapter seven, they do not seek their redress at the Center.

For many Congolese refugees, issues with documentation require them to frequent the Refugee Center and confront the challenges and discomfort entailed. "Dealing with documents," Lionel, a Congolese refugee in his mid-twenties, says, "is not easy. It is always complicated." "In Brazil," Lionel continues, "you never get anything on the first try." Not all refugees, however, are subject to such complications that compel them to return again and again. Syrians and others from the Middle East are not among those who must regularly navigate and wait at sites of asylum like the Refugee Center.

Depriving the Stomach

Deprivation at the Refugee Center largely falls along racialized lines. The sustenance provided those who work at the Center looks very different from that given to those who wait. Nina, the staff cook, with a warm olive complexion and dyed blond hair, prepares a daily lunch buffet for officials and volunteers composed of two meat options, black beans, rice, a green salad, and juice. Lunch is supplemented by frequent snacking, and eating is a constant topic of conversation among staff. "There's never more than 30 minutes that goes by without someone eating something," lawyer Melina remarks. "All the time we're talking about food." Volunteers bring boxes of sweets for the office, and staff take afternoon trips to the corner store for coffee and confections. Nina bakes cakes for staff birthdays. On days the legal staff stays late, Lucas, a senior lawyer at the Center, prepares indoor picnics of bread with dried tomato spread and raspberry jam, and lots of fruit—bananas, guava, papaya—to keep spirits up. Officials keep their stomachs full, eating frequently and freely.

The Refugee Center is a site of legal assistance but also social aid—where migrants seek financial subsidies, language training, and help finding jobs and housing. Though refugees often miss meals while they wait and struggle with food insecurity, it is not a soup kitchen. While officials eat lunch from a buffet table of options, Emanuelle, a staff member, sets out baskets of store-bought, generic-brand cookies for those waiting outside. Refugees do not receive a proper meal nor have the luxury of choice. For those like Rosine from the Congo, or Ibrahim from Nigeria, what they have to eat, they get from the Center. While the cookie allotment is a designated five packets a day, the money earmarked is insufficient to cover the whole month. According to Lucas, "the money for cookies only lasts ten days." Those waiting will go without until the next month. The staff lunch, on the other hand, is never skipped.

The refugee experience is marked by hunger. After I finish orienting Loide, from Namibia, on the asylum process, I tell her she can complete the application at the Center or fill it out at home and come back another day. "I'll probably take it home," she tells me. "I haven't eaten all day." For Mariatu and her husband from Sierra Leone, "The money we had for food today, we spent on the transportation to come here." A Congolese woman asks me if there are any more cookies, touching her fingertips to her chest, declaring one word in her limited Portuguese: "Hunger."

"There's no food here?" a pregnant Angolan asylum seeker probes. She continues: "It is a long time."

Asylum seekers and refugees protest that there are not enough cookies, and that cookies are not enough. Iuwine, an Angolan asylum seeker, asks me: "Lunch? Any lunch for me?" I respond about there being cookies. He motions to his body, signaling how that will be unsatisfactory to maintain all that he has. Later, he asks me again about lunch: "I am going to fall over." Throughout that same day, staff try to get me to eat lunch. When the receptionist Antonio comes to tell me that the Angolan group I had been assisting is ready for me to review their asylum applications, he tells me, "But please, please, go eat some lunch first." Later, when I finish with that group, I ask lawyer Guilherme if I can help with anything. "Go, rest for a second, eat," he answers. When I see the Center coordinator, Adriana, who had asked me to translate a spreadsheet into English, she bellows: "Go *eat*! And then do it." Many concernedly fuss over me eating. They are less preoccupied with the work than with making sure I am fed. Though I say nothing of hunger, staff are acutely attentive to the fact that I have not eaten and try to cajole me into doing so.

Food is not just a substance that fuels the body, it is replete with social meaning. It creates community, and foodways speak to how we see and value others. This pestering communicates care for me and my well-being. In contrast, busy with work, some days staff forget to set out the cookies. Despite Iuwine's clamoring "Lunch? Any lunch for me?" there won't be any lunch for him. And he knows the staff will be fed while he is not.

Organizational procedures in place to maintain fairness and consistency keep asylum seekers and refugees hungry. There are strict rules against volunteers supplementing the designated cookies. During a volunteer orientation for those who will teach the Portuguese classes, Priscila stresses the importance of adhering to these policies. "Sometimes good intentions create problems. For example, one of your students is falling asleep in class, and you ask them what's wrong. And they say they didn't have breakfast. So, you want to bring them breakfast. *Do not* bring breakfast for them, because we have a *system*. If you give a snack to one and not the others, they will come to the Refugee Center and quarrel. They'll say, 'They're racists!'" Priscila underscores the importance of maintaining the order of the system that determines the distribution of food. As black asylum seekers and refugees declare special concessions "racist," they name and recognize racial norms guiding who is subject to hunger.

Lawyers occasionally deviate from protocol, tempering such disparities by sporadically providing treats. Guilherme offers the last slice of birthday cake to an asylum seeker who has not eaten that day, and Lucas shares the picnic spreads he prepares with applicants when he eats in front of them. This rule bending occurs primarily when food is within view, the gaps in sustenance no longer obscured by the walls of the Center. And it happens with cake, pieces of fruit, snacks—not a proper meal.

As the refugees who quarrel with Priscila suggest, racial preference informs when and how officials deviate from food policies. When Hamid, a light olive-skinned Palestinian Syrian refugee, first came to the Center to apply for asylum and seek housing support, Eduarda invited him to eat lunch with her in her cubicle. He was touched by the offer, and it endeared her to him. Camila is a white Uruguayan asylum seeker who suffers from paranoia. When Lucas tells her that the Center offers psychological help, she responds that she doesn't want to see a psychologist. She only wants a plate of food. While Iuwine has no luck when he pleads for lunch, Camila's request is granted. Hamid and Camila do not eat the trifles designated for refugees; instead, Eduarda and Lucas offer them the food officials eat. In doing so, they extend an exceptional line across the sustentative chasm that manifests between officials and refugees.

The other direction of food exchange, when forced migrants share food with officials, is racialized as well. Rossi, from Venezuela, travels from Búzios to the Refugee Center to apply for asylum—a roughly three-hour journey if done directly by car. She has a medium skin tone and wears her straight brown hair with blond highlights. As we sit in the legal office, reviewing her application, she is afraid to be sent home. "I was supposed to fly back on Tuesday." She is relieved when I tell her she cannot be sent back while her asylum claim is pending. She tells me her anguish is mental, not physical. "If I get sent back, and my son isn't there, I'll kill myself." She takes her index finger and draws it horizontally across her throat. "Seriously," she says. With her, she has a box of meringues. She offers them to me, and I eat one. Twice she encourages me to take the rest. Even in her state of anguish, she thinks to share the sweets she brought with her on the long journey to the Center. Earlier that same day, multiple asylum seekers proclaimed their hunger from hours of waiting, imploring staff for cookies to no avail. A tall African man in a yellow jersey comes into the reception area, declaring he wants cookies. "No, man," Antonio responds. "You have to wait outside." While officials dismiss requests for meager sustenance to temper empty stomachs, Rossi generously offers me what she has.

Other asylum seekers and refugees are similarly charitable. Mustafa, a refugee from East Africa with a warm brown complexion, never comes to the Refugee Center empty-handed. He brings staff plastic bags full of *esfiha*, savory pastries filled with chopped meat. Alejandro and Yamile, a light-skinned Colombian couple, gift more esfiha to Guilherme and me than we can consume. Natasha, a young woman from Russia, brings staff the cake pops she made with her mother for Easter. Hayyan from Syria offers me two boxes of cookies. "These were for the person who assisted me yesterday," he tells me. "But since you assisted me today, they are for you." Another applicant brought esfiha and Arab cookies for the legal office the day prior. While not expected, neither are such treats uncommon, and staff cheerfully enjoy them when they appear. As we snack on their gifts, lawyer Ana notes the absurdity with a slight chuckle: "We can't even buy them a coke." She begrudgingly accepts the discrepancy. Such inequality is taken as an irresolvable part of working at the Center.

Except for Mustafa, himself an unusual case in other ways, it is non-African applicants who gift food to staff. It is those rarely subject to the degrading pittance of cookies that think to offer such treats. For the predominantly black African asylum seekers and refugees who regularly endure hunger as they wait at the Center, such an act is not practiced and likely unimaginable. When applicants offer food, they largely do so inside the office, out of sight and beyond the purview of those waiting out on the patio. In so doing, they try to build a personal bridge with officials, differentiating themselves from others and crossing the social abyss between official and refugee. Because officials happily accept the food such applicants bring them, they are successful in this regard. As anthropologist Marcel Mauss proposes in *The Gift*, because a gift is tied to its giver, the act of gift giving and receiving creates a social bond between giver and recipient.[11] Food carries pronounced social and affective weight. Sharing food is an intimately social act that bonds people together in a relationship of care and attention. And, in such encounters at the Center, it also carries racial political significance. Such food shapes and signifies connections with officials, and it signals a closeness to power in the hierarchies that manifest there. Social recognition is forged through the act of gracious acceptance, a relation rarely furnished between officials and black African refugees. Food reveals both social ties and distinctions. Through the provision and exchange of food, and concern with nourishment, officials socially bind themselves to each other, and to asylum seekers like Camila, Natasha, and Hayyan, while denying asylum seekers like Iuwine such ties.

Demanding Deference

I head to the reception office and ask Antonio if he needs help with anything. "No," he says, "I just need you to sit here with me, I've been alone here all day." As I keep him company, an Angolan woman comes in. She asks Antonio, "Can I have the phone number for here?"

He responds, "Let's do that again. You already started wrong." He makes her repeat after him:

"Please." "Please."

"May you." "May you."

"Give me." "Give me."

"The number." "The number."

"For here." "For here."

After she does, Antonio gives her the number.

I ask Antonio, "Why did you do that, if she is Angolan?" In other words, given that Portuguese is her native language. "Because she spoke wrong," he says, "beyond that she said it without even 'please.'" "But maybe in Angola, it's right however she said it," I respond.

"But it's not right here. So, I correct her."

For black African asylum seekers and refugees, seeking assistance at the Center entails not only physical discomfort, but compels their deference in words and temperament. "Just as the individual can be required to hold his body in a humiliating pose," Erving Goffman writes, "so he may have to provide humiliating verbal responses."[12] This appears in starkest relief in the reception office, where contact between officials and asylum seekers is mediated.

Racialized notions of worth shape how the receptionist engages with refugees, and whom he reprimands to wait outside. As Prince, a pensive Congolese man, tries to ask questions in the cramped lobby, Antonio ignores him. Antonio does not look at him, pretending to be occupied with paperwork. Standing behind his oversized desk, Antonio exclaims, "You can wait outside, okay? *Okay?*" As Antonio fidgets with papers with one hand, he gives a big, assertive thumbs-up with the other. In a loud, firm tone he asserts, "*Beleza?* [All good?]" Prince exits the reception and goes to wait outside. Denied recognition, he leaves with his head down. "Here," Congolese refugee Lionel reflects, "I feel totally without identity. I can't complain about anything, I can't say anything, I can't . . . I don't have a voice." Such encounters entail a denial and degradation of the political self before the state from which they seek and obtain safe haven.

Experiences of compelled deference and humiliation appear beyond the Refugee Center. Frederic offers support as a guide and mediator for those recently arrived, assisting and translating for them throughout the process. Frederic tells me that officials at the Federal Police Office "try to make life difficult for refugees." His interactions there entail "moments of humiliation." When he tries to accompany asylum seekers from the waiting room into the back-office space, officers rebuke and demean him. On one such occasion, Frederic tells me, an officer yells: "Hey, hey, where are you going?! What do you think this is here?" Frederic tries to explain himself, but the officer continues to yell: "I don't want to know! You liar . . .

Get out! . . . Get out of here!" Frederic says, "I had to leave." "People try to humiliate me," he laments, by "not letting me in."

In contrast, Syrians and others from the Middle East do not experience such patterns of humiliation at the Federal Police Office or Refugee Center. While Lionel declares that the Federal Police are "nobody's friend . . . because they have a problem with us being [in their country]," Hamid experiences it differently. He goes to the Federal Police Office more than he must because he likes to talk with the officers, particularly Cecilia, whom he calls his "friend." Nizar is a Syrian asylum seeker in his early thirties, with a widow's peak and black-rimmed glasses. For Nizar, his visits to the Federal Police "have been very casual. I didn't feel like I was at a police station. Officers were laughing, making jokes." It's one of the things he likes about Brazil: "Even if you're at the Police, they're making jokes." I ask Nizar if anything has been frustrating or difficult about his experiences at the Federal Police. "No." I follow up if there was a moment where they were ever rude or mean to him. "Not at all," he answers.

Experiences also differ in the lobby at the Center. As I walk into the reception office, I see Antonio casually chatting with Yousef, from Syria, something Antonio rarely did with those from Africa. Nor was Yousef made to wait. He arrived at 2:30 p.m. to the Center, and the legal staff assisted him six minutes later.

While Antonio belittles those who address him "wrong" in Portuguese, he also reproaches Africans who speak to him in French. When they do, Antonio retorts: "Speak Portuguese." He is less demanding with English speakers, however. Contrary to common perceptions about bureaucracies and their offices, such demoralizing conditions are not uniformly imposed upon those who navigate them.[13] Speaking English, most common among applicants from the Middle East, provides such applicants a respite from the push to speak Portuguese correctly and deferentially. Antonio has an affinity for English he does not have for French, primarily spoken by Africans at the Center. He watches music videos on YouTube by US bands like Creed with the subtitles on, practicing the sounds and asking me the meanings. When an English-speaking applicant says to Antonio, "I am trying to learn your language, so you should try to learn my language," Antonio answers, smiling, "with urgency." Rather than oblige deference, such an exchange builds social proximity.

Antonio's behavior is a source of frustration among lawyers at the Center. For them, his demeanor is begrudgingly tolerated as something that cannot be helped. Among staff broadly, it is accepted as the way things are, understood as part of maintaining order under the hectic conditions of the Center. As black African applicants encounter the refugee regime, they experience acute and subtle forms of such interactions that compound to enact racial lessons. Those exchanges leave those like Frederic feeling humiliated, while Lionel learns he doesn't "have a voice."

Suffering Time

Thus far this chapter has examined racial conditioning in the circumstances of bodily comfort and domination. Yet this begs the question of what makes this possible; the arrangements of time and space provide for habitually defiling the black political self. Waiting before the state is not empty time—it is politically productive, conditioning subjects and forming the relations between them and the state.[14] "Something about Brazil," Frederic learns, is that "you have to wait." For the predominantly black African asylum seekers and refugees who wait at the Center, enduring time makes possible their subjection to racial lessons of devalued political worth.

To wait is to be at the behest of others. In coming to the Center, refugees' time is taken out of their hands. They are subject to the temporal will and whims of others. Officials decide when they work and when they provide support. Though the Refugee Center opens at 9 a.m., and applicants arrive at that time, lawyers often do not arrive before 10 a.m. Volunteers arrive late, leave early, and skip shifts. Staff take long breaks. After eating lunch, rather than resume assistance, they may nap, go for walks, or chat leisurely as their food settles. Others play violent videogames together in the administrative office, while those fleeing war and persecution wait outside. Waiting is something marginalized subjects, as sociologist Javier Auyero writes, are "constantly forced to undergo in order to obtain what [is] rightfully theirs."[15] As we discuss the schedules officials keep, volunteer Fernanda observes: "It is because the client is not the boss. It's not the client to whom we are really accountable."

Refugee time is tacitly assigned less value than of those who make them wait. They can be temporally disciplined just as readily by young volunteers as by seasoned staff. Rodrigue, an asylum seeker from Benin, comes for the 2 p.m. appointment that Julia, a volunteer, has scheduled with him. Rodrigue arrives on time. Julia does not arrive until 2:30 p.m. When she does, she utters: "I have to go reread his case first." At 2:55 p.m., nearly an hour after the appointment time, Julia calls Rodrigue from the patio into the legal office. Julia makes no comment and provides no apology for making him wait an hour for an appointment she herself had scheduled. If, as sociologist Barry Schwartz asserts, exercising control over time is essential to power, the inability to control one's time engenders a sense of powerlessness.[16] Waiting disentitles those ensnared. Disregard for refugee time, at the Center and elsewhere, denigrates the political subjecthood of applicants like Rodrigue.

Such encounters of waiting before the state are replete with racial meaning. Lionel first grasps the political significance of his blackness in Brazil while waiting in line at a public employment center. Everyone around him is pushing and shoving, but the public official tells Lionel he has to wait in line. Lionel asks why. The attendant retorts back: "You haven't seen yourself?!" For Lionel, the racial degradation entailed in those words is devastating. He explains, "That was the first time I realized I was black." Before this, "I just thought I was a man, like everyone else." These forms of "racial prejudice," as Lionel calls them, "are the embarrassing moments of my life." As he claims his right as a refugee to employment assistance, he is subject to humiliation. In that waiting, forced to put his body in line and wait quietly, Lionel learns his racial place, uniquely subject to an embarrassment of his political being. Lionel realizes what it means to be black in Brazil, and he carries that racial understanding with him as he navigates the refugee regime.

While black African asylum seekers and refugees may attempt to shorten their wait—by pleading they are in a hurry or calling on any official they see to assist them—they rarely express irritation with the very fact of being made to wait. While Julia does not excuse herself for her tardiness, neither does Rodrigue demand redress. At the Center, Congolese refugee Yornella notes, "you have to be patient." While waiting at the Federal Police Office, Lionel learns how he has to behave. "You cannot rush them," and you cannot complain about waiting "a long time." He learns he must swallow his pride. "You speak softly so you can get your rights and go home," Lionel explains. "You have to be endearing [*carinhoso*]—even when angry, even when hungry."

At the Refugee Center, the workflow is organized through a triage system of small assistance cards, called *fichas*. Upon arrival, the person seeking assistance communicates their basic information and reason for coming to the reception office. While assistance cards have the time of arrival, they do not note the time of assistance. There is no system for tracking how long people wait.

One Friday in the legal office, as we snack on *paçoca*, a candy made of ground peanuts, I remark about how the Center does not collect data on wait time. "It has the times they come in," I note, "but it doesn't say the times they are assisted." "Doing so would provide some sense of how long people are waiting," I continue, "because I really don't have any idea." Ana is enthused by the suggestion of capturing wait times, and keenly eager to implement the change. "That would be good," Ana responds. "We could see about adding that to the paper." She would like to improve this, and twice she tells me to remind her on Monday. Ana has a sensitive, thoughtful demeanor, and takes care to consider how to improve the circumstances and experiences of the refugees she assists. She is the only lawyer who consistently starts work on time, and she notes how taking a full lunch hour would "produce in me a crisis." But with Monday comes another busy day of assistance. Lost in the struggle to keep up with those newly waiting, I do not remember, nor does she. The suggestion is lost in the immediacy of the demanding whirlwind of the Center.

Structural conditions at the Center lead officials to make, accept, and sometimes prefer that refugees wait. Officials accept waiting as an unfortunate reality without resolution; there are just too many refugees and not enough staff. Refugees like Michele similarly learn and internalize these dynamics; as she compliantly notes, "They receive a lot of people. You have to wait your time." Taking one's time, or wasting time on Facebook, forestalls the specter of breaking down from exhaustion. Making refugees wait is understood as part of doing the work well. Guilherme doesn't come to work at 9 a.m. when the Center opens because "If I do," he says, "I am tired all day, and it affects the quality of assistance." Guilherme fears he would make a mistake or lose his patience.

Refugee waiting is also prolonged by organizational precarity. Work conditions at the Center make efficiency exceedingly difficult. In early years, Lucas typed on a keyboard so old the letters had worn away from use. Technological problems are frustratingly common. Not long after I return in 2016, Guilherme tells me the computer network is down. "Does this happen every day?" I ask. "Every hour," he answers. "Great work conditions." We both laugh to appease the sense of impotence. The network and internet often crash, for short or long periods, throughout the day. The printers break down, get stuck on every third page, and sporadically print blank pages. As Lucas struggles with the printer, he complains, "We spend more time on this than assistance." How quickly work is accomplished is subject to the erratic functioning of the printers, internet, and computer network.

Yet not all refugees must experience the powerlessness engendered in waiting. Wael is a lanky Syrian refugee in his mid-twenties, with angular eyebrows and a scruffy beard. He teaches Arabic and studies chemistry. When I ask Wael about his visits to the Center, he explains why they are few and far between. "If you need something," he tells me, "you are going to spend the whole day waiting to be able to speak." "I am not going to humiliate myself," Wael continues. "I will depend on myself, and I will manage. I achieved various things because of the government, but I think I went to [the Refugee Center] three times in the past four years, when I really needed to go." For Wael, to wait at the Center would be humiliating. But he does not have to. Since Wael must rarely go, he is not subject to the bodily conditions that humiliate and exhaust the political will of those who do.

For applicants like Wael who rarely wait, they respond differently to the temporal domination entailed. While it is uncommon to see white people waiting at the Center, when they must, a palpable agitation—an expression that the temporal suck is unjust—appears. Alexander, a Russian asylum seeker, approaches me indignantly after waiting two hours. It is shocking to see him. I had never seen someone that white seeking assistance at the Center. Antonio and Yasmin, a volunteer, refer to him as *o loiro*, the blond man. As Alexander demands to know how much longer he will have to wait, he speaks with a tone of annoyance that surprises me. Over time, such expressions of indignance appeared in my interactions with lighter-skinned refugees, and I came to realize that applicants like Alexander and Wael expressly rebuke the sociopolitical humiliation of waiting. Less likely to be subject to it, they have not normalized it as the way things are. The racial conditioning entailed in the degree and form of state encounters shapes how refugees think and act in them. Their responses are a "product of the internalization of the [racial] structures of that world."[17]

This racial conditioning would be missed if I focused my sights on who obtains asylum and who does not. Centering legal status would underappreciate how forced migrants are incorporated into the racial political order.[18] Racial conditioning occurs through ensnaring domination in Brazil, rather than only political exclusion.[19] Both Syrian Wael and Congolese Michele are recognized refugees, yet only Michele frequents the Center. Recognition does not provide respite for black African refugees, as legal inclusion is underwritten by racialized hierarchies.

Constructing Boundaries

The unequal conditions at the Refugee Center are a product of a stark demarcation of space and access. Staff and volunteers have liberty to come and go as they please throughout the Center. In contrast, the movement of asylum seekers and refugees is highly controlled. Regulating access is central to the daily functioning of the Center, but it also creates racialized divisions. Restricting spatial contact produces two separate worlds that exist alongside each other, a mere wall between them, and yet they feel radically different.

Great efforts are taken to keep asylum seekers and refugees from accessing the inside of the building. Asylum seekers and refugees are prohibited from entering without authorization. A sign on the outside of the patio door printed in all caps, underscored with pink highlighter, repeats in French, English, and Portuguese: "Entry only with lawyer authorization." In a staff meeting, administrator Renato reminds everyone to keep the door closed because "if they see the door open, they'll want to come in." Maintaining these dynamics is so important that rules regarding spatial access are part of the basic training given new volunteers before they start at the Center. At orientations, staff instruct volunteers that they cannot go through the inside of the building with applicants, nor pass through the multipurpose room with them during lunch.

Kept physically distant, so too are refugees denied the power of sight. Posters are taped over the glass insets in the patio door to stop those waiting from seeing inside, blocking what refugee eyes can see. Ironically, these UNHCR posters depict portraits of refugees, declaring: "It takes courage to be a refugee." Such organizational acts of spatial control doubly veil refugees, removing them from view while denying them a line of sight. They can neither see nor be seen. The spatial qualities of such arrangements deny proximity, disavowing social and political recognition.[20] Spatial and social marginality are intertwined.[21] The prolonged, repeated exposure to spatial distance at the Center falls largely on racial lines.

Those who wait are not passive subjects; this racial domination is negotiated. Black African asylum seekers and refugees employ a range of tactics in an attempt to mitigate these conditions. While they may sporadically soften their edges, those conditions remain structurally intact. When Congolese and other Africans breach these spatial barriers, they are rebuked. Some try to wait in the multipurpose room by accompanying loved ones being assisted inside, slowly filling out forms, or lingering as they wait for assistance. Such tactics to garner unfettered access to comfortable seating and air conditioning precipitate bubbling tensions. Micaela, a black social worker who likes to joke about looking like Michelle Obama, exclaims in a loud, assertive voice: "Those who are here to be assisted: Leave this room and wait outside!" Antonio similarly bellows at a Congolese woman in the multipurpose room for not waiting outside on the patio: "You have to wait out there to be called!" Maintaining spatial distance requires constant maintenance. By coming inside, asylum seekers and refugees find respite from the harsh elements on the patio. In attempting to change the conditions of their waiting, they challenge the demarcation of space and the racial power dynamics embedded in it. Yet their attempts are rendered futile. Maintaining order at the Center and elsewhere, as with Frederic's experiences at the Federal Police Office, is a priority, central to keeping the work moving. That Micaela behaved similarly to Antonio underscores how the racial project of asylum manifests through practices shaped by organizational conditions, rather than individual ill intent.

Not all are so harshly rebuked. While staff scold Africans who attempt to wait inside, they can respond differently to others. As Farid, a Syrian refugee, and his Syrian friend wait to be assisted, they linger in the reception office. They carve out spaces for themselves in the cramped room, standing in nooks between the door and filing cabinets. At the time, I am surprised no one asks them to wait outside. Space is in short supply in the lobby, much more so than in the multipurpose room. On a different day in the reception office, Antonio declares his frustration with Congolese and other Africans trying to wait in the multipurpose room. He extends his arms out, motioning to the small lobby around him, and adds in a serious tone: "Here, in the reception, they won't [try to wait]." Antonio suggests he won't stand for that in his office. Yet Farid and his friend do not leave their spots until they are assisted. Antonio does not ask them to wait outside, as he does with Prince. While Syrians are largely exempt from these spatial norms because they do not frequent the Center, when they must come, neither are they pressed that their rightful place is outside.

When Africans are given a pass from these temporal and spatial dynamics, it is because they are seen individually as exceptional, often women. Those universally adored like Jainaba, from Gambia, and Grace, from Togo—notable for the grave particularities of their cases, coupled with gendered perceptions of their cheery temperaments and warm demeanors—are intermittently allowed to jump the waiting queue or offered respite from the patio. On the other hand, while Farid and his friend are likewise exempted from such treatment, they are not known characters nor uniquely endeared to those at the Center.

Spatial boundaries provide for the physical deprivation of refugee bodies. Food and its consumption are hidden from those seeking assistance. Space and time are organized so that meals occur off stage, out of sight. The kitchen, where all food is prepared, is expressly off-limits to asylum seekers and refugees, and they must wait outside while officials lunch. The multipurpose room is, indeed, multipurpose. It serves as a space for assistance. It is where team meetings, public events, and volunteer orientations are held. It is also the lunchroom. During lunch, it becomes inaccessible to applicants and the Refugee Center is closed. Bounding space provides for the racial conditioning entailed in the unequal material conditions experienced by those who work and those who wait.

On her first day as a volunteer, Sofia says she is going out to get a snack, "because it's not good to eat in front of them, right?" Such comments and behaviors highlight the extent to which disparities in consumption are tacitly acknowledged. Yet they are assuaged through their obfuscation rather than their amelioration. Maintaining spatial distance makes the discrepancies in sustenance bearable for officials and volunteers. Those at the Center care deeply about assisting refugees; for many, it is an area they have actively sought out. For those like Sofia, that inequality contraposes the desire to help refugees that brought them to volunteer. By keeping themselves out of sight while they eat, staff do not have to directly confront the inequity in which they participate, and the dissonance that involves. Indeed, I did the same.

Spatial boundaries also limit contact. During a volunteer training, staff advise new volunteers how to avoid those seeking assistance. The most direct route from the legal sector to the reception office and social sector wing, which legal staff frequent throughout the day, is through the patio outside. But staff prefer a more circuitous route. Guilherme introduces new volunteers to this tactic. "When you walk through the door [to the patio] . . . you will, even you, will be grabbed by a bunch of different people to be assisted. So, we have a tactic here, a very good tactic, of going through the inside. It's very important that you do not pass through there with asylum seekers—because Nina is cooking, because there can be more private conversations." Eduarda emphasizes, "But never with an applicant, only the team."

Forced migrants try to wait less time by imploring anyone they see for assistance. In response, staff develop their own tactics of spatial avoidance to maintain order and keep the work manageable. These organizational arrangements are precipitated by the strain and overburden of the environment in which they work. I likewise went through the inside of the building and avoided the patio. But evading those seeking assistance also keeps those outside waiting in discomfort. Denying access to staff signals the social power of those who assist over those who wait.[22] The organization and structure of physical space produces social distance, stratifying "applicant" from "the team," and symbolizes and manifests a racialized political hierarchy.[23]

These logics of separation, which sociopolitically differentiate officials and volunteers from asylum seekers and refugees, extend beyond the Center. Although those assisted frequently ask, staff and volunteers are not to accept Facebook friend requests, share their personal phone numbers, or communicate directly with refugees via the commonly used social platform WhatsApp. The social distance between officials and refugees emerges as chasmic.[24] Friendship between staff and refugees is off-limits. There is also one formal way the movement of officials and volunteers is restricted: They are not to invite refugees to their homes, nor go to theirs. By extending rules of spatial and social distance beyond its walls, the Center not only maintains a set of work dynamics, but also distinguishes between seemingly different types of people.

These rules are not always respected. Lucas goes out for drinks with Adnan, a Syrian refugee and pharmacist, and other officials also casually socialize with Syrians outside work. Though Congolese come from similar class backgrounds as Syrians, such offers of friendship are not extended to them. Miguel, an asylum official in São Paulo, is close with Arabs in ways he is not with Africans. With Syrians and Palestinians, he gets together outside the office, eats lunch at their homes, and chats over WhatsApp. When I ask why he thinks that is, he reflects that it's hard to relate to Africans. "They are different. Their culture is very different, they're different . . . It's something that to this day, I don't know . . . It's a little different." In discretionarily deviating from those rules, officials tacitly enact social ties of proximity and likeness entailed in a shared whiteness.

Overburden and Beyond

When I first started doing assistance at the Center, I was very attentive to the *ficha* cards. When I looked at them, I would compare the time of arrival on the card with the current time, calculating how long that person had been waiting. It produced in me a consistent anxiety. I sometimes saw this same disquiet in new volunteers. When Sofia first starts, she anxiously asks if anyone has assisted a person, going over the cards, reminding those in the legal office that people are waiting.

Later, I experience a shift. On a particularly difficult day, I gain a visceral appreciation for why officials do not concern themselves with the time and number of those waiting. On that day, I struggle to attend the many seeking assistance. I do not stop to eat, despite officials cajoling me to do so. I do not stop working. I do not pause to use the restroom. Staff keep telling me to stop, to pause, to rest, to eat something. I do not.

By the day's end, I am made to realize this pace is untenable. Around 5:30 p.m., Lucas comes into the legal office. "Can I speak with you for a moment?" he asks. This is the only time Lucas ever sits me down to critique how I am working. He begins: "I am the last person who should be saying this, because I am the most stressed-out person in the world, but we have to look after our rhythms. Not to fall into indifference, but the work here is like this every day, you can't act like that. Everyone has their days. I have realized this. Every day someone is having one of these days. And we can't do that." He tells me, "That is not sustainable." He continues, "You cannot save the world." He repeats those words: "You cannot save the world." Guilherme joins in and reiterates Lucas's sentiment, adding, "You start to miss things, or make mistakes, or do a bad job because you are trying to do something too fast." Lucas echoes him, noting that we have to think about the quality of assistance.

After that day, things change. I adapt myself to the work conditions. I stop focusing on the time of others. Making refugees wait, and disengaging from how and for how long they do, I come to understand as central to longevity in this place. Before this, I watched skeptically as officials delayed assisting those outside as they played videogames, chatted leisurely, perused Facebook, and relaxed after lunch. My own preconceptions about how someone invested in refugee support would act and work, and my earlier sense of their seeming "fall into indifference," were challenged as I came to recognize them as shaped by the work conditions. The consistent feeling of being overwhelmed, struggling to tread water, wears officials down.[25] It stifles preoccupation with the waiting of others. Working with many applicants each day, every day, also complicates the possibility of social recognition. "I don't even remember," Lucas tells me over beers, "whom I've met before." I would come to have that same experience. Overburden can lead even those dedicated to refugee assistance to become numb to the proximate struggles of those in search of safe haven.

That it was Lucas who told me "we have to look after our rhythms" is not surprising. Nobody knows better than Lucas the toll that working at the Refugee Center can take on someone, and nobody has survived—figured out how to survive—it longer than him. For almost 10 years, Lucas has worked as a lawyer at the Center—leaps more than anyone else. Over the years, his salt-and-pepper hair has become more salt than pepper. When he first started at the Center, Lucas became disillusioned as he realized no one else wanted to "fight against the system." Lucas feels acute indignation over the absurd legal and bureaucratic injustices to which he sees asylum seekers and refugees, primarily Congolese, subjected in the asylum process.

Lucas has a range of habits and demeanors that help him cope with the fact that working at the Center feels like so much, all the time. He moves and speaks slowly and thoughtfully; neither his body nor his words ever seem in a hurry. He finds sanctuary in swimming, yoga, and meditation. He drinks tea, never coffee, and snacks on raw whole cloves. He compulsively tidies up the office. Yet despite these dispositions, given the many difficulties entailed in this work—from bearing witness to trauma and injustice, to maddening work conditions that leave him wanting to do better than he feels he is able—Lucas remains on edge. As Guilherme jokes, "We have to breathe, not be like Lucas."

Over the years, others join the Center who share Lucas's assessment that the asylum system has dire wrongs in need of redress. Yet, as Lucas and others fight against a daily wave of legal injustices, the seemingly mundane bodily inequalities around them fall outside their purview. Caught up in resolving the latest missteps by the Federal Police, or preparing for the next CONARE plenary, the racial project inculcated in their immediate everyday surroundings eludes them. As officials see the asylum world from their vantage points inside the Center, they are more apt to recognize and respond to injustices that originate from outside it than within. Prolonged habituation normalizes the inequalities ingrained in their proximate milieu. Whether unthought as the self-evident status quo, regrettably recognized and intermittently subverted, or taken as necessary, it is understood as the way things are.

Local explanations for these social arrangements—work overburden, institutional precarity, quality of assistance, maintenance of order— abound. These free-floating rationales provide a meaningful language of ad hoc explanation for why officials must be fed, why spatial and personal distance must be preserved, and why refugee time must be deprioritized. Yet these are vocabularies of motive rather than causal explanations for why such dynamics emerge; they are rationalizations, not root rationales behind the practices seen therein.[26] Transcending the sense-making of those on the scene brings new lines of sight into other driving forces, as readily visible narratives hide "the invisible which determines it."[27]

While organizational constraints and strenuous circumstances make possible the corporeal dimensions of political domination seen at the Center, they are insufficient explanations in and of themselves. Racial logics regarding who matters—not structural conditions—explain why officials eat a bountiful lunch while black African refugees endure hunger, and why no one remembers to turn on the patio's misting fan during hot days. They cannot explain why those who seek assistance wait outside without proper seating in harsh weather conditions, while those inside have cushioned chairs and air conditioning. When the UNHCR invests more funds into the Center's infrastructure, these monies are allocated to upgrade chairs inside the building, rather than providing proper seating outside. Physical abasement results from the scarcity of resources, but also their distribution. Refugees know this, and some protest how resources are allocated; they declare that the money used for lunch should be for the refugees, not staff. Yet such requests go unheeded. Moreover, while structural conditions are consistent, treatment varies. These social arrangements are not uniformly imposed. Accounts readily circulating at the Center cannot address why Antonio asks Prince to wait outside, but not Yousef or Farid. Though many are invested in justice for refugees—or, at the very least, want to help them—what that looks like in practice is underwritten by racial norms of sociopolitical worth and belonging.

Officials are not sinister masterminds; this racial domination has no strategist, and no single official pulls its strings. These patterns emerge from organizational norms and accumulated racial understandings—born from work and interaction within that context and beyond—regarding how the state works, what it provides, for whom, and how. State bureaucracies, as anthropologist Michael Herzfeld notes, are not impervious to the social meanings that circulate in the world beyond; they incorporate popular sentiments regarding race and nation in their routines of action and interaction.[28] Broader racialized norms of political worth underlie what officials take for granted, and how they carry out the work they do. Despite the intentions of those working to aid and support refugees at the Center, such dynamics mark the signification and reproduction of a largely unthought, engrained racial order regarding who matters in Brazil.

The question of waiting—its racializing uncertainty and arbitrariness—will be returned to in chapter five, which addresses decision timelines. In the next two chapters, I continue through the asylum process as the state determines whether someone qualifies for refugee status, focusing on the interview and case evaluation. The chapter that follows examines ways of seeing: how officials perceive asylum seekers and their claims. It delineates core cognitive prisms through which officials make sense of asylum seekers, and how those prisms are racialized. While questions of credibility and gravity figure prominently in the minds of officials as they adjudicate claims, how they make sense of who is believable, and who has suffered enough to warrant asylum, is neither universal nor random—it is shaped by and extends racial meanings.

3

Seeing

MAKING RACIAL SENSE OF CLAIMS

Alicia is a white, late twenties asylum official in Brasília, responsible for interviewing and evaluating applicants throughout Brazil. She shares how she feels about her job as we chat in the government building where she works, the walls lined with shelves brimming with folders full of files and documents. Prior to becoming an eligibility official, she had interned with human rights nonprofits. "It anguishes me, sometimes," she tells me, "to be on the side of the government." But she believes the trade-offs worth it. "It's something I believe in. Really, it's a job that doesn't pay in financial terms, but it's a job that I love. I come here happy to work. It's a subject I like, and I feel that I'm making a difference somehow."

Alicia cares deeply about the work she does and believes in asylum as an institution of protection. She invests energy in wanting asylum to be as fair and just as possible, and that drives how she sees her work evaluating claims. "I have to apply the Convention," she says, "to stay true to the law and the Convention." Alicia continues: "As much as I want a person to be recognized, if I don't believe that the person is really a refugee, I have to recommend rejection."

When I ask Alicia what about her work has most stuck with her for the wrong reasons, her mind turns to Africa. "When you know that the person is lying. It's horrible," she responds, "I don't know how to explain it to you, but you know, by the *feeling* . . . It happens a lot with some countries in Africa." She continues, venting: "I can't explain to you exactly, but you know that the person is lying. And that they are going to benefit, unlike another person that you know is telling the truth." She pauses. She calls this a "feeling of injustice."

In the face of her investment in the sanctity of asylum, Alicia is deeply unsettled that she feels Africans have learned to game the system. She cannot articulate why she thinks this, she just knows by "the *feeling*."[1]

When Alicia told me this, most applicants were African. They came from over 30 countries with heterogenous experiences of persecution at

the basis of their claims—from ethnic and religious to grave and generalized human rights violations. Yet Alicia ascribes a broad-swathed lack
of truth-telling to Africa. In this, she was not alone. Disbelief and doubt
imbue how officials see black African asylum seekers, interview them, and
evaluate their claims. Officials uniquely sought out and scrutinized a range
of questions—such as an asylum seeker's sexuality, travel dates and routes,
or languages spoken—in racialized and racializing ways. Even when officials believe the system unjust, or that a Congolese asylum seeker deserves refugee status, a specter of suspicion influences how they perceive
black Africans.

In contrast, officials assume—rather than doubt—the credibility of
Syrian and other Middle Eastern asylum seekers. Because of this, their
interviews take on a different tone. While Congolese refugees described
their interviews like interrogations, Syrians recounted they were short,
friendly conversations. Racial ideologies configure who is seen as believable, and they can also shape who officials think needs refugee status.

Turning to what happens after asylum claims are filed, this chapter
and the next address how officials adjudicate cases. In examining how
they make sense of claims, here I capture how the form and substance of
thought in asylum screening is racialized. While Alicia affirms the need "to
stay true to the law and the Convention," the law does not readily speak
for itself.[2] "There is always a subjective exchange," Clarice, an asylum official in São Paulo, recognizes, "between the interviewer and the asylum
seeker."

This chapter examines the frames through which officials perceive
asylum seekers as they determine who is a refugee. Frames are how we
process the world: they enable us "to locate, perceive, identify, and label."[3] They guide how people process information and make judgments.[4]
The work of the state necessitates such cognitive filters in order to distill
and make intelligible the variations of social life, and in the process it
constitutes and orders our worlds.[5] Turning to "ways of seeing" entails
an analytical shift from what officials interpret, to the racialized sense-
making entailed in *how* they interpret.[6] These cognitive dispositions matter because they guide action in asylum—with crucial ramifications for
who is determined to be a refugee and what that experience entails. As
black Africans seek asylum, and even as they ultimately obtain it, they
encounter a state that does not believe them. In their encounters with
officials, they learn that to be black in Brazil means having your integrity
and right to belong questioned.

After a claim is filed, the asylum seeker is interviewed. This is the crux
of the legal process. In interviews, officials gather information to evaluate
the credibility and eligibility of an asylum claim, assessing if the applicant

is believable and their narrative plausible, and if their claim falls within the qualifying criteria for refugee status, respectively. In what follows, I focus on race-making through two key frames through which officials interpret asylum claims as they conduct interviews and write up opinions: credibility and gravity. Credibility refers to a perception of trustworthiness and reliability, while gravity entails an evaluation of the severity of an asylum seeker's claim and experiences. While not the only frames through which officials perceive claims, they are principal and fundamental to asylum.

In examining how officials understand those they confront in their work, this chapter captures everyday cognitive workings integral to the racial project of asylum.[7] Racial notions of believability and deservingness structure how officials perceive, concomitantly racializing refugees and incorporating them into the racial political order. Exposing how racialized hierarchies shape credibility and gravity brings to the fore how racial political domination is produced as asylum actors evaluate forced migrants in Brazil.

Obtaining asylum depends greatly on how officials perceive a claim.[8] Officially, the National Committee for Refugees (CONARE) meets in a monthly plenary to vote on all asylum cases in Brazil. While asylum officials make recommendations, the final decision lies with CONARE. Nonetheless, CONARE does not meet applicants and decisions rarely deviate from that recommendation; of the approximately 1,300 cases decided between September 2015 and April 2016, only 15 claims—roughly 1 percent—had their decisions reversed from the official's recommendation. As such, how officials understand asylum seekers and their claims drives decisions. While ways of seeing matter for the official outcome, perceptions also matter because they shape how officials interact with applicants, and thus how asylum seekers and refugees encounter the state and experience their relationship to it.

Credibility

Credibility assessment hinges on officials evaluating whether the narrative, as well as the asylum seeker, is trustworthy—whether the facts presented are to be believed, and thus considered in determining refugee status. To assess claims, as Bohmer and Shuman write about the United States and the UK, asylum officers often descend into a "search for the truth."[9] Adjudicating credibility is enshrined in UNHCR procedural guidelines and pervades refugee status determination globally. The everpresent specter of lies, and determining who is lying, is paramount in asylum and positions refugees as "untrustworthy subjects."[10]

However, deceitfulness is far from a blanket ascription. Asylum seekers are not treated with equal skepticism or scrutiny in Brazil. Not perceived as a racial other, Syrians are not confronted by a system that does not believe them. In a group discussion about "who has credibility" during a legal meeting at the Refugee Center, a Brazilian volunteer reflects on how credibility is racialized. "Syrians in the United States are not going to be considered white," she notes; "on the contrary, in Brazil there is not this idea that he is an other because of color."

In CONARE plenaries, policymakers frame Syrians as credible, genuine refugees throughout the process. When a Justice Ministry representative discusses a Syrian man who applied in 2014 and never formally received refugee status, but had nonetheless obtained and been renewing the corresponding identity document, she explains it as the fault of a government procedural mishap rather than the Syrian, who is "considered a refugee in good faith." She continues, declaring that from the Syrian "without a doubt there was no bad faith in any moment."[11] There is no discussion of possible deceit.

In contrast, questions of credibility play powerfully in how officials evaluate Africans. In short, they can see them as lying. Alicia does not believe, for example, Africans who come from countries where homosexuality is criminalized and identify as gay. "He knows that if he says he's homosexual, he will be recognized," Alicia explains, "because he's been told so." Alicia's frustration stems from her sense of impotence to disprove and thus deny such claims she believes born from a concocted ring of deceit. "It is a specific claim that is very difficult to substantiate," she tells me. "There is no way to say that a person is homosexual or not. Even though I ask millions of questions . . . when you realized you were homosexual, if you've had partners . . . I will never know for sure" because that "won't tell you anything"—"it is a claim that you cannot prove." So, in the end, Alicia begrudgingly notes, "I have to recommend them for asylum." Even though such refugees obtain recognition, their intimate lives are intensely scrutinized in the process.

Homosexuality is not criminalized in all of Africa, nor are African countries the only ones that persecute homosexuality. Countries like Bangladesh, at the time a major asylum-seeking population in Brasília where Alicia worked, has up to a life sentence for homosexuality.[12] Often a legal legacy of British colonialism, homosexuality is criminalized throughout Asia, the Caribbean, and the Middle East and North Africa. Yet it is to Africans alone that Alicia ascribes the "feeling" that they misrepresent their sexual identities to take advantage of rights she does not believe they are entitled to.[13]

On the other hand, homosexuality is not criminalized in the Congo, and perceptions of disbelief manifest differently with their claims. Sara is a white asylum official in Rio de Janeiro. She previously volunteered at an NGO working with Congolese refugees, and she has written about their experiences of forced displacement and integration in Brazil. She is thus reasonably knowledgeable about and sensitive to conflict in the Congo, though she has never been there herself. At the same time, she can perceive Congolese as lacking credibility because she takes their accounts as fabrications, noting issues with coherence and consistency. Sara reflects about one such case, a Congolese woman Sara hesitated in denying even though Sara thought she was lying. "Though [the woman] tells me she comes from Kivu," Sara remarks, "for me she has never ever been there."

Sara's sense of the grave situation in the Congo leads her to waver in rejecting the claim. "To reject Congolese is always really difficult for us. For me, especially. How am I going to say that someone can return there?" She continues: "If you research the country, you will see that the situation in the country is worse today than it was three months ago, and that it only tends to get worse." But, thinking the woman "said this out of necessity," Sara still does not believe her. With the Congo, officials do not doubt that the violence happened, nor its gravity. They doubt the *asylum seeker*— whether they were there, whether they are lying.

UNEVEN INTERVIEWS

Racialized presumptions regarding credibility impact how officials conduct asylum interviews, how long they take, and the questions they pursue. I ask Alicia if there's any country infamous for taking the longest to interview. "The Democratic Republic of the Congo takes forever, *always*." Congolese refugee Frederic tells me he was destabilized by how the official asked questions during his interview. I ask Frederic what he means, and he clarifies: "It's like, they ask you something, you respond, and then a minute or two later, they come back to the same thing. The types of questions that you begin to ask yourself: 'Does this person believe me, or are they trying to find a fault?'" Though Frederic obtained asylum, as he recounted the violence that led him to flee, he felt the official didn't believe him. Lionel says his interview was like "an interrogation, I felt like a convict." Years later, as Lucas reviews a different Congolese claim at the Center, he frustratedly laments how officials "ask questions in such disgusting ways," admonishing attempts to catch Congolese asylum seekers lying during interviews.

Not all have their testimonies questioned. Because there is an assumption—rather than a doubt—of credibility with Syrians, their interviews took a different tone. This difference was notable before CONARE declared Syrians *prima facie* refugees and eliminated their asylum interview. Adnan obtained refugee status before that change. Though there was no mandate to treat Syrians differently, Adnan's interview diverged significantly from the experiences recounted by Frederic. Adnan's interview was pleasant and brief.

"It was very relaxed actually," Adnan recalls. "The person was a gentleman," he recounts. "He was smiling, and asking friendly questions really. It was not in a way that, investigating, it was more conversation." Adnan notes he was not questioned as if he were a criminal. He continues: "It was really . . . just general questions, why did you decide to come to Brazil, how did you enter Brazil . . . for me, it was short. And for other Syrians, it was the same for them. I think maybe for other countries it was a bit longer. But for us I think it was a bit shorter."

Wael, another Syrian refugee, similarly recounted that his interview "was very chill, very relaxed. It wasn't tense, in any way." For Adnan and Wael, their interactions before the state were warm, friendly, and welcoming. Syrians do not have to recount experiences of suffering before the state, nor do they have those testimonies interrogated for inconsistencies or insufficiencies. Officials do not perceive them as incredible; there is no credibility test. And Adnan recognizes that how the state treats Syrians is different and easier than others.

Syrian interviews were also abridged. "It was very, very brief," Adnan tells me, lasting "not more than 15 minutes." For Wael, his interview took "30 minutes—because it had to be translated." Interviews usually take an hour to an hour and a half. "Less than an hour for me," Sara notes, "that's an interview of a Syrian."

Some at the Center both understood the later decision to stop or streamline Syrian interviews and yet saw it as unfair. While discussing their cessation, a volunteer at the Refugee Center questions: "Why Syrians and not Congolese?" Others chime in: "It's a problem of racism," "racist understandings of credibility."

EVALUATING CLAIMS

After the interview, an official, often the same who conducted the interview, produces a case opinion (*parecer de elegibilidade*) based on the applicant's written and oral testimony as well as research on its claims. Evaluating that primary and secondary material, case opinions recommend recognition or denial of refugee status.

Pierre, from South Kivu in the Congo, fled after rebels from Burundi attacked his village. He was in church when the rebels attacked, and they persecuted Pierre's ethnic group. The ensuing massacre led him and his family to flee to Kinshasa, the nation's capital, from where they flew to Brazil and applied for refugee status.

After asylum official Bianca interviews Pierre, she drafts her recommendation. While Bianca knows of mass human rights violations and rebel-driven conflicts in the Kivu provinces, she opens the possibility of denying Pierre through a sense of disbelief. To do so, Bianca makes notes in Pierre's case regarding internal and external indicators of credibility. Officials are trained to do so, and assessing such indicators guides their work: how they conduct interviews and the lines of questioning they pursue, how they craft case opinions, and how they make and substantiate recommendations.

Internal indicators refer to evaluations of the sufficiency, consistency, and coherence of an asylum seeker's narrative. As an asylum official writes in a case opinion: "The applicant's narrative was constructed by way of sufficient and specific details about his personal experience and demonstrated internal consistency. The applicant could recount the facts in a coherent way, explaining the points questioned, in a way that it was possible to understand that his narrative satisfies the internal indicators."

As Bianca notes that Pierre does not know the name of the church where he was when the massacre began, nor of its pastor, she questions the internal credibility of Pierre's claim. Bianca does not note, however, that when Pierre was finally interviewed, it had been a year and a half since he applied for asylum, and almost three years since the attack. Nor is the impact trauma can have on memory recall considered.[14]

It is not with Pierre alone that tests of internal credibility figure prominently. With Congolese, officials give close, painstaking attention to the words said in interviews in search of incongruences. While assisting Motombo, a Congolese asylum seeker, at the Refugee Center, Lucas pulls up the draft opinion for Motombo's case in the national database. It has timestamps noting when, in listening to the interview recording, a thought, question, or comment came to the official. Such drafts, Lucas says, show "what they are thinking." "It has here all the questions they want to ask," Lucas tells us, "and all the things they think are lies."

On the other hand, there is a lack of concern with credibility when evaluating Syrian claims. As I sit in the multipurpose room at the Refugee Center, I go over the application of a would-be Syrian asylum seeker before it is submitted to the Federal Police. The asylum seeker's uncle has come on his behalf. While the application states his nephew served in the military, the questions in the form regarding what that military service entailed, and its duration, are left blank. I confirm with the uncle, "He did military service?" "Yes, without a doubt," he answers. As I ask him what his nephew did and for how long, I start to feel uncomfortable having someone else fill out these blank responses. I want him to take it back to his nephew to complete; I have been trained that individuals should not fill out applications on another's behalf. Any discrepancies between what the uncle writes and what his nephew may later recount in an asylum interview—a marker of inconsistency, an internal indicator of credibility—could be used as a reason for denial.

Guilherme, a lawyer at the Center, gets involved and interjects. With a large arm gesture, he exclaims: "Just let him fill it out!" While I worry any inconsistencies could bode poorly for the nephew, Guilherme is unfazed. For Guilherme, my request would be a waste of their time. He does not imagine a world in which Syrian credibility is doubted.

An alternative reading could suggest these differences to be a function of country of origin alone, not racialized. But, while seen most starkly with Syrians, such differences extended beyond them. Among Middle Eastern and Afghan cases more broadly, questions of credibility were not foregrounded in either interviews or case opinions in the ways I documented for Congolese and other Africans. I never heard or saw a shadow of doubt cast on an Afghan case of persecution by the Taliban, for example, analogous to what I found with Nigerians claiming persecution by Boko Haram. While not only black African applicants were subject to doubt, they were acutely so in ways I did not find with other asylum seekers in Brazil.

Because of a sense of certainty that asylum officials would not doubt or question Middle Eastern claims, legal representatives largely stopped doing interviews or case opinions of them altogether. At the Refugee Center, lawyers schedule intake interviews with asylum seekers after they submit their applications at the Federal Police. Those interviews serve the dual purpose of preparing the asylum seeker for their eligibility interview with the asylum official from CONARE, and for the Center to garner their own account of the claim. They provide the most crucial ammunition lawyers have to debate its credibility and eligibility. Lawyers mobilize those accounts when they perceive a case as wrongly set for denial. However, as noted in chapter two, lawyers rarely scheduled Middle Eastern or Afghan interviews. Because lawyers did not worry that asylum officials would burrow into their cases in search of lies or discrepancies, they did not feel inclined to prepare them for the eligibility interview nor to collect their own narratives.

As set out in UNHCR guidelines, external indicators of credibility include, on the other hand, "consistency with family members' declarations and with externally available information." As Pierre's family also applied, Bianca wrote notes to herself to use their narratives as tests against each other, to compare what each said was their religion, the name of the church, and their ethnicity; and to compare their statements about the attack in the church, the escape, and coming to Brazil—the airport, for example, she notes. By questioning the airport, Pierre's travel route gains significance in testing credibility, though legally immaterial to evaluating the merits of his claim.

Nor is it with Pierre alone that travel routes gain such import. A sense of disbelief is a well-worn cognitive canyon with Congolese migratory paths. Frederic vents about this based on his years translating in asylum interviews. "The first thing that I think is wrong with asylum," Frederic says, "is that they ask all these travel questions, about how they traveled." "You don't even remember what day you traveled," he continues. "People err with this. That shouldn't enter." He knows how inappropriate and unsensible it is to ask such details to test credibility, but finds it happens prominently with the Francophone Africans he translates for. In such ways, details irrelevant to eligibility can be used to discredit asylum seekers. This is so common that, in the intake interviews they schedule, lawyers at the Refugee Center orient asylum seekers that their travel dates and routes will be part of how the official tests if they are telling the truth. In contrast, when Syrians were interviewed, officials did not compare their family members' statements, they did not scrutinize whether their narratives were coherent and consistent, nor did they pursue details about their travel in order to search for lies.

Credibility can also provide a cognitive shortcut for quickly denying Africans, even when substantial evidence signals the gravity of the claim. Emmanuel suffered violence in his home country and fled to a refugee camp in Benin. The camp was frequently attacked, and Emmanuel endured more violence. The camp was destroyed. Emmanuel had "documentation of basically all that he lived," Ana tells me, including photos from the camp. Nonetheless, Emmanuel was denied based on credibility. The case opinion asserted that his narrative was not credible because he had failed to prove his nationality. Because Emmanuel got a passport when he was already in the refugee camp in Benin, he had a Beninese passport. Inside, it declared his actual nationality. But, Ana shares: "The state didn't check the inside of the passport. They saw that the passport was emitted in Benin, but didn't see that [inside] it shows his birthplace." The case of Emmanuel stuck with Ana, "not because of the case itself," she tells me, but "because of the response of the state." Emmanuel was denied and awaited a decision on his appeal. Because racial notions shape who is assumed readily incredible, Africans like Emmanuel can be denied even with corroborating evidence. On the other hand, Syrians are recognized without any at all.

Officials can also perceive black asylum seekers as lying because they see lots with the same story. While consistency with compatriot accounts could suggest credibility, racialized sense-making could lead to the opposite. During research, I documented no instances of officials doubting clusters from outside Africa. Bianca, who interviews predominantly Congolese and other Africans, reflects about hearing clusters of similar stories: "I think what was almost scary was that the stories were almost identical. Many stories that the asylum seekers would bring were the same thing, and eventually you would hear the same thing always, all the time . . ." I ask Bianca how she handled that, and she responds: "I was a bit desperate because . . . on top of thinking that the stories were lies, you are kind of trying to rescue the asylum seeker from that repeated plot . . . It was like I was trying to say: 'Help me help you. Please tell me something that is a little different.'" A perceived lack of novelty leads to questioning the veracity of the claim. "We always hear the same story, from the same city—30 times," Guilherme similarly notes, and "you begin to discredit."

"I even discovered later," Bianca continues, "that there is a name for this: *credibility fatigue*. It's when you're tired of hearing the same story." That's when Bianca asked for a break because, "as much as I don't want to, I'm going to end up violating someone's rights." Bianca cares deeply about trying to do right by asylum seekers. She asks for a break because she is anguished that she may not.

Internal and external indicators of credibility mark a relatively recent conduit for racialized impressions of disbelief in Brazil. In 2014, a UNHCR consultant from Canada was brought for a training that institutionalized credibility as a criterion. "The whole world went there to study credibility analysis," Guilherme tells me, and "it started being taken up." He continues: "There was a whole restructuring of the work of CONARE." With that training, credibility became formally incorporated into official procedures, including as one of the three sections in a case opinion.

While such mandates help structure the form anti-blackness takes in the minds and practices of officials, they are not its root. They do not explain why disbelief comes to the fore when officials encounter black Africans, nor why they closely interrogate the claims of Congolese like Frederic, Pierre, or Motombo. Moreover, officials sought out lies and incongruences long before credibility became formally codified. Frederic's interview occurred many years prior. Lucas worked in asylum long before that restructuring. Yet, he reflects, "When I first started, I got training I didn't like." He continues: "They wanted me to look for lies, to see if people were lying, like a detective." At that time, the vast majority of asylum seekers came from Africa. Rather than mark a top-down imposition, such reforms gave new structure to preexisting racialist tendencies involved in the forming of what asylum official Hugo called an "official's impression."

In Lucas's telling, CONARE had in his early years always been led by people who were conservative, who looked for whatever reason not to believe the applicant. While, over the time I know him, Lucas holds out hope that a range of political and institutional shifts will change this proclivity to doubt, they do not. It continues across changes in government and rotations of officials and representatives. Driven by racial ideologies of worth and belonging pervasive in Brazil—rather than party politics—meant change came instead from encountering Syrian refugees.

The training officials receive cannot alone explain racialized ways of seeing in asylum. There was no formal orientation for asylum officials until 2015, when a two-week training was instituted during a massive restructuring. That training, co-led by CONARE and the UNHCR, covered the governing laws and procedures, as well as how to conduct interviews and evaluate asylum claims. There is also an annual end-of-year training on a designated topic, such as exclusion clauses. Multiple officials lamented having called on the *coordenação*, responsible for overseeing the process, for more training to no avail. As Daniela, an official in São Paulo, attests, the two-week training was "pretty little for all the work that it would be to run an office without anyone in charge."

Nor can it be explained as a top-down imposition from administrators. As Daniela signals, officials work with great autonomy. Rarely has someone overseen their work. The position of eligibility coordinator, who reviewed officials' case recommendations, was relatively short-lived, and the offices in Rio and São Paulo did not have on-site administrators. In a year and a half, the *coordenação* changed four times.

Furthermore, it is not a consequence of individual prejudices. The disbelief of Congolese and other Africans is pervasive, seen diffusely across the refugee regime. For example, asylum officials, lawyers, and volunteers alike think some who say they are Congolese are instead Angolans trying to pass as Congolese in hopes of obtaining asylum.

Guilherme asks Frederic, "How do I say 'thank you' in Lingala?" Frederic responds: "I don't know in Lingala, but in Kikongo." Lucas quickly retorts: "You wouldn't pass the credibility test!" The room breaks into laughter. Though both languages are spoken in the DRC, Kikongo's status as an official language in Angola as well calls into question whether its speakers really are Congolese. As Lucas's retort signals, language is another way racialized disbelief manifests in officials' assessments.

Lawyers and volunteers at the Refugee Center likewise doubt Africans are who they say they are, using language to judge incredibility. "People will say they are Congolese," Guilherme notes, "but with Angolan accents in Portuguese." Volunteer Matilde comments about a woman she thinks is Angolan pretending to be Congolese. Matilde notes: She didn't interact with the people from the Congo, "you could tell she understood" Portuguese, and she translated for others. Though the woman translates between Portuguese and French—the latter an official language in the DRC but not Angola—her familiarity with Portuguese is used to discredit her. So too is her decision not to socialize with Congolese, though there are many reasons why someone would not. Moreover, decades of protracted conflict in the DRC and Angola have pushed both groups back and forth across the border, explaining why some Congolese speak Angolan Portuguese.[15] Nonetheless, while known to the lawyers at the Center, such alternative explanations do not register. Though aware there could be other reasons—and they have no way of truly discerning—the disbelief remains. To Matilde's doubt, Lucas mentions none of this. "Yeah," he assuages, "there are definitely times that happens. Sometimes they just lie."

Lucas, however, sees nothing wrong with lying. He rationalizes it as a reasonable response to an unjust system.[16] Deceit before the state does not produce a "feeling of injustice" for him as it does Alicia; it is instead asylum itself that causes such sentiments. He does not take refuge as sacrosanct. He deeply believes it needs to be totally reimagined for refugee justice and autonomy. And, consistently confronted by official evaluations of Congolese as incredible liars, Lucas prioritizes getting Congolese recognized above other claims.

Lucas was not alone in normalizing perceived African lies. So too did Sara think that the Congolese woman she believed lied to her "must have had a reason for doing so." Lucas and Sara saw lies as understandable responses to the limited model of refuge that confronted them. They continued to see Congolese claims as grave and eligible, and wanted them to get refugee status. Nonetheless, Lucas and Sara still thought they could be dishonest.

In sum, anti-blackness structures credibility. It does so in ways both configured by and that transcend mandates and trainings, individual proclivities and positions, and institutional epochs. Notions of black deceitfulness, present in the world beyond asylum in Brazil, take on particular shapes and meanings through the cognitive frames of that field, as officials alone and together figure out—through thought, practice, and interaction—how to make sense of those before them.

Gravity

While credibility hinges on believability, gravity entails making sense of who needs and deserves protection. I use the gravity frame to refer to an evaluation of severity, in type or degree, of an asylum seeker's past experiences and future possibilities—their characteristics, experiences, or circumstances. It has multiple manifestations, such as perceptions of whether an asylum seeker has suffered severely enough to warrant refugee status, has migratory options beyond asylum available to them, or presents a threat to national security. It appears most often in how asylum actors perceive the type and degree of violence or persecution underlying the claim. In this way, the gravity frame is key to how officials evaluate whether an asylum seeker is eligible for refugee status, as inscribed in international and national definitions. Such assessments uphold the ideal of asylum as an exceptional category of protection, but they also take on a range of roles that limit applicants' access to asylum and shape the racial political domination that manifests.

VULNERABILITY

Marie, from Central Africa, applied for asylum based on many years of domestic violence at the hands of a family member. At a Previous Studies Group (*Grupo de Estudos Prévios*, or GEP) meeting to discuss the cases slated for the CONARE plenary that month, officials and representatives debate the merits of Marie's case. "If it was a case of forced marriage," Paolo, Foreign Relations Ministry representative, says, "I might understand. But here she doesn't even say he beat her that much."

Paolo does not dispute that Marie suffered gender-based violence, which could legally qualify her for asylum based on persecution as a member of a particular social group. He does not perceive her as lacking credibility. He believes her. But Paolo does not think the account violent enough. He disputes whether the violence she experienced is sufficiently grave to warrant asylum, as is his mandate. Gravity appears as a cognitive prism through which to evaluate the gender-based violence Marie suffered.

However, gravity also constructs and channels a broader evaluation of Marie's need and deservingness to question her claim. Others at the meeting pointedly note the lack of suffering in Marie's life more generally. "But her [relative] helped her pay for her studies," the CONARE coordinator retorts, "so she had to be grateful for that." "In [her country]," the coordinator continues, "it's not just any woman who makes it to university." An asylum official notes that Marie had been in a good position back home, because she had worked in an international NGO. In such statements, members display that they perceive Marie as unsatisfactorily vulnerable— because she went to university and had a stable job.

While the question of gravity follows from the law in evaluating the gender-based violence she suffered, officials and representatives debate the severity and magnitude of her suffering more broadly. Escaping beyond the bounds of the law, officials come to evaluate not only the gravity of the violence at the basis of the claim, but the whole circumstances of the life she fled. Through the expanded domain of gravity as a way of seeing asylum seekers, and not just their claims, Marie's socioeconomic status—though legally irrelevant—obtains meaning in determining her claim. Marie is recommended for denial.

It is principally with black Africans that such filters of socioeconomic gravity open the possibility of rejection. It is not in Marie's case alone that questioning a lack of economic vulnerability, legally immaterial to refugee status determination, appears. In 2012, during a slow day in the cubicle at the Refugee Center, Lucas says that if asylum seekers show up with an earring, or a cellphone, officials are likely from the start not to listen to them and to deny the application. At the time, most asylum seekers came from Africa, and Lucas refers to African applicants in his telling. In such instances, judging a lack of economic vulnerability provides for rejection—regardless of the violence or persecution their claims may detail. As we see in chapter six, however, a perceived lack of economic need among Syrians is imagined as a positive asset for Brazil, not a reason to cast doubt on whether they are truly refugees.

Gravity as a cognitive filter also involves questioning the merit of the *type* of vulnerability at the basis of the claim. The refugee definition is exceedingly narrow in the types and experiences of suffering that fall within its mandate—even with the expanded definition seen in Brazil's Refugee Act. While asylum actors judged Marie and other Africans for not suffering economically, on the other hand, when they express economic motivations for migrating, such applicants are seen as demonstrating the wrong type of vulnerability.

However, seeking economic stability and fleeing violent persecution can coexist in the minds and lives of any refugee. Frederic speaks on the impossibility of disentangling economic motivations among those who flee as refugees, "because," he articulates, all refugees—whether "Syrians" or "Congolese"—"are normal people who have strategies. They do all the stuff people do." He continues: "You will not be able to find a person who wasn't also here for economic reasons." "This separation," Frederic says, to distinguish the refugee from "the person who searches for better living conditions," is impossible. "Always part will be about better living conditions—it will always be part, because it is *human*." Even officials recognize the difficulty of disentangling economic and other motivations. "Congolese have always shown us," Lucas notes, "that this distinction between refugee and migrant is arbitrary. We will never have sufficient tools to make those determinations."

Frederic knows that it is not with Congolese alone that economic concerns imbricate the decision to flee, and recognizes this with Syrians as well. Though Frederic knows multiple drivers underlie the displacement of any refugee, he also knows—and I found—that economic motivations of Syrians and other Middle Eastern refugees do not appear in how their claims are adjudicated. Questioning the economic vulnerability of Arab applicants—whether having too much or not enough—does not inform the evaluation of their claims as it does with Africans like Marie.

At the Refugee Center, Firas, from Syria, turns his asylum application in to me so I can review it before he takes it to the Federal Police. As I do, I see that in response to the most important question on the form—"Please explain why you decided to leave your country of origin or habitual residence and seek protection as a refugee in Brazil"—he wrote only that he wants to work. He does not name any violence or conflict as driving his migration to Brazil. Firas breaks the assumption that all Syrians obviously have the right type of vulnerability, or, in the language of the refugee definition, that they have a fear of persecution. In his application, Firas does not articulate the gravity sought after by officials in African claims. Because economic motivations are not pursued as a reason for Syrian denial, Firas will undoubtedly receive refugee status—regardless of the narrative he presents.

INTERNAL DISPLACEMENT

Gravity, at its core, is about evaluating whether someone is in desperate need of international protection. While it guides a focus on type and degree of suffering, as with Marie, it also leads to evaluating whether the individual has other migratory options available to them—in other words, if international asylum alone will bring them safety. This involves questioning if an asylum seeker could have, in the eyes of the official, found protection by fleeing internally to another part of their own country, rather than seeking refuge outside that country's borders. Case opinions include a question on the alternative of internal displacement. It asks: "Does the applicant have the possibility of returning to any part of that country and living reasonably without fear of persecution or undue difficulty?" Formally embedded into the structure of the case opinion, it is seemingly a prism through which to evaluate all claims.

However, questioning whether an applicant can avail themselves of other alternatives does not come up in all cases. The option of internal displacement appears as a filter for denial primarily in African claims. During my fieldwork, Nigeria, Mali, and the DRC were the only countries for which that filter was discussed or employed. I ask Lucas if internal displacement as a reason for rejection "has ever been used in relation to the Middle East? Pakistan, Afghanistan? Or only African countries like Nigeria and Mali?" He cannot think of such an instance for the former. The possibility of internal displacement appeared as a patterned path for denying African asylum seekers.

While the option of internal displacement sporadically peppered the evaluation of Congolese cases, and appeared with Malian claims, Nigeria epitomizes how this came to play in asylum in Brazil. Nigerians fleeing Boko Haram are perceived as having other options for safe haven—the country conditions are judged insufficiently grave for refugee status. Most Nigerians applied for asylum based on persecution by Boko Haram, a violent insurgency organization that has killed tens of thousands, engaged in bombings and massacres, and became infamous after its mass abduction of 276 schoolgirls in 2014. By 2015, the conflict had displaced over two million. Boko Haram operated primarily in northeastern Nigeria. This made, in the minds of officials, the rest of the country safe.

Reflecting on a GEP meeting she attended where all Nigerian cases up for debate were slated for rejection, Sabrina, a lawyer at the Refugee Center, notes: "They don't want to pass Nigeria . . . They always decide the cases of Nigeria saying they had the option of internal displacement." Even if an applicant lived in eastern Nigeria, Sabrina recounts, she was still perceived as having the option of internal displacement because "she wasn't born there," so the analysis was "she could go back to her place of birth." Or, "if she was born in eastern Nigeria," they said she could instead go back to where she lived. There is a consistent questioning if Nigerians need to be in Brazil. This perceived lack of needing international protection made them deniable. Two-thirds of Nigerian asylum seekers were denied asylum in Brazil during the height of the conflict.[17]

Though officials recommend denial in Nigerian claims when they did not first attempt to migrate internally, this rests on shaky legal and empirical grounds. The law does not mandate that an individual first seek safe haven within their country before availing themselves of international refuge. As Sabrina notes, it is "only a supplementary criterion." The Refugee Convention does not require refugees first dislocate internally before they look for asylum elsewhere; it does not have to be an option of last resort. But, in the face of Nigerians, the interpretation of the Brazilian government is different; they are expected to migrate internally and deny them believing they have no need to come.

With claims from Nigeria, the possibility of internal displacement was applied stringently and liberally. While concentrated in the Northeast, Boko Haram had engaged in violent attacks throughout Nigeria and in neighboring countries. According to the UK Home Office, Boko Haram expanded its attacks outside the north to Abuja, Lagos, and other states in the South—holding partial control of more than 15 areas of the country.[18] As Ana writes in a northern Nigerian case opinion: "The US State Department publicly recognizes that places outside of Northeastern Nigeria are targets of violence and attacks perpetrated by the group Boko Haram . . . the extremist group expands its targets of attacks to regions beyond northeastern Nigeria, which is in line with the expansionist principles of the group's activities and with news broadcast in local and international media."[19] The US State Department recognized that Northern Nigeria was "not a region free of the religious conflict that plagues Nigeria." While reports from other countries' state departments affirm the violent and volatile situation in regions outside the Northeast, officials saw even neighboring states, including those in the North, as sufficiently safe.

"I don't know why, really," Sabrina reflects, "Brazil didn't want to receive Nigerians." "I don't know if it's because there existed some fear of many Nigerians coming here, or if it was drug trafficking." She continues, "which shows that asylum decisions are also very political: Who do we want in the country." She reemphasizes this point: "Today my impression is that the Brazilian process, it is much more political than legal." It is political, and those politics—"who do we want in the country"—are racialized. While evaluating gravity is crucial to adjudicating who is a refugee in Brazil, anti-black racism shapes how that frame manifests.

GRAVE AND GENERALIZED HUMAN RIGHTS VIOLATIONS

Brazil's 1997 Refugee Act expanded the refugee category beyond the 1951 UN Convention. It includes not only those fleeing individual persecution, but also contexts of grave and generalized human rights violations (GGHRV)—whereby the local circumstances from which applicants fled are understood as grave enough to warrant protection. It can be used as a motive for recognizing individual cases, applied to a specific country region, or a blanket extension to an entire country—the latter of which has occurred with Syria, Venezuela, and Afghanistan during the last decade.

During a legal meeting at the Center, Lucas discusses the criteria CONARE employs to determine GGHRV. He incisively reflects: They use "skin color, too, though they never want to admit it [*nunca querem assumir*]." He's just returned from a plenary session where GGHRV was discussed for Mali and Palestine, and those conversations proceeded very differently. Lucas senses that color impacts when CONARE determines

GGHRV applies. Racialized hierarchies that imbue color differences shape the ease or hesitancy with which officials and representatives adjudicate who experiences broad enough conditions of gravity to merit asylum.

CONARE has been disinclined to extend GGHRV to Africans or Haitians. Beyond Venezuela, it has appeared principally with refugees from the Middle East. Excluding Syria and Venezuela, which had seen blanket extensions, among individual cases recognized under GGHRV from 2016 to 2020, 82 percent were from the Middle East versus 15 percent from Sub-Saharan Africa. Few Congolese refugees were recognized on this basis during that period (7%), while it was the primary reason of inclusion for refugees from Palestine (72%) and Iraq (65%).[20]

This reluctance became palpable in discussions about Mali in 2016. Over several months, asylum actors engaged in contentious debates about for which years and which regions Malians qualified under the GGHRV mandate. That year, CONARE planned to reject dozens of Malian claims, judging the country conditions now safe enough for their return. This included applicants who arrived in 2013, during the height of a violent armed conflict that displaced almost half a million, one of the most acute in the world at the time.[21] Facing pushback, Mali was removed from the plenary for further review and discussion. Civil society representatives argued that CONARE recognize 2013 claims under GGHRV given when they fled, so as not to penalize them for the delay in adjudication. Claims made after, participating civil society organizations proposed, should be evaluated based on the specific region and year of application, with GGHRV variably applicable. Officials and representatives also debated whether GGHRV applied broadly, or only in the North. While the CONARE coordinator initially agreed to recognize 2013 claims under that mandate, a few months later CONARE changed its position, and set to rejecting cases from 2013 onward. Civil society representatives pushed back that they at least be reinterviewed, arguing their initial interviews were premised on GGHRV, and thus did not explore possible inclusion due to individual persecution.[22] In the end, all were rejected.

No legal procedure demands restricting GGHRV regionally or temporally in such ways. For Syrians, Afghans, and Venezuelans, that extension was not tempered or restricted. When CONARE determined that conditions in Syria constituted a generalized state of violence and human rights violations, there was no discussion whether there was any safe place where Syrians could go inside national borders, as seen with Mali. Afghanistan was recognized, without spatial or temporal restrictions, as a context of GGHRV in December 2020, months before the political upheaval seen with the United States' withdrawal. Notably, in contrast with Syria and Afghanistan, the recognition of Venezuela as a situation of

GGHRV in 2019 was arrived at begrudgingly in practice, following years of discussion in CONARE meetings. While ultimately celebrated as affirming Brazil's vanguard position, representatives noted GGHRV could be revoked at any time.

At the same meetings Malians were ultimately denied such protections, officials and representatives also discussed extending recognition to Palestinians in the Occupied Territories under GGHRV. Those conversations proceeded quite differently. There was general agreement that Palestinians qualified under that basis, without temporal or spatial restriction. As GGHRV applies to everyone within a designated area, the primary question was instead about whether every person—including Israelis—in the territory would be recognized. "The thing is," a UNHCR representative tells me following that meeting, "GGHRV has to be for everyone." The issue was not about restricting Palestinian access, as with Mali, but that all and only Palestinians qualify for that protection. That year, Palestine was the second largest nationality recognized under that mandate, after Syria; though the DRC was the top recipient from Africa, double as many Palestinians as Congolese obtained asylum on that basis.[23]

NATIONAL THREAT

The Federal Police participate in the asylum process and have a vote in CONARE. How the Federal Police see gravity differs from the forms of evaluation seen among other officials. Rather than perceive gravity through an asylum seeker's suffering or vulnerability, the Federal Police see it in the threat they pose for national security—whether their presence makes the nation-state vulnerable. The Federal Police focus on the possible threat an applicant poses rather than on the gravity of the circumstances of the claim. Frames do not exist uniformly across the minds of participating actors, as they are dynamically entwined with the domains and positions from which they are formulated and enacted. Motivated by different perspectives, investments, and dynamics, the form and content of ways of seeing vary. Among the Federal Police, the primary concern is a racialized fear of who is coming and what threats they bring.

While the 1997 Refugee Act is broadly progressive, it includes exclusion clauses. Asylum cannot be invoked in Brazil if the refugee is considered a danger to national security or the public order. The Refugee Act provides for denying refugee status due to participation in acts of terrorism or drug trafficking. These are present concerns among the Federal Police. As Samuel, a participating UNHCR officer, tells me: "This is something the Federal Police brings."

Notably, in earlier years, Federal Police officers did not perceive Mid-

dle Easterners or Afghans as a national threat. "The idea that Arabs are security threats in need of surveillance," as anthropologist John Tofik Karam
writes, "does not resonate in Brazil."[24] In 2013, Wahed, an Afghan engineer, who contracted with international companies, applied for asylum
following persecution by the Taliban. While conversing privately about
his case, Lucas pontificates about how the Federal Police will not treat him
like the Africans they usually see, because of Wahed's different profile—
his class and because he is "white," Lucas notes. Rather than fear they will
respond to him poorly or think he is a terrorist, Lucas presumes Wahed
will experience unusually favorable treatment. Lucas was right. The police
officer instead found it humorous Wahed was applying for asylum in as
violent and dangerous a country as Brazil. The officer pulled up his own
shirt, showing scars of bullet wounds. He saw Wahed as under threat in
Brazil, rather than a threat to it.[25]

However, external influence from the United States led to a radical
shift. Ahead of the 2016 Olympics, American law enforcement and intelligence services became highly involved in the Brazilian government's
security preparations. Federal police and other units received counterterrorism trainings from the United States for many months prior, with
dozens traveling to the United States to observe security efforts at events
like the Super Bowl, the US Open, and the Boston Marathon.[26] "They
went to some talk," Guilherme retorts, "and now they're crazy about terrorists." How the Federal Police perceived some from the Middle East
and Afghanistan transformed. They pushed for Syrian interviews to be
reinstated to screen for terrorists. This reconfigured cognitive frame was
triggered with others from the region as well.

As I assist an Angolan asylum seeker at the Federal Police Office in Rio,
an officer explains to her why the police have the screening procedures
they do. "We have people from Iran, Iraq, Afghanistan," so we have to do
um filtro bonito—a good filter—so "we don't cry later." By this he means
to make sure they aren't violent militants. This "good filter," present after counterterrorism exchanges with the United States, included visits to
homes. Sima, from Afghanistan, obtained refugee status with her husband
and daughter because of persecution by the Taliban. She comes to the
Refugee Center in shock that the Federal Police came to her house and
took pictures of her documents, wanting to know how many people lived
in her home. As Sima recounts her consternation, Guilherme adds, "They
are doing that now with Syrians." They also went to Father Benicio's par-
ish, which has offered shelter to predominantly Syrians but also asylum
seekers from around the world. "They are crazy," Guilherme responds.
"That is our Federal Police." Through a reconstituted racialized frame of

national threat, the Federal Police began to equate refugees like Sima and her family with the dangers they fled.

The fear that nationals from the Middle East and Afghanistan would make them "cry later" was not endogenous to Brazil. As Wahed's experience suggests, that racialization of gravity by the Federal Police was not always present among them. Geopolitical influences transformed how they perceived and interacted with such asylum seekers.

Given the nature of its external introduction, the sense Arabs and Afghans were possible terrorists was not diffuse across the refugee regime.[27] While Federal Police officers came to see them as security threats, others perceived them as refugees. Grant rates among such groups are high: Syria (98%), Iran (88%), Iraq (98%), and Afghanistan (94%).[28] As volunteer Fernanda prepares to orient a new Syrian asylum seeker at the Center, she asks Guilherme if there's any particular information she should give him. "It's really just about cases of exclusion," Guilherme responds. He explains: "CONARE says exclusion cases include people who were military, or those who come from regions without conflict." But he signals with his tone that it really doesn't matter. "Even so they are passing."

While the perception of such forced migrants as a national threat appeared after being introduced from abroad, asylum actors have often evaluated black Africans as endangering the nation. With the Ebola outbreak in West Africa in 2014, the Federal Police came to see Africans broadly as a threat to public health. In August of that year, the Federal Police put together a list of African countries they would not assist because of Ebola. Included were countries that had not registered a single case of the virus, like Ghana.[29] In doing so, they restricted such nationalities' access to the asylum process, as it is at the Federal Police Office that an asylum claim must be filed. "When they arrived at the Federal Police, the entity to which refugees are sent on their arrival in the country," as Serricella writes, "they had difficulties being served due to the fact that they are Africans."[30] The Ebola outbreak produced a diffuse sense of threat among police that led to discrimination in the face of diverse African nationalities.

In contrast to the seeming possibility of Arab terrorists, which appears as a concern among the Federal Police, other asylum actors likewise perceived Africans as a threat due to trafficking. Though neither are noted in the law, the Refugee Act's exclusion clauses expanded in practice to include involvement in arms and human trafficking. In 2012, a notion emerged among asylum officials and CONARE representatives that Senegalese were engaged in arms trafficking. As Lucas frantically retorts, now everyone "has the idea that anyone from Senegal, you have to tell the Federal Police!"

In 2016, fears of a human trafficking network emerged after a few African applicants provided largely identical green identity certificates declaring they were born in the same place in the Congo. Legally, neither entry with false documents nor irregular entry should come into play in asylum screening in Brazil, with the understanding that individuals flee under whatever possibilities are available. Nonetheless, the specter of a smuggling ring appeared. "Fuck," Lucas says, appalled by the leap in judgment. "What do they have in their heads?!" Guilherme and Lucas sit side by side in the lunchroom at the Refugee Center, conversing in hushed tones about the accusation of smuggling. Lucas says: "If they keep looking for this trafficking ring—which they are not going to find—nonetheless they are going to produce crime . . . If someone pays, it is because the system is unjust." Lucas continues: "If they do this investigation into the ring, everyone is going to be thrown into the same bag."

Drug trafficking, formally included as an exclusion clause, is another example of how refugees are seen as a potentially grave threat to the country. How that filter materializes, who and what is imagined as participating in drug trafficking, however, highlights how anti-black notions of threat underlie its enactment. How this plays out in practice is with Africans.

Daoud is an asylum seeker from Mali. The Federal Police add an addendum to his application declaring he served time in prison for drug trafficking. Daoud had been found in Rio with a kilo of cocaine seven years prior. He spent four years in prison. Though Daoud served his sentence, the Federal Police foregrounded his criminal antecedents as the way to perceive him—as an unending threat to the public order.

While drug trafficking concerns configure how officers perceive Africans from multiple countries, principally Angolans, it does not drive how Latin Americans are filtered. This is surprising because Brazil emerged over the last decade as a vital transit point of cocaine smuggling from Latin America to other regions, given that Brazil neighbors three major producing countries, Colombia, Bolivia, and Peru, from which more than half of the cocaine seized in Brazil has originated. As specialist Paula Miraglia attests, "Drugs for these violent markets are supplied principally via Brazil's land borders."[31] Empirically, then, fearing Latin Americans as drug traffickers would make more sense as a generalizable fear. At the time, they made up 8 percent of asylum decisions, and represented 25 percent of immigration to Brazil over the decade prior, for which the Federal Police are also responsible.[32] Yet the specter of such criminality principally followed Africans.

Such forms of discrimination—the perception of Africans as a national threat due to imagined arms, human, or drugs trafficking—are not a fact to which those refugees are unaware. When someone asks Frederic about prejudice from other refugees, he doesn't know how to answer the question. "There is much more prejudice from the Federal Police than from other refugees."

Racial ideologies and hierarchies shape, and are reproduced through, the cognitive frames through which asylum actors perceive asylum seekers and interpret their claims. Such frames are integral to how refugee status determination unfolds. They inform who is interviewed, how an interview proceeds, and how cases are evaluated. Racial notions—of believability and morality, worth and deservingness—are refracted through the ways of seeing in Brazil's refugee regime, and in ways irreducible to individual discretion or what is written in law. Through cognitive frames, asylum actors bring abstract policies into being. While formal policies help structure their implementation, investigating such policies through the perceptions that constitute their enactment shows how the shape and form of those policies shift in racialized and racializing ways.[33] These frames racially situate and differentiate foreign newcomers before the state from which they seek safe haven, in ways entwined with and separate from the legal outcome.

Continuing through the asylum process, the next chapter turns from ways of seeing to practices of knowing: the techniques of knowledge production and evaluation entailed in asylum. It addresses how the epistemic practices employed reproduce a white logic, as officials make knowledge claims from nowhere that know no bounds.

How are you to prove the obvious
when proof thirsts to loot self-evidence
like a pirate thirsting for a lost ship?

The obvious is defenseless like a gazelle
stabbed by safety, like you.

Like you in this field wide-open to armed archeologists
who never cease to interrogate you:

Who are you?

You check all your body parts and say: I am myself.

They say: Where is the proof?

You say: I am.

They say: This is not enough.

MAHMOUD DARWISH, "In the Presence of Absence"

4

Knowing

"It's the reliving," Yornella, a Congolese refugee, recounts. "To tell the bad things you went through. It's like you're reliving everything." For Yornella, her interview was the most difficult moment of the asylum process. When the asylum official started asking questions, Yornella reflects, "I became very emotional. I couldn't get myself to speak. I became very scared, and I started to live everything that happened there. I was living that movie. Everything got mixed up in my head, and I couldn't. I wanted to just sit on the floor, I couldn't bear it. It was very intense for me."

It was the interview that did it. "Before, I didn't even have any emotions. I wasn't afraid, not at all ... My emotions were from having to speak. It was that pain. To speak of the things that I had lived, that I live. It was just, I was reliving the memories, those moments, those bad moments that happened." The interview forced Yornella to confront emotions and memories she otherwise managed to keep at bay.

To be recognized as a refugee, Yornella had to expose her inner world of painful memories to the state for its dissection. The encounter of the asylum interview—by forcing a bureaucratic confession, calling her to open herself up to relive traumas she did not want to—dominates rather than empowers refugees like Yornella as they submit themselves before the state. On the other hand, Yornella does not even know the name of the official who interviewed her.

Her asylum interview was an exposure of a particular kind, focusing in on what was individually felt and experienced—precisely what was so difficult for Yornella. "It was very emotional. She was asking the questions and I was just there to answer . . . It took a long time. It took a long time because she had a lot of questions, to know what it was like. 'And you were where?' and I'd answer. 'What was your path like?' and I'd say all the way I went until when I arrived here." The asylum official controlled the narrative path of the interview, reshaping and reorganizing Yornella's memories as they saw fit. Yornella did not have the autonomy to share her testimony in her way. She instead felt she was only to answer the questions she was prodded with.

In the Congo, Yornella worked as a project manager for an NGO focused on improving the lives of those in vulnerable conditions. She has a bachelor's degree in International Relations from the best university in the country. In her interview, the official asked Yornella what the weather was like as she fled and about the details of how she made it to Brazil. She did not, on the other hand, despite Yornella's skills and intellect, ask her about the context that led her to do so—a subject about which Yornella is well versed academically and professionally. By constricting questions to her body—what it felt, where it was, what it went through—the interview limits her being and shrinks her humanity as she seeks to claim a stable place in the world.

This chapter addresses the practices of knowing in asylum: how officials produce and search for truth to determine who is a refugee. It focuses on the relationship between race-making, knowledge, and the body as officials conduct interviews and produce case recommendations, as they extract and analyze asylum seeker claims regarding what happened to them. Racial political meanings are embedded in the disparate treatment of bodies and knowledge in asylum. As officials delimit who can know what, those epistemic boundaries produce racial meanings, disempower racially othered newcomers vis-à-vis the state, and reinforce white racial domination in Brazil—even in the face of those who obtain refuge as Yornella did.

The pursuit of truth is racialized, and a white logic structures the epistemic practices of (dis)embodiment seen in asylum in Brazil. In the process of constructing and evaluating knowledge, asylum seeker knowledge is constricted, while white official knowledge is not. As noted in chapter one, almost all asylum officials self-identify as white. In the face of predominantly nonwhite asylum seekers, official screening practices particularize their knowledge and seek out their embodied experience, pursuing truth as found in and from their bodies.[1] Rather than take seriously the knowledge of those most closely affected, organizational procedures disallow such asylum seekers the right to analytical thought and deny them claims to general knowledge. Yet not all refugees are subjected to reliving their trauma in the ways Yornella was. Such epistemic practices can be bent or reimagined. Refugees racialized as white in Brazil often did not have their bodily experiences pursued, nor their knowledge tested or particularized in the ways black African asylum seekers did.

While officials compulsively embody nonwhite asylum seekers, devaluing and circumscribing what they know to their bodies, they concomitantly disembody themselves and lay a monopolistic claim to knowing and seeing without bounds. In doing so, they practically enact the epistemological privileges of whiteness—as officials demand to see while remaining invisible, as they decide what is and is not knowledge, as they claim an unbounded authority to know and be unknown.

These practices form part of the epistemic logic of asylum, constitutive components of its *raison d'être*—determining who among asylum seekers is a refugee.[2] Questions of truth and knowledge are central to asylum: who has the authority to know, how one knows, and what signifies legitimate proof. Officials are not mere analyzers of evidence. They do not simply establish facts. As they carry out their work, interviewing applicants and making evaluations, officials construct the meanings of knowledge and define what counts as truth. "How different claims to truth are adjudicated," as sociologists Claudio Benzecry and Monika Krause write, produces a particular "kind of social order."[3]

How officials produce and analyze information is underpinned by a white logic whereby truth and racial power are mutually constituted. A white logic, following sociologists Tukufu Zuberi and Eduardo Bonilla-Silva, exists when white supremacy defines "the techniques and processes of reasoning," and the epistemic tools and practices employed support a racial hierarchy. In such contexts, the foundational principles of knowledge grant "eternal objectivity" to whites, while condemning nonwhites to "perpetual subjectivity." A white logic fosters a "debilitating alienation" that marks racially oppressed people as "incapable of meaning making" while cultivating in whites "a sense of superiority, a sense they know things."[4]

Epistemic practices of (dis)embodiment play a vital role in how a white logic manifests in asylum in Brazil. The body, its differential treatment and visibility, is crucial to the operation of racial power between states and migrants.[5] (Dis)embodiment captures an arrangement of separate yet interrelated practices of disembodying and embodying knowledge whereby different epistemologies govern different populations, demonstrating what Miriam Ticktin calls a "dual regime of truth" in asylum integral to racial political domination.[6] Embodied knowledge refers to "knowledge that cannot be easily dissociated from the personal qualities of its bearer," while, in contrast, disembodied knowledge is that where the producer of knowledge is understood as irrelevant.[7] Extending Donna Haraway, I find that asylum seekers are racialized as they are taken as "embodied others, who are not allowed *not* to have a body, a finite point of view, and so an inevitably disqualifying and polluting bias in any discussion of consequence."[8] In stark dichotomy, officials enact a "conquering gaze from nowhere . . . that mythically inscribes all the marked bodies . . . claim[ing] the power . . . to represent while escaping representation."[9]

Rather than the consequence of a particular subculture or individual prejudice, these epistemic practices permeated asylum across individual officials and institutional epochs. Sometimes they followed from procedural guidelines, other times they were deviations. While officials strove to work in ways to not marginalize applicants, the epistemic practices of asylum construct racialized subjects. To echo Scheurich and Young, it is not that officials are "involved in a racial conspiracy or moral bad faith, but that these individuals can only name and know from within the social context . . . in which they live [and work]."[10] As the racial political order is refracted through the asylum process, white supremacy shapes its practices of knowing—even as the state grants safe haven.

Official Bodies

The asylum interview is a crucial moment of contact between officials and applicants, and officials learn how to handle their own bodies during such interviews. How asylum actors carry their bodies and tactically interact with asylum seekers is seen as important enough to be part of the sparse training they receive. This training includes how to navigate physical touch when an asylum seeker cries, and how and when to establish eye contact. Bianca tells me she was also trained "to imitate the [asylum seeker's] body, to be like a mirror." How officials handle their bodies is seen as shaping the quality of an interview. As Sara tells me: "[The asylum seeker] must have confidence in you . . . if not, the person is not going to tell you what you need to find out. I think this is only through contact. Through that contact when I look at her . . . In some way, I need to connect with that person . . . I would try to laugh about something, to show I wasn't a robot." Officials are keenly aware of their own bodies during interviews and consider how they handle their physical presence crucial to an interview's success. This is why Sara tells me, "I am so against interviews done by videoconference, I think I would refuse to do one."

Officials also recognize the impact such work has on their bodies. When I ask Isabela, an official in Brasília, about her work experiences, her thoughts turn to her own body. She neglects her body to carry out the number of interviews required of her. "We didn't manage to eat, to get up. We couldn't drink water." Isabela continues, "We avoided drinking water so we didn't have to get up [to use the restroom]." Officials also understand and receive training on the emotional impact of conducting asylum interviews. During a workshop with a psychologist, Sara learns "to see that, in the end, many feelings are involved in all these activities." She continues, "Even if you must maintain a distance, you are going to absorb something from that person's story." It is not women officials alone who feel the impact. "Every time I hear a story," Hugo, an official in São Paulo, shares, "it touches me somehow . . . you get a little broken [*você fica meio quebrado*]." As Bianca notes: "My primary problem is at home . . . these thoughts keep invading my mind. There's even a manual . . . that had a funny test I kept sharing with other officials if the applicant's post-traumatic stress impacts you. The questions were: 'Do you have invasive thoughts? Do you feel depressed? Do you feel tired?' All the answers we marked were yes." "We also need a therapist," Bianca adds. Officials were aware of the deeply intimate impact their work had on them—their bodies, feelings, and thoughts.

Yet, while officials were cognizant of their own bodies and emotions during interviews—navigating physical contact, making a point to laugh, ignoring the need to use the restroom, neglecting hunger, or learning how to handle their emotional responses to asylum seekers' narratives—they omit themselves from the case documents they produce, enacting a white epistemic privilege of disembodiment in the work. This can have negative consequences for how asylum claims are perceived and evaluated.

Disembodying Officials

Officials enjoy the privilege of a non-corporeal identity as they adjudicate claims. Refugees know little about the officials who interview them—they may not even know their names. Expunging themselves from documents, officials obtain a screen of invisibility. Early on, they did not write their names in the recommendations they produced because there was no designated line for them to do so. The official's presence in an interview is effaced in case files. When officials transcribe and summarize interviews, they do not capture their own words or record their conduct in them. Officials do not document their physical engagement with asylum seekers—when or how a hand is touched, a laughing joke introduced, eye contact maintained. They do not record their somatic state—whether it was the last interview of the day and so they were tired and worn down. Nor do they note limits in their language skills or knowledge of situations referenced—whether they were unfamiliar with a word used or event mentioned. Though officials engage many of these issues in trainings, and reflected on them in our conversations without prompting, they are not included in case files. There is no documentation of the official's somatic state, interpersonal engagement, or subjectivity. Not including the questions asked during interviews, or other details about the official, impacts how a claim is perceived. Subsequent readers do not know whether details were spontaneously given or elicited and how.

These practices can have deleterious impacts. Stephanie, from Nigeria, was set to be denied. When Sara interviews Stephanie, Sara feels she is unable to establish that personal connection she finds so important to a quality interview. Stephanie does not go into detail. "I tried to draw out her story," Sara recounts, but "she would only say to me: 'That stuff with Boko Haram, that stuff with Boko Haram.' But she didn't develop that at all." Sara recommends rejection because "based on the account she gave . . . there was no way." But, as they discuss Stephanie's case at the GEP meeting, Ana shows that Stephanie's interview at the Refugee Center had been quite different. It had been a much fuller account. Based on that discrepancy, Stephanie is withdrawn from that month's plenary and scheduled for a reinterview. Her second interview with Sara goes very differently. As Sara recalls: "It was a day that I was alone in CONARE . . . And I thought, well, I am going to use this to my favor. I chatted with this woman for like 40 minutes before starting the interview, with the recorder turned off. I asked about her life, how she was doing . . . all that conversation to create the ambiance . . . And then, finally . . . she told me, for real, what had happened to her. It was in fact a case of gender violence, a very delicate topic." Sara writes a new case opinion and, "thank God," Sara says, Stephanie is recognized as a refugee.

As case opinions do not discuss interpersonal dynamics—to do so would entail inscribing officials in files—the practices of official disembodiment preclude reflective consideration of any difficulties in establishing a personal connection in an interview. This issue appeared acutely for women asylum seekers, given the intimate nature of gendered and sexual violence that appeared at the basis of many women's claims. At the same time, men could likewise struggle to recount the torture, violence, and degradation they experienced. Because details on the rapport established are not included in case opinions, they are not considered in determinations, easily leading to the rejection of refugees like Stephanie. Sara's first case opinion recommended denial, not a second interview. Though officials know these dynamics matter, standard bureaucratic procedure leads officials to speak from nowhere—an epistemic privilege of whiteness—and trumps the possibility that they would be considered as officials determine who is a refugee.

Officials expunge not only their bodies but also their words, though here too, they know their determining value. As Sara tells me: "In the training, they were very emphatic in trying to pass on to us the way of asking the question. In a way to not induce the person, and to make the person understand exactly what we want." UNHCR guidelines note that officials should maintain detailed interview transcripts including the precise questions asked. Yet, officials' questions are not documented in case files.

Their verbal presence in the interview exchange is not recorded. This occurs even though interviews are not structured or uniform; officials do not use interview guides. And it happens although officials drive the flow, order, and structure of that interaction—deciding the line of questioning, what to ask about, in what order, and when to elicit more detail. Officials do not include their own words in either the interview summary reports or case opinions they produce. In interview summary reports, officials only record asylum seeker responses, beginning each new line with "that"—"that he has two sisters," "that he was born in Kinshasa," or "that with the money he earned, he heard talk of a boat going to Brazil." In case opinions, officials summarize asylum seekers' statements without noting how that material was elicited. This erasure continues throughout the case opinion; when officials include quotes from interviews in their analyses, they remove them from their context in the interview. These were standard bureaucratic practices of the work, seen across officials no matter their role or background. Officials erase their own prompting words and questions, regardless of the gender or class position of the asylum seeker they evaluate, enacting a white logic that provides officials the unique power of invisibility and disembodiment.

When asylum seekers' words are divorced from the prompting questions, they can contain multiple meanings that come to bear in case evaluations. In an interview report for an African applicant, official Vitor writes "that he wants to work." In reviewing Vitor's interview summary, Maria, a legal volunteer at the Refugee Center, becomes flustered and frustrated. Maria volunteered at UNHCR prior to coming to the Center, and recalls how important it was for UNHCR to know, as a participating member in CONARE, whether something was asked or if the person offered it up. Maria continues: "If someone says, 'I want to work in Brazil' it's very different than if Lucas says, 'Do you want to work in Brazil?' and the person responds, 'Yes, I want to work in Brazil.'" Without situating it within the interview exchange, in other words, without the words of the official, it is unclear how to evaluate that information. The statement may have emerged unprompted. Or Vitor possibly asked, "Do you want to work?" and the applicant responded that he does. That might seem the appropriate answer. Expressing a desire to work could indicate the asylum seeker does not wish to be a burden on the state. As Mimi, a refugee from the Ivory Coast, put it, in reference to her subsidy assistance: "I don't want $300 *reais*, I want employment!" Yet, because officials' practices disembody and erase their own determining participation in cases, it is unknown whether a question produced this response. Writing "he wants to work," without context, frames the applicant as an economic migrant and thus seemingly not a refugee. Expunging an interviewer's words could instill doubt in the motives of asylum seekers. Though Maria pushes Lucas to get officials to clarify in interview summaries whether such statements were solicited, her requests go unheeded. Despite Maria's apprehensions, such erasures were a standard epistemic practice across the sites of asylum during my years of fieldwork.

At the same time, such practices could be bent for forced migrants racialized as white in Brazil. For Syrians, these issues and concerns do not appear. When they stopped being interviewed, there were no official questions to erase and their cases could not be undermined through such practices. Yet it is not for Syrians alone that such exceptions could be made. Wahed, an engineer from Afghanistan, was persecuted for contracting with the Afghan government and North American entities. After the Taliban assaulted him in his home, he fled with his wife and traveled aimlessly throughout Latin America before eventually applying for asylum in Brazil. As noted in chapter three, Lucas affirmed that, in Brazil, Wahed was white.

For Wahed's interview, I was instructed to produce a word-for-word transcription. It is a five-page, single-spaced document. We deviate from standard procedure as I am guided to record the words of the interviewers and inscribe them in the text. The transcription includes full exchanges, including the interviewer questions, such as "You owned your own company?" To which Wahed responds, "Yes." When confronted with an applicant racialized as white, officials can be more reticent to disembody themselves in ways unthinkingly done when interviewing racially othered asylum seekers.

Embodying Refugees

Epistemic practices of (dis)embodiment triumph through the written word. While officials omit and invisibilize themselves in case files, they take note of nonwhite asylum seeker bodies and make them exceedingly visible in text. Officials document not only their words but their corporeal and emotive responses. They expect such asylum seekers to speak from and with their bodies, foregrounding them as they carry out their work. While UNHCR standards encourage documenting relevant observations of demeanor and behavior, how this manifests in practice signals how the epistemic privileges of whiteness mark asylum seekers as racial others disallowed the disembodiment that bureaucratic procedures afford officials.

The bodies of nonwhite asylum seekers are highlighted through a line of questioning ("Was it hot?") and the inscription of bodily responses into interview reports (noting whether an applicant "starts to cry" or was "laughing"). Through such practices, as Miriam Ticktin writes, officials

construct the asylum seeker's body "as a site of truth and authentica-
tion."[11] Officials could seek truth not through asylum seekers' claims, but
through their bodily demeanor. In the interview report for a Congolese
asylum seeker forced to live as a sex slave, for example, the official writes
"that she does not show emotion when speaking about that." Seemingly
objective and innocuous descriptors are anything but, as they provide an
avenue to question asylum seekers' claims to refugee status.

These practices are not aberrations, but instead a standard part of,
as lawyer Guilherme notes, "the criteria by which they will be judged."
Lawyers at the Refugee Center inform nonwhite asylum seekers that not
only what they "say" is relevant in interviews, but also how they "act."
Emotions and "whether they give *sensorial* details," lawyer Ana explains,
enter evaluations. "It is necessary," she advises, "to explain about what
was seen, but also what was heard and felt." Like whether it was hot or
cold, Guilherme notes. In the search for precision and conclusiveness,
in the face of irresolvable uncertainty about eligibility, officials engage
in racializing practices that ascribe truth to the asylum seeker body.[12] As
Guilherme explains during a volunteer orientation at the Refugee Center: "The law says that you cannot require refugees to provide any documentation; so, since that cannot be a process of proof, a mechanism was
constructed . . . that ends up creating a certain model of a refugee . . .
Eligibility has to do as well with the person's behavior. If the person is
smiling while telling a sad story, this will be considered. It values the person's suffering . . . our role is to prepare people to know what will be the
criteria by which they will be judged."

Not all asylum seekers are subject to lines of questioning and evaluating that constrict truth to their somatic selves. Even before Resolution 17,
Syrians were not obliged to speak from their bodies or confess intimate
histories of violence in interviews. After it, they became largely exempt
from interviews altogether. However, in this Syrians are not alone. Other
Middle Eastern asylum seekers also experience such procedural bending.
As noted in chapter two, Middle Eastern and Afghan interviews were
rarely scheduled at the Refugee Center. In deciding not to carry out interviews with such applicants, they were exempted from having to relive
their traumas—precisely what Yornella felt to be the most emotionally
disturbing and challenging part of the process. Lawyers at the Center did
not worry that CONARE eligibility officials would burrow into the embodied details of those claims in the search for truth. Because of this, they
felt no need to prepare them for it. Such practices of knowing through the
body were tacitly recognized as particularly present with black Africans.

For applicants racialized as white in Brazil, bodily responses can be
muted and downplayed rather than foregrounded. While Syrians most

starkly demonstrated the racialized underpinnings of the epistemic logic of asylum, it is not for them alone that practices would bend. Mark, a Christian Palestinian who lived in Israel, applies based on experiences of hate and discrimination. He says he was derided as an "Arab" and "traitor," was almost arrested for having the wrong documents, and had guns pointed at his face and was forced to remove his clothing at checkpoints. The asylum interview entails no questions about the sensorial details of those encounters—he is not asked what he saw, heard, or felt—nor does the official take note of how Mark acted as he recounted them. There is no mention of his physical state, emotional behavior, or embodied presence in the interview report or case opinion. Mark's body—in either his lived experiences or during the interview itself—is not inscribed into his case file as a site of truth in the ways I documented with black Africans.

This racialized discrepancy occurred at the Refugee Center as well. As we interview Wahed, he begins to cry. I write in my field notes: "He rubs his eyes. We wait a few minutes together in silence . . . The wife exits . . . He gets out a hanky and wipes his eyes with it," and "the whole time, [his wife] is crying." Yet, there is no mention of either's emotional state in our lengthy interview report. This diverges from standard procedure at the Center. When I ask Ana and Guilherme how they respond when someone cries, they both note that they inscribe it in the interview summary.

Increasingly perturbed by the role such evaluations play in the adjudication of Congolese and other black African claims, Lucas writes an email to Guilherme, Ana, and me: "We need to include in the conversation with applicants that they must be prepared for the expectations interviewers will have in relation to many things, which are not just discursive . . . in addition to talking about what interviewers assume with true speech [*discurso verdadeiro*]—fluency, coherence, motivation—we have to talk about expectations about expressions—emotion, physical expression, etc.—and also about what they expect about their profile (including the clothes they wear)." Lawyers at the Center did not have such conversations with Middle Eastern applicants, because lawyers did not worry they would be subject to such expectations.

The pursuit of the body in interviews led to irrational practices. If the asylum seeker flew to Brazil, Bianca asked what they ate on the plane. On reflection, she knows this is absurd. It has no legal relevance for determining eligibility. Yet she couldn't stop herself from chasing such details, thinking she would "find the meaning" (*resgatar o sentido*) of the asylum seeker's claim. Months later Bianca would pick back up interviews, she tells me, and they wouldn't make any sense. She would spend so much time testing credibility through such questions, she'd later discover she didn't have the real "content," as she put it, that mattered. More focused on the airport someone flew through, or what was served on the plane, Bianca compulsively pursued bodily experiences to the extent she neglected the real basis of claims. The white logic permeating asylum screening in Brazil led Bianca to engage in unconscious habits of seeking truth through the racially othered body that, upon later contemplation, she realized was immaterial to her legal objectives as an official.

Though similarly irrelevant, travel routes and trajectories are foregrounded in interviews, particularly with Congolese and other black Africans, as noted in chapter three. Vitor is infamous for asking "absurd questions," as Adriana, the coordinator of the Refugee Center, puts it, about travel itineraries—time, duration, dates, layovers. Adriana explains why she thinks these questions are unfair: "You know, sometimes people are in the bottom of boats, in the dark. Sometimes they have no idea where they are going or where they've been through until they arrive here. Sometimes people sleep! You don't know how long you were in the plane—you slept!" Exceedingly hard to remember, such interrogations can leave asylum seekers feeling off-kilter and like they do not know what the official is signaling truly matters. Adriana continues her vent: Vitor has no shame "in being racist." By calling those practices "racist," Adriana intuits who is subject to them. This is so common that, in the orientations they schedule, lawyers at the Center alert asylum seekers that travel dates and routes will be part of how officials pursue the legal meaning of their mobility. Mark, the Christian Palestinian, on the other hand, was not asked such questions.

Such practices of burrowing were not unique to Vitor. Lucas vents to me about how traveling has entered into adjudication. "You have no idea how much time is wasted on that," he shares, recalling a discussion at a GEP meeting about a Congolese asylum seeker who had gone to China. "They spent so much time going back and forth, trying to figure out: 'What do you think he was doing in China?' 'Well, I think . . .' 'Well, maybe it was . . .' 'And how did he get to China?' 'What do you think he did while he was there?'" As Lucas recounts it, he imitates the curious, gossipy tones with which officials prodded together into details of the man's life irrelevant to their task at hand. "What does how they escaped," as Guilherme reflects during a volunteer orientation, "have to do with establishing a well-founded fear?" Nonetheless, Guilherme adds that he likewise asks how they came, even though "it doesn't make much sense." The focus on travel—irrelevant to establishing the merits of a claim—displays the practical emphasis on locating predominantly black bodies in time and place.

This search is not innocuous. The operation and experience of the interview affects the political subjecthood forged, and the relations the state establishes with those seeking its protection. For many, the asylum interview is the only time forced migrants personally encounter the governing body that decides their fate. In the penetrating pursuit of truth from their bodies, asylum seekers lose control over who knows and what is known about the intimacies of their lives. They are racialized and politically dominated as their reserves of the self must be exposed and violated to obtain asylum—even for the many who do.

The compulsion to bring the body into being in files also means asylum seekers must complete applications in their own handwriting. With Congolese and other Africans, this requirement was incessant. Frederic had been helping Africans fill out the form but, when Frederic's handwriting became recognizable by CONARE officials, this became a serious issue that threatened to undermine their claims. I and others at the Center were instructed to "get them right as they come in and make sure they know they have to fill out the paperwork."

Many experience this as humiliating. Raimundo, from Guinea-Bissau, comes to apply for asylum at the Center. He asks if his Guinean friend, who attends university in Rio, can help him fill out the application because of Raimundo's limited schooling. "I only finished second grade," he admittedly pleads. "My writing is horrible." The idea of doing it himself provokes a feeling of incompetence. In this, Raimundo was not alone. After her claim is denied, Anália, from Angola, comes to complete an appeal. She asks me meekly, "Can you write it?" She is embarrassed by her penmanship; "My letters are so bad." I check with Guilherme whether this is possible. "No," he responds, "she has to write it." Rather than empowering, the moment when applicants enact their right to claim asylum can trigger a sense of public shame and personal inadequacy. They are forced to do something they do not want to do, that they feel as an acute mortification of the self.

Failing to do so can be a basis for rejection. At the beginning of interviews, officials ask whether the applicant filled out the form. Gabriel fled Nigeria after Boko Haram bombed where he worked. But, because Gabriel said he did not fill out the application himself, the official disregarded it entirely and recommended Gabriel be denied. The weight placed on writing in your own hand signals the disquieting epistemic meaning attached to the asylum seeker body, one of the multiple ways it was materialized and inscribed in files.

However, that practice of embodiment could also bend. In contrast to the experiences of Gabriel and other black Africans, Syrians did not have to submit claims in their own hand to be seen as genuine refugees by the state. Sama and her Syrian family applied for asylum three months after fleeing to Brazil. In the case opinion, the official writes that his recommendation is "based on the analysis of information contained in the asylum application filled out in her own handwriting." This is dubious. Though the family affirmed they did not speak Portuguese in their declarations at the Federal Police, each form was completed fluently in Portuguese and appears written in the same hand. It is doubtful Sama and her family completed their applications. Nonetheless, this is neither noticed by nor of consequence for the adjudicating official.

More generally, Syrians are not forced to be visible or confess their truths to obtain asylum. In their applications, Syrians often leave whole pages blank, decidedly declining to fill out the information requested. One of my primary tasks at the Refugee Center was to review applications after asylum seekers filled them out, noting questions left blank or filled out inaccurately. We then would go through the form together and I would have them complete each question left insufficiently addressed. But, with Yasser's almost blank application form—itself composed of 20 pages with roughly 65 questions—I only request that he confirm he is Syrian and whether he has been accused of a crime. Given CONARE's efforts to streamline the process and grant Syrians asylum, I knew Yasser did not have to render his inner fears and personal history visible to obtain refugee status. In an analysis of refugee claims filed nationally, other researchers similarly found Syrian refugee applications and case files uniquely and notably incomplete, and how "many of the questions on the forms were left blank."[13]

Constraining Refugee Knowledge

Kemi is from Nigeria. After Boko Haram burns down her house, she flees to Brazil and applies for asylum. In her interview at the Refugee Center, Lucas asks Kemi what her job was, the violence she experienced, and if she could identify the attackers. He asks about her religion, and whether she had ever been to or knew anyone in Brazil. Lucas does not ask Kemi about the sociopolitical context of Nigeria, Boko Haram, or the passing of recent legislation—all central to her case. Although Lucas had no prior knowledge of Boko Haram, and knew little about Nigeria, he did not ask her anything beyond her personal experience, even though Kemi had the language skills, political awareness, and education to do so.

While officials focus on the bodies of nonwhite asylum seekers as the site of truth—asking applicants to explain the physical attacks or threats they experienced; and the dates, times, locations, and details of those events—they concomitantly constrain, particularize, and devalue their capacity for thought. Officials do not ask applicants about the wider contexts that give meaning to their experiences of violence and persecution. Not asking such questions marks an important epistemic practice: You are not allowed to teach us. You have no knowledge of value to this process beyond your first-person account. The conduct of the interview is geared toward the asylum seeker sharing what they witnessed and experienced at the level of the body, not what they know at any abstract level. In doing so, such forced migrants are encountered and interacted with as if they know nothing of substance.

As we sit at a table in the CONARE office in Brasília, Alicia reflects on how she conducts interviews and the types of questions she asks. If she has to ask about political persecution, she establishes whether they belonged to a political party; if so, which party, their role, and if others recognized them as a member. One of the ways of getting at that, Alicia explains, is asking about "the clothes they wore." To evaluate such claims, Alicia does not tell me she asks what they know about the party—its political platform, history, organizational structure—but instead how they adorn their bodies. Such epistemic practices neither engage asylum seekers as thinking beings who know things, nor provide space for refugees to assert themselves as such.

Unbounding Official Knowledge

Unrestrained by their bodies, officials' evaluative practices enact the white privileges of knowing and seeing without bounds. They become panopticons. No information, knowledge, or claim to epistemic authority seems off-limits.[14] Officials prod deeply and intimately into refugee lives, and they work as if all knowledge falls within their reach.

Those who work in asylum have an unbounded panorama of sight. There is no limit to who can access case files. Volunteers alike have free rein, often including the national database that extended beyond the cases they worked. Fernanda, a white legal volunteer at the Center, was responsible for producing case opinions and acutely considerate about accessing asylum seekers' files. In the beginning, she kept asking permission to print a case opinion and take it with her, or to access SEI, the national database, from her home. She would ask with a tone of uncertainty, feeling it was something she did not know if she had a right to be privy to, given the sensitive nature of information in files. In this, Fernanda was unusual. Her attentive concern genuinely surprised me. Lucas's response was always positive: "You may, you may." Over time, Fernanda came to realize that unfettered access to the lives of others was standard practice. Lucas had moments when he worried about this, but it was part of how the refugee regime worked, how the work got done.

The power dynamics of this visibility are not benign. When the delicate details of human life are "collected and recorded in a dossier [readily] available to staff," as Erving Goffman writes, it entails "a violation of one's informational preserve."[15] When asylum seekers cannot decide who can cross into their lives and access their intimate details, it marks an invasion of the boundaries of the self. Because Syrians and other Middle Eastern refugees were not obliged to offer up such intimacies in case files, their beings were not violated in such ways.

Jonatan applied for asylum in Brazil after fleeing Eritrea. He deserted the army from which he was conscripted to attend his father's funeral. When he was found, he was tortured and imprisoned. He managed to escape. If he returned, his desertion could lead to further torture, arbitrary imprisonment, or forced military service—as has been the case for others in Eritrea.

CONARE denies Jonatan's claim, based on Vitor's opinion recommending rejection. In his few-paragraph analysis of the case's merits, Vitor writes that Jonatan says he was conscripted into the army and was in charge of other soldiers. Yet, Vitor writes, Jonatan does not know the name of his gun and, when naming his rank, calls himself a "soldier." Vitor asserts that any military in the world has a competent hierarchical structure whereby mere soldiers are not in charge of units of men, and that all military men of the world would have the minuscule competence to know the name of their guns. Vitor calls this "the universal professional level of the armies of the whole world."

While Jonatan's interview was conducted in English, without the aid of an interpreter, his English is quite poor. "The reality for many asylum applicants," as anthropologist John Campbell notes, "is that while they may speak a number of languages, they do so only partially and imperfectly."[16] In preparing his appeal, I discover Jonatan's limited vocabulary in English does not include captain, lieutenant, or any other term denoting a higher military rank. Jonatan's language skills lead him to approximate his post with "soldier." Nor did Vitor consider that Jonatan knew the name of his weapon—just not in English. In a follow-up interview for his appeal, Lucas asks Jonatan to name his weapon. Jonatan responded that in his country they called it a "Kalashi." He then draws a detailed sketch rendering of an AK-47, or the Kalashnikov.

"Could it be that with disembodiment," anthropologist Michael Taussig asks, "presence expands?"[17] Disembodiment provides for a white epistemic authority without bounds, denying the recognition of official knowledge as partial or incomplete. The practices through which this manifested in Jonatan's case were multiple. Vitor does not imagine a military could work any other way than how he says it does, and he does not think Jonatan could know more than him in this regard. Vitor allows for himself a universal knowledge regarding militaries that was not restricted to his own experience, nor does he evaluate the particularities of the Eritrean context. Vitor does not ask Jonatan about the situation in his country or the nature of its military, even though Vitor does not seem to think language would impede Jonatan's ability to do so. Practices of official disembodiment allow for bombastic claims. While officials constrain what such asylum seekers can know to their bodies, in contrast, they can make definitive, authoritative evaluations about matters on which they have no studied expertise. Echoing Aimé Césaire, when asylum officials believe they "alone know how to think" and racially othered newcomers are "incapable of logic," they enact a racist epistemic logic that marginalizes asylum seekers—even when they obtain asylum.[18]

Devaluing Asylum Seeker Truths

In case recommendations, officials enact a hierarchy of knowledge that places the declarations of nonwhite asylum seekers at the bottom rung— their truth and reliability inherently, readily, and easily brought into doubt. To evaluate asylum claims, as Alicia and others told me, "we try to separate the material facts." They take the dates and places specified, and look for evidence—from a variety of electronically available sources, with varying degrees of validity—to confirm, or discredit, that the threat identified by the applicant existed in the time and place indicated. Any source that questions those "material facts" can bring the request for asylum into ill repute. While in interviews officials engage asylum seekers as somatic vessels of embodied experience—but not of general, abstract knowledge—as they produce case opinions, they privilege their own and other disembodied knowledges. The authority to decide what is ultimate truth is an entitlement of whiteness. Taken together, these practices of knowing engrain a relational, racialized epistemic line of political domination.

To research claims, officials rely heavily on Refworld, a website database of reports "carefully selected and compiled from UNHCR's global network of field offices, governments, international, regional and nongovernmental organizations, academic institutions and judicial bodies."[19] The reports available on Refworld are produced by government and nongovernmental entities such as the US State Department, the Immigration and Refugee Board of Canada, Human Rights Watch, and the UN Security Council, among others.

Officials rely on a wide choice of other materials as well, including media reports, academic sources, and seemingly anything on the internet. While officials do not prefer any particular news organization, they generally limit their sources to news in languages they speak. These include the *New York Times*, BBC, *Pakistan Today*, or an op-ed published in a local Colombian newspaper. Clarice, a white official in São Paulo, tells me she has used gender theorist Judith Butler in opinions, and another cites postcolonial theorist Edward Said. Any internet source can be employed, including sites of unverifiable caliber, rigor, or political intent, such as: the Cuban Communist Party website, the online sociocultural Cuban magazine *Convivencia*, the Girls Not Brides campaign website, or Radio Okapi in the DRC. Lucas admits to having used personal blogs in recommendations. Officials also cite Wikipedia. Emiliano, a legal volunteer at the Center, heatedly critiqued how officials substantiate case opinions. "It seems like they're doing homework for elementary school. Because you grab someone's case opinion, and there are three Wikipedia articles there? Like, are you kidding me?! [*Está de sacanagem com a minha cara, né!*]"

A lack of institutional oversight provides for loose and idiosyncratic practices in case analysis. Consistent, however, is that seemingly any disembodied knowledge—any knowledge claim uncoupled from its producer, where the actor responsible is unknown and their subjective position unknowable—can be used to prove or discredit asylum seekers' accounts. While civil society representatives were unlikely to recommend cases for rejection, I found little difference in the research practices employed across Refugee Centers or CONARE offices in Brazil. Despite their possible biases, such sources are taken as legitimate and objective at the moment of evaluation. Though officials learn in their two-week orientation training "what is information and what isn't," as Luis, a white official in São Paulo, puts it, and "what can be used for the case opinion and what cannot," in practice, I found that seemingly anything on the internet could be mobilized as information. While Alicia tells me, "It is a lot more difficult to do a case opinion of rejection" because "you have to argue very well the denial," I did not find this to be the case in my analysis of case opinions. While some officials recognized the problems regarding interviewing practices noted above, I registered little consideration of the fallibility of these sources as avenues to evaluate claims.

The Refworld database is unresolvedly incomplete and at times dated. As anthropologist Anthony Good attests, State Department reports "tend to repeat themselves year after year, and are not sourced."[20] Nonetheless, they are presented as truth in case files. That officials can singularly assert them as such marks another epistemic privilege of whiteness in asylum; as they declare such sources to be knowledge, they practically become what officials proclaim them to already be: undeniable fact.

These epistemic practices ignore inequalities in internet usage and knowledge production, and the geopolitical interests that influence the production (or lack thereof) and character of such documentation. Some conflicts receive more attention by human rights organizations and news outlets than others, while the unequal distribution of internet use globally also determines what knowledge and how much becomes available through such searches. As political scientist Bruno Magalhães writes, in places like the North Kivu province in the Congo, "human rights violations can go on for weeks, without a single report to confirm that they ever took place."[21] And "official sources," as Guilherme notes, often "provide 'cleaned' information." Guilherme references the political motivations of US State Department reports, which skew and impact what information they note and how it is framed. There are many reasons to be concerned that such sources are held as more authoritative than the accounts of asylum seekers. Nonetheless, it is how the work of evaluating who is a refugee gets done. When I produced case opinions, my research practices were analogous; I reviewed Refworld and tried to find anything on the internet to substantiate an asylum seeker's account.

The epistemic practices of case production and analysis work in tandem to devalue nonwhite asylum seeker knowledge. I take notes while Lucas interviews Djo, from the Congo. Lucas does not ask him questions beyond his experience. Rather than learn the violent political context of Djo's city from him, organizational procedures entail looking for such information elsewhere. The resulting case opinion uses reports from the UNHCR, Integrated Regional Information Networks (IRIN), UN News Service, Amnesty International, BBC News, and Human Rights Watch—which confirm and thus legitimate what Djo narrated. The recommendation discusses the use of violence against civilians, particularly rape; limitations on journalist freedom of expression; and the state of general violence and fear in his province. No one asks Djo about these topics, though central to his case. Lucas does not ask Djo how to spell the names of the cities Djo references, instead guessing their spellings in hopes of later finding them online. When Djo references the "rebels" in his interview, Lucas does not ask him the name of the group. Internet searches, not Djo, clarify who the rebels were. Guessing this information in the meantime conceals the bounded, limited nature of officials' knowledge—that there are things they do not know. Disembodied digital documents, not Djo, confirm that the conflict happened and his case is worthy of refugee status.

These epistemic practices can lead to a different outcome. During his interview, Benjamin, from Nigeria, explains in great and consistent detail his experience of being at a church when it is bombed by Boko Haram. But the adjudicating official finds no external corroboration. Because the official finds no news coverage of the bombing, he doubts its occurrence. The official recommends Benjamin be denied because, even though his claim is not refuted, neither can it be confirmed. Benjamin is rejected and files an appeal. In this, as detailed in the following chapter, Benjamin was not alone. Other black Africans similarly shared his fate when officials were unable to find reports confirming the violent incidences that catalyzed their flight. Indeed, they are also denied when they exist aplenty.

On the other hand, for claims from the Middle East, officials often proceeded under the presumption that they were credible and confirming evidence would be found. Recognized as *prima facie* refugees, Syrians do not have the merit of their claims individually evaluated. Yet, even before this designation, their claims were tacitly recognized as irrefutable truth not subject to close interrogation and triangulation. This was the case for Sama and her family. Her case was adjudicated before Syria was taken as a context of grave and generalized human rights violations.

The official's opinion, which recommends recognition, claims it is based on the information presented in Sama's application. Instead, it is a boilerplate opinion with no proof the official read or evaluated her file. Sama writes that they are killing everyone in the war in Syria—especially intellectuals, lawyers, and doctors—and threatening the lives of her children. She's a lawyer, while her children are students, doctors, and pharmacists. Her daughter says her school was a target of bombs and missiles, and many other students have been killed or kidnapped. Another daughter survived a bomb that went off at her workplace. For these reasons, they fled to Brazil.

Not yet declared a situation of grave and generalized violence, the recommendation underscores "that the objective situation in the country of origin, *per se*, is not the only nor a sufficient element to satisfy the granting of refugee status; it is necessary, therefore, that it negatively impacts the applicant's life." Despite this, the official does not assess how Sama and her family claim the conditions in Syria affected their lives. No interview was conducted, so the official does not know where and when the attacks happened, which went unclarified in their applications. In the opinion, the official makes no mention of any details at the basis of Sama's claim. It vaguely affirms the emergence of grave crises in Syria since the Arab Spring movement began, and mentions the Syrian government's violent repression of protests—though none of the family wrote they participated. It does not reference any source confirming the targeted persecution of those in occupations like her and her family, nor the school or work bombings they mention. Indeed, not a single source is referenced at all. While black African asylum seekers have their claims summarily devalued, brought into question in the face of seemingly any other knowledge claim, no external sources are mobilized to confirm let alone discredit the truths Sama and her family presented.

Alejandro, a Venezuelan asylum seeker, asks me if he might share news coverage about the current situation in Venezuela with CONARE because, in his words, he sees local sources CONARE may not see. Alejandro informs me that he had been told officials were asking for such contextual information. I check with Sara about this possibility, and she responds: "I don't know what exactly he means . . . We only ask in case they want to add something for their own individual case . . . This is *only evidence presented by him* . . . We will not necessarily come to use that source in our case opinions. Because the sources [we use] must be impartial . . . [emphasis added]." Material presented by an asylum seeker is determined *a priori* as biased and unsuitable as objective evidence. It is not the document itself that signals its utility in determining truth, but who mobilizes it. As the epistemic logic constricts asylum seeker knowledge to their bodies and experiences, Alejandro's desire to provide general information beyond his individual case, to inform CONARE about the situation in his home country, is refuted. The determining "truth" must be found elsewhere and by officials. It is their own process of discovery that makes it knowledge. Through such practices, officials claim the white epistemological entitlement to determine what is true and why in asylum.

In this chapter, I have shown how a white logic structures why officials do not believe Jonatan was a conscripted military officer, do not ask Kemi about the legislation that led to her persecution, and deny Benjamin because there was no online news coverage of his church's bombing. Rather than aberrations, these examples represent not the bias of a particular official but a formally and informally constructed epistemic logic, enacted through a series of practices that constrict and constrain what nonwhite asylum seekers are rightfully understood to know.[22]

These practices can provide the justification for rejection, making certain pathways to legal exclusion uniquely likely for black Africans. But, regardless of whether the state extends refugee status—Kemi and Djo received asylum, while Benjamin did not—the process of adjudication politically devalues their ability to claim to know their own histories. As officials' practices privilege their own ways of knowing and establishing truth, and extend epistemic privileges to some refugees, while concomitantly circumscribing and questioning the knowledge claims of other asylum seekers, they produce a racialized hierarchy of epistemic (dis)empowerment before the state. This monopoly on epistemic authority incorporates refugees into a racial political order, even for those deemed worthy of protection.

In the next chapter, I turn to the asylum decisions that follow. Chapter five addresses the racial project entailed in ultimately determining who among asylum seekers is a refugee. Focusing on asylum recognition rates and decision wait times, I show how the racialized nature of outcomes in and priority for adjudication produces racial domination through processes of both legal inclusion and exclusion in the face of black African forced migrants, in ways not seen with others.

FIGURE 4 CONARE Plenary–Brasília, Brazil. The National Committee for Refugees (CONARE) decides all asylum claims and formulates policies in Brazil. Most representatives never meet the asylum seekers whose cases they decide, and refugees rarely appear at a CONARE plenary. CONARE representatives are often men, and none are black. Photo by Isaac Amorim/Agência MJ.

5

Deciding

At the Refugee Center, I sit on a bench on the patio with Joseph from Nigeria. He fled to Brazil after Boko Haram bombed his village. Though external reports corroborated Joseph's story, CONARE denied his claim. I sit with him while we finalize his appeal. A legal volunteer had prepared a 15-page supplement on Joseph's behalf, and I guide him as he fills out the last questions on the form. As we work together, he is stoic. But as we talk, his responses betray a sense that he holds within a deep frustration with the decision, acutely upset by the slight of having to appeal the state's rejection of his claim to refuge.

As I explain to Joseph the next steps, Antonio, the receptionist, interrupts to tell me about Hassan, a Syrian asylum seeker, and "what he needs." Hassan wants to know about the RNE, the identity document for refugees, and Antonio asks me to explain it to him. "Yeah, actually," I say to Antonio, "I already talked to him."

I call Hassan over and reconfirm what I had told him. Hassan has piercing blue eyes, his skin golden from the sun, with tousled wavy curls. I reiterate that there is no way for him to get the RNE until he is recognized, and I clarify it is very difficult to open a bank account without the RNE, one of his primary inquiries. "You have to wait until you are recognized."

"For how long do I have to wait?" Hassan asks.

"This month," I respond, "there were cases decided from 2012, 2013, 2014, and 2015."

"I don't understand." He presses, "How long?"

"I really don't know," I say. "It's random, it's not chronological."

He says, "So I just have to wait?"

"Yes. Syrians are being recognized faster," I continue. "But I don't know exactly how long."

Though I have already addressed Hassan's concerns, Antonio interrupts me to prioritize Hassan's needs over Joseph's. As my conversation with Hassan continues, I feel increasingly awkward. As Hassan stands before me, we discuss not *whether* he will be recognized—but *how long* it will take. Irrespective of whether Hassan has experienced persecution, and regardless of whether he fears its possibility, as I found not all Syrian refugees did, I know Hassan will be recognized and quickly. The question is only how fast.

In contrast, Joseph is still beside me, his claim recently rejected. Despite the horrors he experienced, Joseph sits holding his appeal papers in his hands. As Hassan and I speak in English, Joseph understands the whole encounter. He does not look at either of us. He looks down at the ground. And he does not say a word.

This chapter addresses the racial politics of the asylum decision. It is about decisions, who waits for them, and why. While the prior two chapters attended to what goes into evaluating claims, chapter five turns to the decision itself. Capturing the racial project in who is recognized and how long it takes, it shows whose lives the state sees as a priority and how the racial order shapes the disparate experiences of refugees like Hassan and Joseph. With Congolese refugees, while most are ultimately recognized as refugees, they wait years in legal limbo and precarity. Regardless of the outcome, as Congolese and other black Africans wait for an answer, they learn the state pays their lives little importance as those decisions are deferred.

The unequal racial order in Brazil also shapes who makes those decisions. Once a month, representatives from the different entities that comprise CONARE gather to decide who is a refugee. Though CONARE recognizes most who apply, racial political domination manifests in how and when that happens. One year, Frederic was invited to speak at a CONARE plenary in Brasília, where case decisions are formalized. It was the first time a refugee ever attended. "Imagine, they are there discussing asylum," Priscila says, "and never had a refugee there." Frederic's presence at CONARE marks another first. Priscila continues: It's the "first time there was someone black."

Recognizing, Rejecting

From 2013 to 2021, Brazil recognized 92 percent of asylum claims. Syrian and Venezuelan decisions augmented the recognition rate in some years. Yet in 2014, for example, the recognition rate excluding Syrians was still 84 percent. Given the size of recent Venezuelan forced displacement, their adjudication as *prima facie* refugees had a significant impact, with recognition rates going from 40 to 98 percent in 2019, and from 66 to 98 percent in 2020, when including Venezuelans.[1] Making sense of these high aggregate approval rates requires recognition that, in the words of Lucas, asylum "is not a technical decision but a political one." Other officials and refugees alike shared Lucas's sentiment. Such high overall rates present Brazil as an exemplar of humanitarian welcome for refugees.

However, racialized hierarchies underlie who among asylum seekers is recognized as a refugee. During fieldwork, I compiled an individual-level dataset of all asylum claims decided nationally in Brazil between September 2015 and April 2016. One night over beers, Guilherme and I discuss that dataset, and what analyses would help guide the Center in its work. "It would be really, really great," Guilherme interjects, "to do the acceptance rates by race."

Disaggregating Brazil's lauded high approval rates by nationality and region suggests racial discrepancies in whom the state declares to be a refugee. In what follows, I dissect patterns found among the top six countries represented among asylum decisions in my dataset: Syria, the Democratic Republic of the Congo (DRC), Pakistan, Nigeria, Ghana, and Guinea-Bissau. Each accounted for at least 5 percent of decisions during that period (see table 1).

Congolese have been an African anomaly in terms of recognition rates. While racial domination happens insidiously through inclusion for Congolese, it manifests more commonly for other African nationalities through outright legal exclusion—without notably impacting Brazil's highly celebrated overall tendency toward recognition. Based on my dataset, non-Congolese Africans are much less likely to obtain refugee status compared to others. The relative similarity among the top African asylum-seeking countries other than the DRC—Ghana (18%), Guinea-Bissau (3%), and Nigeria (18%)—in unlikelihood of recognition, contrasts sharply with the vastly more favorable outcomes not only for Syria (100%) but also for Pakistan (75%).[2] Relative to Ghana, for example, and while controlling for other characteristics—gender, age, and single versus family application—Guinea-Bissau and Nigeria are slightly less likely to receive refugee status, 90 percent and 35 percent, respectively. Pakistan, on the other hand, is 1,200 percent more likely to be awarded asylum (see table 2).

Such rates and estimates demonstrate the state's disfavoring of African asylum seekers relative to others, a pattern also seen at the regional level. From 2014 to 2020, approval rates for major applicant regions were as follows: Middle East and North Africa (93%, or 74% excluding Syria), Latin America and the Caribbean (99%, or 62% excluding Venezuela), South Asia (42%), and Sub-Saharan Africa (30%, or 17% excluding the DRC).[3] Despite Brazil's high rates of recognition overall, the unlikelihood of recognizing Sub-Saharan Africans as refugees exists to a degree not seen with any other region. Such patterns expose a racial project in asylum decisions, uniquely subjecting black Africans to legal exclusion, while being mystified by Brazil's celebrated image as a bastion of refugee protection. These disparities exist despite such applicants making legitimate claims to asylum.

The cases whose evaluation and adjudication consistently deviate from official procedural standards and guidelines—those judged unfairly and wrongfully recommended for denial like Joseph—are from Africa. The legal team at the Refugee Center, as a participating member in CONARE, is responsible for representing not only cases from the state of Rio de Janeiro, but claims filed throughout the country.[4]

In preparing for one GEP meeting, where officials debate cases before the CONARE's deciding plenary, the legal team at the Center reviews case files for the 53 asylum seekers within their jurisdiction slated for rejection at the upcoming plenary. Two-thirds of those listed are African, with others from Latin America, Europe, and South Asia. Of the six of those 53 cases deemed ill-judged by the team, all are from Africa: Nigeria, Mali, Mauritania, and Senegal. We found issues with asylum officials not pursuing possible reasons for recognition in their interviews and case opinions, and evaluating eligibility criteria in distinctively restrictive ways. Such problems, which provided for their rejection, jeopardized those African cases. Those issues were not found with the claims recommended for denial from Cuba, the Dominican Republic, Italy, Pakistan, Portugal, or Venezuela; we did not find those latter judgments to be out of line with official mandates for how to interview asylum seekers and evaluate their claims. Altogether, Africans were doubly undermined: by being strongly represented among those planned for rejection, in line with above, but also by being principally among those whose denials were made possible by careless or exclusionary work practices, practices we did not see with others denied at that same time. What follows are the stories of those six.

Seydou from Mali applied in Rio.[5] As I review his case, I see that the interview was poorly conducted, with little effort shown to gather information relevant to the case, and that the discussion of the claim's merits is disconnected from the particularities of Seydou's narrative, suggesting a template case opinion. I advise we argue he be removed from the plenary and reinterviewed.[6] Similarly, Malick, from Mauritania, gave accounts of racism in his home country that were unexplored in the official interview. Malick is ultimately denied.

Olatunji applied for asylum in Mina Gerais. In Nigeria, Olatunji suffered arbitrary imprisonment and penal mistreatment. In a statement taken when Olatunji filed his application at the Federal Police Office in Brazil, the police officer notes they believe the arrest was politically motivated. Nonetheless, the case opinion recommends rejection, declaring that "asylum is not for people who have had problems with justice." Though perturbed, the legal team decides not to challenge the decision because Olatunji had already received permanent residency, most likely through marriage or childbirth, when CONARE finally sets to adjudicate his claim—four years after he filed.[7] Olatunji is denied.

Ousmane, from Senegal, applied in Rio Grande do Sul. Ana reviews Ousmane's file and finds it a possible case of gender-based persecution that went unexplored by the interviewing official. She notes the under-development of the interview, including material facts of the applicant's claim the official did not ask about. At that time, officials did not record interviews, but instead produced limited summary transcripts. In the interview transcript, Ousmane notes being persecuted for having a homosexual relative. He declares that he left with his family after they suffered threats because of the relative's sexual identity, and "that his [sibling] had been physically attacked because of this." Yet, as Ana writes in the civil society report she prepares for the GEP: "There is no indication that the applicant has been asked about the threats . . . the period in which this occurred, or the content of the threats" that appear in the "applicant's asylum request." She cites how this runs counter to UNHCR procedural standards, which declare that "the interview should be used to . . . complete accounts regarding material facts." While officials could pursue lines of questioning that called into doubt the credibility of African applicants, the case of Ousmane shows how neglecting details regarding a case's eligibility can also lead to negligent recommendations for denial. Ousmane is ultimately rejected.

Gabriel, from Nigeria, applied in Paraná. In his interview, Gabriel, an Igbo-Christian, says the Christian market where he worked was bombed. After the attack, Gabriel recounts that he did not return to Abuja, where he lived two hours from his work, because of fear. Abuja, the nation's capital, had been a focus of attacks by Boko Haram. After the attack, Gabriel fled to Benin City, where he lived until he made it to Brazil. Benin City had also experienced attacks by Boko Haram.

In the case opinion, the official decided to disregard the entire application and declaration forms because in the interview Gabriel said he had not filled them out himself. Though Gabriel asserted in his interview his ethnic-religious identity, and he recounted the attack at the market and the fear it produced in him, the merit of ethnic and religious persecution as a basis for recognition was not explored by the official. The official slated Gabriel for rejection.

After reviewing Gabriel's file, Ana writes the civil society vote arguing for recognition in Gabriel's case: "The ethnic-religious background of the conflict in Nigeria is undeniable . . . at least 71% of the deaths perpetrated by Boko Haram have been of the Igbo ethnic group in recent years, due to their involvement both in churches and commercial spaces in cities. Which means to say that just by belonging to that ethnicity, the applicant would be more susceptible to be a victim of the conflict and, moreover, recognized as Christian, a target of the extremist group." Ana cites local and international news and government reports corroborating these facts. "Igbo people have been killed by the group en masse . . . [with] ethnic cleansing perpetrated by Boko Haram . . . the year in which the applicant suffered the attack . . . the main reason for his asylum request." Experts and US State Department reports also confirmed the religious conflict driving Boko Haram attacks in all three cities where the applicant worked, lived, and originally fled, and that those "locations may be the target of future attacks." As Ana concludes in the vote: "It would be unreasonable to assume, therefore, that the applicant could return to these locations safely, without being subject to rights violations." She also notes the applicant's demonstrated fear of persecution, a criterion for recognition, as he declared in his interview that "he would not find peace if he was forced to return to Nigeria." Despite Ana's defense of Gabriel's claim based upon various external sources, he is rejected by CONARE the following month.

Williams is also from Nigeria and applied in Rio. Williams is an active Christian who volunteered as an assistant pastor. He fled after he suffered an attack in the commercial center where he worked, where Boko Haram detonated several bombs and cut off power in that region of the city. Williams lived close to his work and, when he fled, he thought his family was killed in the attack.

Even though regional ethnic-religious conflicts lie at the basis of Boko Haram's attacks, Williams's ethnicity is not asked in his official interview. In the case opinion, the official recommends denying his claim on the basis that his home state in Northern Nigeria did not qualify as a context of grave and generalized human rights violations according to a UNHCR report, and because the official could not find proof of the bombing in the news.

Yet, as Ana writes in the civil society vote recommending Williams, according to the UNHCR and UK Home Office, there were over one million internally displaced Nigerians in the Northeast, almost 50,000 internally displaced in the Center-North, 174,000 Nigerian refugees in the world, and an another estimated 200,000 in refugee camps in neighboring countries. Just the month prior, the US State Department had declared Williams's home state was "not a region free from the religious conflict that plagues Nigeria, based on the actions of the extremist group Boko

Haram," naming his state as among the regions "implicated in situations of human rights violations" because of the group's attacks. Moreover, as Ana asserts, it "is next to the states where there is recognition of serious and widespread violation of human rights according to the UNHCR." Even more disconcerting, Ana writes:

> A survey of previous CONARE decisions shows that there is a tendency to accept cases from [his state]. Among those cases recently designated for approval, 60% were based on religious persecution . . . There is previous recognition by CONARE officials that [his home state] has not proved to be a state capable of protecting people in situations of religious persecution in recent years . . . [and] that in [that state] there are persecutions against civilians operating in commercial regions, which corroborates the applicant's report, as well as that [his state] is a recognized region of conflict, above all of an ethnic-religious nature, led by Boko Haram.

In making her case, Ana cites five cases filed the same year from Williams's state recommended for recognition by officials, and references the very arguments and reports presented in those case opinions, to assert that "the applicant deserves protection for indicating that he is Christian, for working as an assistant pastor, and that he was the victim of an attack at the . . . shopping center, where he also worked; [and for] having a well-founded fear of persecution for religious reasons." Notably, those five case opinions for recognition were done by different officials. By recommending Williams's denial, as Guilherme noted, they were not even being consistent among themselves. That inconsistency in decisions, seen acutely with African claims, disadvantaged Williams and opened the possibility of wrongful denial.

At the GEP, the official responsible for evaluating Williams's claim argued that an attack against an applicant does not confirm a well-founded fear if there is no news about facts that could affect people in that region or of that profile. Lucas and the other civil society representatives countered that the concrete fact of the attack is itself proof that the fear was founded, confirming the need for recognition.[8] Moreover, Ana's vote had detailed the presence of attacks in Williams's home state, particularly against Christians like himself. And to do so, she referenced the case opinions produced by that official's colleagues. The arguments by Lucas, Ana, and others were to no avail. Williams is rejected.

Decisions against those like Gabriel show how Africans are held to higher, more incisive burdens of proof for credibility and eligibility, and how those can have consequential impacts for their legal outcomes. Cases like Williams's show how they are also subject to inconsistencies that preclude them.

At the Refugee Center, Ana becomes perturbed as she reviews the case opinion for Samuel from Nigeria. Though Samuel was in church when it was bombed, the official argued it wasn't his church. Perusing the opinion while sitting in the legal office, Ana interrupts those of us working, "I'm sorry, I'm sorry I have to read this sentence." Ana reads it aloud to those present: Just because the applicant had the unhappy experience of being around bombings, it doesn't make him a refugee because it was indiscriminate. Ana goes off. "You are supposed to *include* not *exclude* types of persecution. If there was political persecution, religious persecution—you add them all together. Boko Haram, if they bomb churches, mosques, newspaper companies—that doesn't mean you say, 'Oh hey, it's indiscriminate so there's no persecution'!!"

Lucas echoes her indignation. "That's exactly what happens in Syria— it's indiscriminate!" He continues: "They don't care who you are." Lucas notes how not all are denied on this basis. He feels that the same claim would be seen and decided differently if it were not Nigerian, but Syrian. If he were Syrian, Lucas reflects, he would certainly be recognized.

Such dynamics are not just about being Syrian, as nationality and race-making intersect. Embedded in the notion of Syrianness are racialized privileges to not be subject to such lines of inquiry and argumentation. Nor did I see such unduly rigorous applications of the law to deny those fleeing the Taliban. It was with Africans that such patterns emerged in adjudications. They are uniquely exposed to demanding standards of evidence, excessive recourse to bureaucratic protocol, draconian criteria for inclusion, inconsistencies in evaluation, and careless neglect—as officials fail to ask them relevant questions, explore and develop their accounts, or pursue possible reasons for their recognition. The racialized nature of such disparate practices and outcomes provides for producing racial domination through legal exclusion in the face of black Africans seeking safe haven.

SPEEDING UP, SLOWING DOWN

Speaking during commemorations for the World Refugee Day in 2016, João Guilherme Granja, Immigration Department director, declared, "We have, in the last five years, a new challenge: growth." While Brazil received less than a thousand asylum applications in 2010, it began to face an exponential growth in asylum claims in the following years (see fig. 6). The institutional setting of asylum became characterized by significant growing pains.

Five years later, Brazil had a backlog of over 25,000 claims. In the face of this increase, the number of asylum officials grew from roughly four to 23 nationally, and new offices were opened in São Paulo, Rio, and Porto Alegre.[9] Yet, as Guilherme attested, speaking on a panel in 2016, having "15 people responsible for doing evaluations is still insufficient to affect the number awaiting decisions." "The structure in Brazil," he reflects, continues to be "limited." While the number of recognized refugees doubled between 2010 and 2015, this did not keep pace with the increase in asylum claims. As Guilherme underscored, "that number does not correspond to the previously 15,000 and now 25,000 awaiting decisions in their cases."

Despite the dramatic increase in applications, and the addition of new asylum personnel, the number of claims adjudicated remained largely the same. While CONARE analyzed an average of 107 cases during its monthly plenary sessions in 2013, that average only increased to 218 claims per meeting in 2016. Despite the backlog, fewer than 2,000 claims were adjudicated that year.[10]

How long asylum seekers waited for decisions steadily increased as the total number of pending claims rose. In the mid-2000s, the average time for analysis was between four and six months and, by the beginning of the following decade, it was seen to take nine to ten months.[11] By 2016, the process time had stretched to average a little over a year and a half.[12] In the words of one official: "It is difficult to keep up . . . CONARE tries, but the fact that you must grow as everything is happening, makes you unable to organize."

Hidden within these average wait times are racial disparities. Because CONARE does not decide cases in chronological order, asylum seekers can wait significantly more or less time, depending on the Committee's priorities. And those priorities are racialized. To wait is to suffer, and such forms of political suffering are acutely experienced by Africans.

Despite the increased backlog, Syrians waited less time to get a decision. Their cases are fast-tracked. According to my dataset, in February and March 2016, the average time to recognition for Syrians was 300 days—less than a year, much less than the average time. This cannot be explained by their *prima facie* status, as that does not formally provide for prioritization. Though most Congolese receive refugee status, their cases are significantly delayed relative to Syrians. Congolese, who had their cases decided in that same period, waited an average of 629 days— almost two years and more than double the average time Syrians did for largely the same outcome. Aggregate government data shows even starker disparities. From 2014 to 2020, Syrian decisions took 1.1 years versus 2.9 years for Congolese.[13] While the vast majority of Congolese are ultimately approved in recognition of the grave violence and weakened state in their home country, their neglect by the state highlights how racial domination can manifest through processes of legal inclusion.

The state enacted this favoring by having Syrians predominate among cases decided. This was made possible by two practices. First, Syrians were overrepresented among those included in plenaries. For example, Syrians represented 6 and 15 percent of asylum claims filed in 2013 and 2014, respectively, in Brazil. Yet, in 2014, 58 percent of claims decided were Syrian. That year, there were 11,200 pending case decisions.[14] In one plenary, July 2014, of the 678 claims decided, 534—79 percent—were Syrian.[15] In my dataset, almost double the number of Syrian than Congolese claims were decided (table 1). From 2013 to 2020, each year, roughly twice as many Syrians as Congolese applied for asylum. Yet, on average, over six times more Syrian than Congolese cases were decided each year during that time.[16] This privileging was made possible by a lack of transparency or formal system for how cases are selected to go forward.

Second, the number of cases decided at plenaries was expanded. Almost 700 claims were adjudicated in that July 2014 plenary, a number higher than any other before 2018, with an average of 289 decided per month that year and with a low of 105.[17] In prioritizing Syrian claims and pushing them through quickly, CONARE produces racialized hierarchies as they signal whom they want to stay and readily make it possible for them to do so.

Racialized differences in wait times transcend Syrians and Congolese. From 2014 to 2021, claims from the Middle East and Afghanistan averaged 2.4 years for decisions, while Sub-Saharan Africans waited 3.9 years. Among other top applicant populations from those regions, Palestinians waited 1.7 years while Senegalese waited 3.7 years, for example.[18] In my individual-level national dataset, Syrians were not made to wait as Africans were, but neither were Pakistanis (see table 3).[19] Relative to the DRC, variations in decision times for Ghana, Guinea-Bissau, and Nigeria were not statistically significant. However, Syria and Pakistan waited much less than the Congo—an average of 12 and 10 months less, respectively. That gap was statistically significant net other captured factors. While Africans are uniquely subject to rejection, they also experience exceptional delays in decisions.

Some asylum officials explain these delays as driven by a struggle to locate applicants. In the words of Alicia: "The great difficulty is finding the person. There are a lot of cases from 2013 and 2014, because the person disappeared." In CONARE plenaries, representatives likewise bemoaned the struggle to locate applicants. At the time, CONARE sent notification letters to appear for interviews through the mail, to whatever address the asylum seeker had last provided. Returned notification letters were common. But that is an insufficient explanation for delays. Ousmane, from Senegal, was added to the plenary five months after his interview. Seydou from Mali was put forth for the plenary almost two years after his interview. Similarly, Williams from Nigeria was interviewed but his case was not adjudicated until 17 months later. Though the state had conducted its interviews, and had all the material needed to make adjudications, providing decisions in their claims was not deemed a priority.

The timeline for Syrians was even quicker a few years prior, generally averaging six months—while the wait times for others concomitantly continued to grow. Wael and Adnan both arrived in 2013, before Resolution 17. Wael waited six months and Adnan only four months. These quick decisions occurred though no formal policy of prioritization existed, and Syrians had yet to be declared *prima facie* refugees, which later entitled them to streamlined processes of recognition. The process for Wael and Adnan was standard; they both had interviews and had their cases judged individually. Yet decisions came swiftly. Hamid applied in 2014, after Resolution 17, and was recognized after just three months. Similarly, due to errors in Wael's father's documents, his father's case was processed as a new asylum claim rather than as a case of family reunification. "So," Wael reflected as he bemoaned to me the bureaucratic hiccup, his father's recognition "got delayed three or four months." While felt by Wael as a frustrating delay, his father received refugee status far quicker than many others.

Asylum officials expressed their difficulties navigating this temporal prioritization of Syrians, particularly as other asylum seekers acutely protested that preference. Sara, an asylum official, reflected on these tensions: "Even though [Syria's] been recognized as a situation of grave and generalized [violence and human rights violations], that doesn't necessarily mean that they would have priority in front of the other cases. Many asylum seekers from other nationalities take issue with this [*questionam isso para a gente*]: 'Why do Syrians automatically receive a document?'" As Sara underscores, there is no policy or procedural explanation for why Syrians receive priority. Even after the *prima facie* designation, it does not in and of itself explain why Syrians would predominate among decisions or have their cases fast-tracked. Making sense of this practice requires looking elsewhere: the racial project of asylum.

Sara was not alone in her struggles to navigate the injustices of Syrian prioritization in decisions and wait times. Emiliano, a legal volunteer at the Center, was surprised he had to traverse these tensions as a volunteer, likewise confronted with asylum seekers perturbed by the disparity. As Emiliano reflects:

> Many who aren't Syrian are very, I don't know if revolted is the right word, but they are very outraged [*injuriada*] with the differentiated treatment that persons coming from Syria have in the asylum process. I've grown tired of hearing people say, "I filed my application more than a year ago and nothing happened, I still haven't even done the interview with CONARE, and his [a Syrian's] [decision] already came." And the [Syrian] person is right beside them, you know? "How can it be!" And what can you say to this [non-Syrian] person? "Really, people who come from Syria, it is much easier for her to get asylum than for anyone from your country." I'm not going to say that to them. If I do, they'll be outraged [*injuriada*] . . . That sucks [*isso é chato*].

At the same time, Syrians presented an exceptional manifestation indicative of a broader set of dynamics that extend beyond them, as black Africans experienced delays in decisions that others from the Middle East, Afghanistan, or Pakistan, as seen above, did not.

Moreover, delaying decisions can also serve as a strategy for denial. The injustices of suffering time and legal exclusion can intersect. Though it is standard to evaluate claims based on the conditions when an asylum seeker fled, in 2016, CONARE officials pushed for rejecting Malian claims based on the argument that Mali no longer represented a context of grave and generalized human rights violations (GGHRV). According to the officials, it was possible to return to southern Mali. However, Mali had been recognized as a context of GGHRV in 2012, and a number of the cases set for rejection were backlogged claims filed in 2013. At the same time, after 2013, other regions of Mali continued to be recognized as contexts of GGHRV up to 2015. Civil society representatives pushed for those cases to not be harmed by delays in the processing of their claims; they argued there should be equal treatment with 2013 claims judged prior and they should not be denied because CONARE took so long to evaluate their applications. Penalizing Malian cases for decision delays provided a mechanism for their occlusion from recognition.

This occurs with other African cases as well. As Fernanda and I walk to the subway, she reflects on seeing this with Togo, a gap between formal mandates and how CONARE works in practice. "They say," I note, "that an applicant should not be penalized because of delays in processing." Fernanda responds: "But they do. I've seen that with cases from Togo, for example. Someone leaves when there is grave political violence and persecution, political party issues, but then the country is supposedly democratic, there are smooth elections, and [CONARE] says there's no issue." She adds: "That was the case of a woman who came into the legal office earlier today I spoke with—she had been rejected for that." Rather than evaluate a case based on the context when an applicant fled, assessing the country conditions when a case is finally evaluated provides a maneuver for denying African claims, as those often delayed.

Those Still Waiting

The gap in wait times becomes even starker when considering claims still awaiting a decision. The wait times for decisions are skewed by analyzing only those who have had their cases decided. Each year, CONARE decided fewer claims than were newly filed—the backlog ever increasing. Though the process was said to average a year and a half, this average only included those cases adjudicated. During fieldwork, I encountered many who had been waiting over three years with their claims still pending.

As the backlog exponentially increased, the gap manifest by prioritization became even more important. "There are about 20,000 asylum seekers waiting for decisions," Lucas says in 2016. "And those, they are not Syrians." Lucas continues: "There are lots of Congolese who are not even getting to the decision." Since his words, this backlog has only grown. And, though Congolese have been one of the primary populations seeking asylum in Brazil, some months they are not even included among those that go up for decision.[20]

Predominantly Africans fall through such cracks. When Mbaye, from Senegal, goes to the Federal Police to renew his asylum seeker protocol, they tell him to go to the Refugee Center to get in touch with CONARE to see what is going on. It's "a long time," Mbaye says to me. Mbaye applied in 2012. When I meet him to check the status of his claim and renew his protocol, it is 2016. It has been almost five years since he applied. On another day, Mbaye returns to check again if he has a decision from CONARE. With him are two other Senegalese applicants, one of whom had similarly applied in 2012, the other in 2013. All their cases remained pending.

One day, after lunch at the Refugee Center, Frederic hands me his cellphone, which displays an asylum seeker's case number. He asks me to tell him what's up with Congolese Tonton's claim filed in May 2014. I look it up in the SEI, the asylum case database, and find that Tonton had been recommended for refugee status based on persecution and grave and generalized human rights violations in September 2015. It is now June 2016. Nine months had gone by, and the case had yet to go before CONARE to have the decision formalized. It is not until August of that year that Tonton is recognized.

His case was not an anomaly. Andre, also from the DRC, similarly applied for refugee status in 2014, and received a positive case recommendation in September 2015. Yet, as of September 2016, he continued to wait for a decision. Even when asylum officials judge them to be refugees, Congolese like Tonton and Andre experienced grave delays in being added to CONARE plenaries. While Tonton was eventually recognized, I do not know what became of Andre's claim—when or if he was finally officially recognized as a refugee.

The extent to which this elongated waiting is a systemic problem for Africans is made clear by a 2016 agreement with the National Immigration Council (*Conselho Nacional de Imigração,* or CNIg), responsible for formulating and coordinating immigration policy in Brazil, to regularize for humanitarian reasons the migratory status of asylum seekers waiting since 2013—already three years.[21] When the legal team at the Refugee Center began collecting names for inclusion in that CNIg resolution, the vast majority—64 of 74—were African. Moreover, two of the six denied African applicants discussed above had applied in or before 2013. They should have been referred to CNIg, but they were not. Instead, they were rejected.

Congolese refugees waited even when they were already entitled to asylum through family reunification. As a right of asylum, the extension of refugee status to family members is an administrative process, not an evaluative one. But cases of family reunification must wait to be included in the plenary to be formalized. Debaba came to Rio in 2015, when his wife—a recognized refugee—brought him through her right to family reunification. Many times, Debaba comes to the Refugee Center wanting to know when he will know. He protests that he has been sick, in and out of the hospital, and lives far from the Center. "When will I know?" he asks. Lucas explains he must wait to be included in the plenary. "Usually, it takes less than a year," Lucas adds, "but now it is taking longer." Notably, this timeline greatly exceeds the few months Wael's father had to wait, or those seen generally for Syrian refugees recognized via asylum who similarly did not undergo interviews. "There isn't any other way for you to make a document for me?" Debaba asks. "No," I answer. "I have been waiting for seven months." Deflated, he adds, "Just wait?" I have no other answer for him. "Just wait," I respond. As the state makes African refugees wait for the rights formally due to them, without clear timelines or avenues for recourse, their political presents and futures are taken out of their hands. Formal inclusion is underwritten by the impossibility of full black political membership before the Brazilian racial state.

Precarity of Legal Limbo

Such delays in decisions mean black African asylum seekers disproportionately wait in societal precarity. While seeking asylum in Brazil provides access to a range of rights and benefits not seen in other countries,
it remains highly insecure. In the words of Eduarda, a social worker at the
Refugee Center: "The law is good. It allows for the right to access, but if
we look at the practice . . ." "There is the law," Pedro, a legal volunteer at
the Center, similarly reflects, "and then the implementation of the law is
something else."

The nature of the asylum seeker identity document signals the dire gap
between formal protections and everyday precarity. Upon submitting an
asylum claim, the Federal Police emits a protocol (*protocolo*) as the asylum
seeker's identity document. The protocol provides an asylum seeker the
legal right to live, work, and move freely in the country while they await
their decisions. Protocols must be renewed every six months to a year,[22]
and can be extended for as long as the asylum claim is pending. However,
asylum seekers experience stifling limits as they try to rebuild their lives
in Brazil with a protocol in hand.

Being black acutely compounds those difficulties and shapes the lived
reality those struggles take. "The protocol makes existing in this city

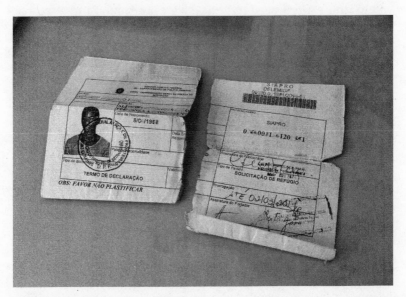

FIGURE 5 Asylum seeker protocol. The *protocolo* is an asylum seeker's official
identity document in Brazil as they await the decision on their claim. This one has
torn at the folds from wear. Image anonymized. Photo by author.

dangerous," and, Pedro adds, "There is a racial question. Imagine: Poor, black, doesn't speak the language. The police questions him, and he shows the *protocol*!" The protocol is a physically precarious document—it is a piece of standard printer paper to which the asylum seeker's picture is attached with a glue stick. Because the Federal Police renews the protocol with a stamp, rather than emit a new one, the protocol cannot be laminated. This only exacerbates its precarity. These pieces of printer paper are the asylum seeker's official identity document in the country, which they should always have on them as it proves their legal right to reside in Brazil. Protocols are folded up and kept in wallets for years. Over time, protocols disintegrate at their edges. Folded creases turn into tears. Protocols turn yellow and gain a permanent dampness, softened from the moisture of living near a person's body in Rio's hot, humid climate. In attempts to assuage the precarity of paper, some asylum seekers developed tactics, like laminating a photocopy reduced to the size of a credit card.

"It is a horrific racism," in the words of Priscila, "that the protocol cannot be laminated." There is no procedural mandate explaining the protocol's delicate nature. Though I was only a temporary resident in Brazil, the Federal Police provided me with a standard, hard-plastic identification card, referred to as the RNE—the same one recognized refugees receive, and which Hassan asks about. Receiving a protocol, rather than a standard ID, as Pedro and Priscila signal, makes black applicants uniquely vulnerable to acute dangers and insecurities before the punitive arm of the state and society broadly. And they are made to wait in that precarious condition longer than others.

Guilherme, speaking on a panel at a lawyers' association, addresses the need to take seriously the conditions of those awaiting their decisions, particularly given the increasing backlog. "We need to think about the *asylum seeker*," Guilherme emphasizes. "They are *hypervulnerable*, even more than the refugee." He continues, "I don't know if you've had the opportunity to see their document, but it's *paper*."

The simple, precarious nature of the protocol undermines its credibility. The lack of authority attributed to a wrinkled piece of printer paper, coupled with a dearth of familiarity with asylum seekers' legal rights, are key obstacles.[23] Brazilians with which asylum seekers interact as they navigate life, and as they claim those entitlements in practice, often do not know what the protocol is or the rights it guarantees. The frail document the state provides makes asylum seekers more susceptible to economic exploitation. I talk with Francois out on the patio at the Refugee Center, and he wants to open a legal case for stolen wages. He says he wasn't paid because of the protocol, because they didn't know what it was. "We don't do that here," I tell Francois, "but the Public Defender's Office does." When

I head back into the legal office, I find out I was wrong. "Actually," Lucas says, "not even the public defender does that." Bruna, a legal volunteer, adds with a self-evident tone: "This is Brazil." The seeming obviousness betrays a sense that, in Brazil, stolen wages and exploitation of black labor are so common it would be unfeasible for the public defender to address it.

After an asylum seeker is rejected, such delays and documentary precarities of legal limbo continue. If denied, the asylum seeker has the right to appeal.[24] If an appeal is approved, the appellant obtains the rights of refugee status. If denied, the applicant would not be forced to leave the country—Brazil does not have a deportation policy—but they would fall into an irregular legal status, living without formal rights. However, as of 2016, CONARE had not adjudicated an appeal in the previous three years. All appellants continued to live in legal liminality with only a protocol to attest to their rights during that time.[25] The state does not make publicly available data on the number of appellants or for how long they have been in that condition.[26] Nor did I come across such data during fieldwork. Given the racialized disparities of rejection rates, and thus those who appeal, the neglect of appeals suggests a further instance in which African migrants are not deemed a priority—neither a population worth tracking nor taking note of—and the lived precarity that produces.

Appellants can be subjected to other legal slights. After Guilherme assists Osvaldo, from Angola, Guilherme is irate. "That's the seventh person," he exclaims, "who has not been given a new protocol when they went to do the appeal. They [the Federal Police] just put a stamp on top of the appeal [application], and they think that's okay!" When Osvaldo went to the Federal Police, they refused to give him a new protocol. As Guilherme's words indicate, in that Osvaldo was not alone. Guilherme is frustrated. He asks me to hand him a plastic folder labeled "Problems: Federal Police," so he can add Osvaldo's case to his growing file.

To Wait Is to Suffer

Waiting not only produces protracted legal and socioeconomic precarity, but is also an emotionally weighty experience. As sociologist Barry Schwartz writes, "delay is not only suffered; it is also interpreted."[27] That condition of uncertainty, of enduring limbo and struggling to make sense of a legal process that is opaque and incomprehensible, can produce emotional turmoil.

Roughly two hours after Obi, from Nigeria, arrives at the Refugee Center, I go outside to speak with him as he sits on the patio. The patio is packed. He has come because he needs a letter confirming that there is still no decision in his case so he can renew his protocol—yet again—at the Federal Police Office. As I confirm with him that he wants to know if there's been a response from CONARE in his claim, he opens up. Obi responds, "Actually, I have many things I want to say—many problems." He continues: "I don't mind waiting, but I want to know what is wrong, what is taking so long. Did I do something wrong?"

It has been three years since Obi applied. And being forced to wait, without reprieve, without explanation, produces in him an acute anxiety and confused desperation. And he worries that it is his fault, that he has done something wrong to be so cast off and ignored.

Others felt similarly. Rasheed, from Ghana, is emphatic: "I want to talk to you. I was looking for you. I want to talk to you. I need to talk to you." He wants to know if there's an answer yet. "What is going on?" he asks. "We were five guys. We all entered at the same time, and all of them already know. What is going on?" As we discuss his case, he speaks over me. Discharging his anguish is more important than the information I could offer.

Rasheed applied in 2014, and he comes multiple times to ask about his claim. A week later, as I assist him in the legal office at the Center, he tries to explain through analogy how he experiences the protracted waiting he has endured, and how little sense it makes to him. "Let me explain to you," he says. "Let me give an example: Imagine . . . we are all in class together. And we take an exam, and the teacher brings the results. All the results are going to come at the same time." He becomes agitated as he verbalizes his confusion that Brazil does not judge cases chronologically. "Why?!" he bemoans. "I don't understand!" He underscores that he knows "others who know"—so why not him? He becomes visibly frustrated as he stresses his feeling of personal injustice. To this, I have no answer. I tell him I do not know why. All I can do is send an email to CONARE to ask what is happening. But this is not an answer, not a resolution, that provides Rasheed a reprieve from what has thus far been two years spent in a state of waiting and unknowing.

As sociologist Javier Auyero details in his ethnography of bureaucratic offices in Argentina, *Patients of the State*, waiting is replete with political meaning and crucial to the production of state domination. By determining when and how rights and services will be fickly provided, the state manifests its power over those seeking its support, as denizen subjects are forced into powerless submission as they struggle to lay claim to what is legally theirs.

In some instances, officials understand waiting as for the asylum seeker's benefit. As I assist Rasheed, in English, Guilherme and Lucas sit beside me. Rasheed wants to know the status of his claim, and standard procedure involves emailing CONARE to follow up on his case, in an attempt to nudge forward adjudication. Guilherme looks over and speaks to me discreetly in Portuguese. "I do not know his case," he continues, "but there is a great chance he will be denied." Guilherme knows Ghanaians are unlikely to obtain refugee status. Guilherme suggests that I should not send an email to try to speed up his case. I respond to Guilherme in kind in Portuguese, continuing to speak in front of Rasheed, about him and his case, while we exclude him from deliberations about issues deeply relevant to him. I ask if Guilherme wants to explain that to Rasheed. Guilherme does not respond, busy with his own tasks. Lucas joins in the conversation and asks me, still in Portuguese, to ask if Rasheed received orientations when he arrived about the possibility of being denied. Guilherme and Lucas are both fluent in English, but Portuguese is more expedient and Lucas was often sheepish to use his English. We do not speak so Rasheed can understand us. I turn back to Rasheed, asking him in English if this was the case. But Rasheed seems confused by my questions and does not respond to them directly.

In such instances, officials make decisions for asylum seekers from which they exclude them. While Guilherme often explained to those he assisted why he may not push to have CONARE adjudicate their claims—that it may be better to wait if denial is likely—this was not always the case, particularly when tasks pulled him in many directions. Even when based in good intentions, hoping to elongate the period an asylum seeker may live and work with a regular status in Brazil, such actions could reproduce the obscurity of the asylum process, and the experience of precarity and political domination it entails.

Later in the day, I follow up with Guilherme about what he thinks I should do in Rasheed's case. Confirming whom I'm talking about, Guilherme clarifies: "The one who was angry?" He says: "I would not send an email, for his own good." Because, Guilherme continues, 100 percent he is going to be denied. I had already told Rasheed that I would email CONARE, so I am apprehensive about not following through. Intuitively, I agree with Guilherme that is the best thing to do. But I opt to look at his application to see whether it is a good case before I truly decide.

A few hours later, at the end of the day, a volunteer from the reception brings me Rasheed's file. It's been hectic, and I already forgot I had asked for it. I read over his application where he recounts familial persecution over land holdings. "Sounds like a strong case," Guilherme says. I look then to see if the Center had put together a case recommendation for Rasheed, and I find that he had been interviewed by legal volunteers the year prior, and they had written up an opinion suggesting he be recognized.

Once I see Rasheed does have a strong case, with which Guilherme now agrees, I decide to send an email to CONARE on his behalf. But when I go into the email account, I realize I had already done this—just the week prior. I had no recollection of having met Rasheed before that day. As I express my shock and dismay at myself aloud, Guilherme retorts: "Welcome [to my world]. It gets worse." "Now I understand," I respond, "why he was so angry with me."

As asylum seekers like Rasheed wait for answers from the state, they are politically demeaned and disempowered. As they voice their feelings of injustice to those tasked with providing them assistance, they experience compounding slights of being unseen, unimportant, and uncared for. The hectic conditions of the Center and the number of people assisted each day make it difficult to remember and recognize them, to provide the quality of assistance asylum seekers want and those at the Center wish they could provide.

This chapter has addressed the racialized hierarchies that manifest in how and when asylum claims are decided. The state rejects black African asylum seekers at rates and in ways not seen with others. Even when the state recognizes them, the process can drag in ways others do not experience. As they are forced to wait in legal liminality, they suffer, degraded by the state from which they seek redress and political standing. In the following chapter, I turn to the racial politics of care and concern for refugees in Brazil.

If we are saved we feel humiliated, and if we are helped we feel degraded. We fight like madmen for private existences with individual destinies . . .

HANNAH ARENDT, "We Refugees"

6

Caring

In September 2015, Alan Kurdi washed up on the shores of Turkey. He drowned in the Mediterranean trying to make the passage to Europe with his father. He was three years old. The photo of his small, lifeless body, facedown in the sand, made world news. In just 12 hours, the photo reached nearly 20 million people.[1] It became a global watershed moment that galvanized interest and support for Syrian refugees—increasing volunteering, campaigning, and donations on their behalf.[2]

It had ripple effects in Brazil as well. With the photo of Alan Kurdi, and news of mass Syrian forced displacement, the Refugee Center in Rio de Janeiro received a flood of donations. "After the visibility fleeing Syrian refugees received in Europe," Adriana, the Center coordinator, notes, "it called attention to the refugee question here."[3] Fernanda, a legal volunteer at the Center, shares: "When I first started it was shortly after the photo of the Syrian boy on the beach came out . . . this appeared a lot in the Brazilian press, and it really moved people . . . there wasn't space for anything because there were so many donations. My first day as a volunteer [when I was supposed to work on asylum cases] . . . I separated and folded clothes, organizing, so they could distribute the donations."

Yet, these donations were not distributed to whom the donors had in mind. While the conflict in Syria mobilized Brazilians to donate, Congolese and other Africans were the primary recipients. They are the main beneficiaries of the social assistance distributed at the Center broadly: financial subsidies, hygiene kits, cookies and basic foodstuffs, volunteer labor, and clothing donations, among them. In contrast, Syrians receive limited assistance at the Center. "There isn't much financial help from the Refugee Center," Wael says. "And there should be . . . I am a refugee here . . . If I were to go to ask them for money, they say they don't have any. [But the money] is in their hands."

This chapter addresses a surprising puzzle. While Wael and other Syrians are favored by the legal arm of the refugee regime, and society more broadly rallied in the face of their plight, they find little social support at the Refugee Center. Conversely, though Congolese experience many barriers on the way to obtaining refugee status, and Brazilians largely did not realize they exist, they are the primary recipients of the social and economic aid distributed there.

To make sense of this incongruence, this chapter uncovers how racialized notions of need, worth, and vulnerability underlie the allocation of charity. It examines racial logics of care and hospitality among the public, and how those intertwine and contrast with the racial logics of vulnerability at work in the social sector of the Refugee Center. Thus far, this book has focused on the legal realm of asylum: the evaluation of refugee status claims, and access to rights and documents. But the refugee regime also entails administering aid, and its different arenas can work in uneven and contradictory ways.[4] While prior chapters addressed how officials produce racialized lines of difference and inequality as they determine asylum, this chapter examines whom broader publics care about and the racial project of humanitarian assistance. The dynamics of aid make racialized subjects, exposing refugees—both those who do not receive support and those who do—to vital racial lessons about who they are imagined to be and what they can expect in Brazil.

Racialized notions of refugee worth exist beyond the refugee regime. Syrian refugees appeared acutely in society's line of sight. Syrians were seen as worthy of support, welcomed as uniquely capable immigrants that reaffirmed Brazilian hospitality. Given the myth of Syrian "entrepreneurial spirit" in Brazil, Syrians were lauded as self-starters and greeted with open arms. They were not seen as hapless poor. On the other hand, the public was largely blind to the struggles of black African refugees in Brazil and afar. Failing to reckon with the Africans in their midst and feel empathy for their plight, the racial limits of public hospitality were doubly enacted and obscured.

While the highly visible Syrian refugee situation catalyzed a wave of donations and volunteers, these charitable acts were not distributed to them because Syrians were not perceived as those in most dire need by those at the Center. Given severely limited funds, where there is always never enough, social workers use criteria to determine aid. They cannot give to all, so they prioritize those seen as most vulnerable. And, as they do, they racialize refugees.[5] Notions of Arab autonomy and capacity, circulating outside and within asylum, meant Syrians were seen as insufficiently vulnerable for such assistance. The racial imaginings that organize how Syrians are perceived led those at the Center to misrecognize Syrian experiences of socioeconomic suffering in Brazil—even as they exclaimed their need for support.

In contrast, while Congolese and other Africans experience difficulties obtaining refugee status, and are invisibilized in the public Brazilian imagination, they are the main beneficiaries of assistance distributed at the Refugee Center. Social workers prioritize Africans because they see them as uniquely vulnerable in the harsh racial realities of Rio. But the support available is meager, and far from sufficient to meet demand. Social workers cannot apportion rights and have severe limitations in trying to provide forced migrants what they clamor for. And seeking and receiving aid comes at a political price. It disproportionately exposes Congolese and other Africans to the paternalism embedded in charity. They become objects of aid, not subjects of rights.[6] Expressions of aid enact hierarchies between bestower and bestowed. By being denied such supports, paradoxically, Syrians are pushed to be autonomous subjects. Aid—inherently a discretionary gift rather than a political entitlement—leaves little recourse for refugees to claim support, and can disempower those who seek and receive it.

Public Visibility and Support for Syrian Refugees

After Kurdi's death, media coverage of asylum seekers and refugees doubled.[7] The images of Alan Kurdi and distant Syrian suffering were imprinted on the collective psyche, mobilizing unprecedented compassion for refugees in Brazil. Within a week of his death, then-president Dilma Rousseff published an opinion piece in *Folha*. "The terrible photo of a three-year-old boy, Aylan Kurdi, dead on a Turkish beach . . . a tragedy of terrible proportions." She reiterates Brazil's openness to welcome refugees. A news article titled "The Syrians Are Arriving" similarly noted that "the rising number of asylum claims reinforces the importance of offering help so people can rebuild their lives and regain their autonomy."[8]

The concern for Syrians triggered unparalleled forms of charitable support in Brazil. "The donations for Syrian refugees keep increasing," a lawyer at the Refugee Center in São Paulo noted, "by much more than 100 percent. We have received messages, phone calls, people that search us out to bring donations . . . hygienic kits, blankets, milk, powdered milk for children, diapers, and also money."

In Rio de Janeiro, the desire to help overwhelmed the Refugee Center. The Center stopped taking clothing donations because it had nowhere to store them all. The growing awareness and concern for refugees catalyzed by Syrian forced displacement also led to an influx of volunteers never seen before. "It must have been right after the time when the photo appeared of the Syrian boy on the beach, that it started," Emiliano, a white legal volunteer, reflects. "How many people came! [The Center] started to receive mountains of resumés for volunteer positions, when before they were just yelling into the wind, searching for people to work there."

I saw this dramatic shift in volunteer interest during my time at the Center. In 2012, when I began fieldwork, I was the first volunteer the Center had received. In 2013, we were two. In 2014, the number had increased to make a sizable team. When I returned in 2016, six months after Kurdi's death, there was a waiting list of 70 people wanting to volunteer. I am not alone in noticing the shift. That year, Priscila, who coordinates volunteers at the Center, addressed the change at an open house for possible new volunteers. "There are now 45 volunteers," she says, "which will only grow with this call. Last year, we had the idea to have 20 volunteers, and we thought that was a lot. So, you have an idea how this work is growing."

Over beers one night, Lucas muses on how dramatically the scenario had changed since he began working at the Refugee Center almost a decade prior. "This topic, now it has gained value . . . . People were never interested in this. When we would go [to the university] to look for help, we needed help, the person: 'Hm . . .' And now everyone wants [to help], right? And that is . . . it's incredible, isn't it?" When Lucas gave talks in classes at universities, he would pass around a piece of paper for people to write their names and emails if they were interested in getting involved. The paper would wind its way around the room and return empty. Within the year of Alan Kurdi's tragic death, school visits became a common sight at the Center, something I had never seen before. Class after class of high school, undergraduate, and graduate students came to hear about refugees and listen to the stories of those who had come to Brazil to seek asylum.

Brazilians also showed a marked desire to house Syrian refugees. While Pastor Benicio had long run a shelter for refugees at his church, he was particularly moved to help Syrians. At times, the church offered food and shelter predominantly to them. Despite the church shelter's official three-month-maximum-stay policy, he allowed Hamid to stay indefinitely in a room for him alone. Other Brazilians would call the Refugee Center expressing their desire to take in Syrians.

This public support filtered into the Refugee Center in other ways. When Naem, from Syria, comes to the Center to apply for asylum, he is accompanied by Benison, a light-skinned black Brazilian, whom Naem met at the Arab restaurant where he works. When Naem returns another day with his completed application, Benison and another Brazilian join him. I initially thought the third man was an Arab immigrant who would help translate—because I had never seen such support. It was rare for a Brazilian to accompany an African claimant to the Center, let alone two. Only later would I realize that that seeming aberration signaled a racialized pattern of public solidarity.

Sometimes this support came from family members, possible because of past Syrian immigration to Brazil. When Munir, a Syrian refugee, comes to inquire about family reunification, his middle-aged niece accompanies him. "I am not a refugee," she explains to me. "I came here as a child with my parents, you can see by my accent." She laughs. She translates from Portuguese to Arabic for Munir and is his incessant advocate, asking me many times the same questions about how family reunification works. "Everything," she asserts, "needs to be known with certainty." She explains that the family is financially supporting Munir, and because of that he is able to bring his wife and children. Munir's family ties in Brazil were made possible by past policies that allowed Middle Eastern immigration, while concomitantly banning and hindering African immigration. Because of historical racially restrictive immigration policies, such established familial ties—and the social and financial supports they provide— are unlikely for African refugees today.

The keen desire to help Syrians appeared poignantly in society broadly. Wael, a Syrian refugee, had tried desperately, to no avail, to continue his university studies in Brazil. Wael's petitions to be admitted were denied, until a professor went to the Rectory and got the decision overturned. Wael started back up his degree. Wael believes he is in the position he is "because I got the help of some people. . . . Probably there are other refugees who deserve a lot more than what I deserve." But, he continues, "the Brazilians here, they really go to great lengths to help us." While Munir was able to bring over his family because of his immigrant familial networks, Wael resumed his degree because of the goodwill of Brazilians without direct ties to Syria. "It is difficult to get help from the government," Wael says, "but society generally helps."

Such exceptional public support was shaped by the lauded attributes ascribed to Syrians and other Arab immigrants in Brazil. They are seen as educated entrepreneurs set to improve the economy. Because of their assumed high levels of educational attainment and economic capacities, as Brazilian professor Cecilia Baeza underscores, there is a sense that Syrian refugees "represent more of an opportunity for Brazil . . . than a burden."[9] Brazilian professor Oliver Stuenkel similarly notes that Syrian refugees "help the country's economy by reducing Brazil's chronic shortage of skilled workers and boosting innovation."[10] Such statements echo discourses that circulated during Brazil's era of whitening policies, that saw such immigration, including by Syrian-Lebanese, as an opportunity to improve Brazil.

As historian Jerry Dávila notes, while in the United States Middle Eastern identity is conditioned by foreign policy, in Brazil "it is negotiated in the marketplace."[11] The stereotype of the commercially astute Arab, which coalesced during the First Republic, was reinvigorated during Brazil's neoliberal turn during the late twentieth century, where those of Middle Eastern descent were framed as possessing positive economic qualities—ethical, shrewd—beneficial for the nation and its economic transformation.[12] This national myth has led Brazil to treat Arabs as immigrants rather than refugees, as anthropologist Leonardo Schiocchet writes, assuming "they would become integrated as Arab immigrants had in the late nineteenth century."[13] This "collective myth about the place of the [Arab] immigrant in the Brazilian nation"—principally based on Syrian-Lebanese immigration during the twentieth century—has shaped responses to Syrian and other Arab refugees in contemporary Brazil.[14]

These racial stereotypes came to the forefront at public events about refugees I attended throughout Rio. At a Refugee Symposium hosted by the Red Cross in 2014, an audience member comments, "These Middle Eastern folks have the advantage that they speak English—How many Brazilians do?," ascribing through language skills a perceived socioeconomic prowess absent from Brazil and to its benefit. At the packed opening of a refugee art exhibit in 2016, the Brazilian owner of the cultural space hosting the event reflects on the moment: "I am a child of Portuguese migration—all of us are migrants. When we see on TV, all those fleeing, we have so much land available . . . our country needs people . . . My own city was beautifully developed because of the migration of Syrians, Lebanese, Turks. Here we need those people . . . Thanks to those who choose our country." In imagining immigration as a shared national ethos, and constructing a seeming bounty of land ripe for development by Syrian refugees and others, he builds ties of community with those forcibly migrating today whom he sees as an economic gain for Brazil.

After the exhibit, Lucas texts me: "Refugees really has become a bourgeois topic." An avowed Marxist, Lucas focuses on class divisions as he tries to make sense of the new world of seemingly cult interest in refugees in which he now finds himself. It is not just any Brazilian who is able to donate their time and wares to others. They come from a patterned position of economic privilege, often living in the wealthiest zones of the city, and attending its best private universities. They are also predominantly white. While a privileged socioeconomic status provides the possibility for such acts, a racialized sense of shared community shapes the desire to do so.

Such support from the middle and elite classes in Rio, in a city marked by no shortage of social issues toward which to give one's time—racial inequality, police killings, severe material deprivation, and a host of social ailments suffered by a vast section of the city's predominantly black and brown inhabitants—is remarkable. Now it seems, Lucas muses, "the whole world likes refugees. I think that's good." "But there's something strange. It seems like the whole world likes the global poor." There's a lot of romanticization and "glamor" involved, Lucas notes, in the growing concern and charity for refugees he sees. "People are now sensitized to the Syrian question," Lucas reflects on another occasion, "but here we had this week a genocide, a genocide in small terms, in the favela. How can we be preoccupied with the situation of the Palestinians, and their occupation, but here we have armored vehicles [*carros blindados*]? There is a military occupation here in this city . . . Not to erase the difference . . . but we have to question . . . the privileging of the foreigner." Lucas incisively questions why the atrocities suffered by Rio's poor do not find the same support and indignation seen for Arab refugees. Racialized notions of worth inform why Syrians and Palestinians may elicit concern—while anti-black police violence in the favelas does not. And it is not just any refugee Brazil seems to care about.

Lack of Visibility and Public Support for African Refugees

When people find out Elena volunteers at the Refugee Center, they ask about Syrians. When she talks about Congolese, they are confused. As we chat in the legal office, she lightheartedly mimics the responses she gets: "What? There are Congolese here? What? There are Angolans here?" We both laugh. "People have no idea that there are African refugees," Elena says. She continues to mimic their unfamiliarity with Africa: "What's going on there? Is something going on there?"

For many who have never been to the Refugee Center, they have no idea Brazil hosts African refugees, let alone that before the Syrian conflict, they were the primary asylum seekers and refugees in the country. They know little to nothing about the Congo or Africa broadly. This is also the case among those who come to work and volunteer there. As Lucas reflects, when he first started at the Center, "I didn't even know what 'a Congolese' was."

When I ask Emiliano, a legal volunteer, what most surprised him when he started at the Center, he responds:

That is something that is very clear. I thought that refugees were people from Arab countries, basically. I was really shocked when I found out that the majority were from the African continent. And that there exist a considerable number of people from Latin America, as well. That was the first thing that was clear to me, that was deconstructed there. I was so surprised when I saw there were so many people from the Congo, because I had never heard anything about the Congo. I had heard of it, but like, never talk about the country, the history of the Congo. Nothing, zero. I didn't even know where it was on a map. And it is, like, half the continent, practically.

As Emiliano laughs at his own past ignorance, I ask him why he had imagined refugees were predominantly Arab and hadn't thought about Africans. "When people hear about asylum, we hear about asylum in relation to war. And we hear that there was war where? We heard that there was war in the Middle East. We never hear of Africa . . . For us, there is like a sheet that covers Africa, and no one takes that sheet off, you know? We only imagine the Middle East, that turbulent place that has a lot of war, so people flee from there." Emiliano continues, thinking pointedly about the Congo, "I discovered a parallel world where there was a war going on that I had never even heard of, not even knowing where to point on a map where that country was."

As Emiliano suggests, the media is a major source of information about refugees. And it has paid little attention to the Congo. In the two years prior, the leading national newspaper *Folha de São Paulo* published 1,112 articles about the Syrian conflict and forced displacement, but only 23 pieces on the Congo.[15] When the major newspaper *Globo* interviews Adriana for a piece on refugees in Brazil, she pointedly mentions Congolese. Yet the article's title erases them: "Number of Syrian refugees in Brazil fleeing war grows."

Racial understandings deeply entangle the visibility of death, concerns with distant violence and suffering, and resultant mobilizations of charity and solidarity. What media coverage and images circulate, what they evoke and the responses they elicit, is refracted through the racial prisms through which people make sense of their social worlds near and far.[16] Kurdi's light skin had an affective power that evoked interest and compassion not seen with Africans.[17]

Congolese know this well. During a meeting with Congolese asylum seekers and legal volunteers, Franck, who fled political persecution in Kinshasa, conjures the picture of Alan Kurdi. "That one child," he says, "and yet how many children in the Congo?" "When that child died," he says, "this went around the whole world. I do not understand the difference between this baby—who was white—and the millions who died in Africa—who are black . . . six million dead in the Holocaust, ten million dead in the Congo. It is not taboo [to say this]. It is discrimination, period." Wilson, another Congolese asylum seeker at the meeting, echoes his sentiment. "It is impossible to deny what is happening in the Congo. I agree with him about the discrimination. Three French die in a terrorist attack, and the whole world mourns. But a massacre in Benin, no one says anything." As cultural theorist Judith Butler writes in *Frames of War*, "one way of posing the question of who 'we' are, is by asking whose lives are considered valuable, whose lives are mourned, and whose lives are considered ungrievable . . . an ungrievable life is one that cannot be mourned because . . . it has never counted as a life at all."[18]

Prior to the Syrian conflict, when most were African, refugees were framed through discourses of criminality and impoverishment that limited the possibilities of Brazilian hospitality. "We live in a society that unfortunately has two labels for refugees," Adriana reflected, "one that they are those wretches there that are dying, or as outlaws [*bandidos*]."[19]

In earlier years, "the refugee" was racially entangled with "the fugitive." A public fear that refugees were outlaws was so prevalent that African refugees mobilized to have their identity document no longer say "refugee."[20] Notions of black criminality filtered into how the then predominantly black African refugee population was perceived. "The prejudices we suffer . . . born of ignorance," Frederic laments, because people "think of the refugee as a criminal." The anti-blackness underlying that prejudice meant that—while it continued to impact how Africans like Frederic experienced Brazil—it was not extended to Syrians when they began to arrive. For refugees racialized as white, that label is not equated with criminality.[21]

During a meeting among legal staff and volunteers at the Refugee Center, we discuss two conservative discourses that circulate about immigration in Brazil. At the time, Syria was not yet prominent on people's minds. While one discourse is an obvious demonstration of xenophobia, the other is more coded. "People say," one participant asserts, "'How will a poor country help other poor people?' . . . because they can't say we don't want any more blacks." This second nativist discourse entangles poverty with blackness and acutely confronts African refugees. "Some say that we are only taking favors," Frederic notes, "that we are indirectly abusing the nationals." Because of the anti-black undercurrents that drive that discourse, Syrians are not made sense of in this way. They are imagined as self-sufficient entrepreneurs, not a burden of hapless poor that Brazil could not, would rather not, bear.

Stereotypes regarding refugee socioeconomic capacity are racialized. Educational attainment, professional qualifications, and English language skills are not the exclusive domain of Syrians. Most Congolese refugees have college or at least high school degrees. This, like Syrians, is above the Brazilian average.[22] Syrian and Congolese refugees have analogous rates of high school and college completion.[23] In their home countries, Syrian and Congolese refugees principally engaged in the same activities: trade and studies.[24] And many African forced migrants hailing from former British colonies—like Nigeria, Sierra Leone, and Ghana—arrive natively fluent in English.

African refugees in Rio mobilized their professional backgrounds toward remarkable acts of entrepreneurship. Michele is a Congolese refugee in her mid-forties. Michele has a bachelor's degree in Business Administration. In the Congo, she was a clothing designer. In Rio, she found work as a janitor at the train station. It was the first time in her life she had ever worked in cleaning. In her off hours, Michele would design and sew clothes in her home, first with Brazilian fabrics, and then began to import African ones. After less than two years working at the train station as a janitor, Michele transitioned to supporting herself solely with her clothing designs.

Many other African refugees could easily be understood as proactive, go-getters. In the Congo, Prince was a math teacher. He fled North Kivu, stowing away on a boat in Kenya that—unbeknownst to him—would bring him to Brazil. His first five nights in Brazil, he slept on the streets. In Rio, he got a job as a salesperson at a sportswear store. Though he had no prior sales experience, after three months he became the store's top-selling employee.[25] Other African refugees, like Oti, from Ghana, came to the Center to discuss how to open a business. As I talk with Edward, from Sierra Leone, about applying for family reunification, he pulls out his wallet and proudly shows me his Itaú business credit card. He explains he is trying to start a business, and he wants to bring his brothers to help him. Despite such examples of entrepreneurial grit, an enterprising spirit is not a social quality associated with Congolese or other Africans. "There are still barriers that need to be broken," Frederic observes. "Just because we are Africans, they think we have no culture, that we are ignorant and uneducated . . . like monkeys, only for being Africans."

Mustafa, from East Africa, is the only African described as commercially astute by those at the Center. He's universally lauded as the most entrepreneurial of any. Previously a civil servant, Mustafa started a food cart business that came to operate throughout Rio. Mustafa's success becomes the topic of conversation during lunch. "He's going to command [*dominar*] Brazil!" Guilherme affirms, and Ana laughs as she quickly echoes him, "He's going to own all of Brazil." But Mustafa's seeming incomparability as an African entrepreneur proves the rule. This quality is not seen to extend beyond him. While Syrians generally are ascribed a go-getter spirit, regardless of their economic realities in Brazil, Mustafa is seen as a uniquely exceptional individual. Cases of economic accomplishment do not drive how Brazilians imagine Africans, in the refugee regime or beyond.

A Lack of Aid for Syrian Refugees

A marked tension existed between how empathy and hospitality config-ured the public response to Syrians, and the ramifications of Syrian racial-ization inside the social sector at the Refugee Center. Racialized ideas of autonomy and capacity—that Syrians can stand on their own two feet—imbued why they are so welcomed by the public, and yet why they were not prioritized for socioeconomic support at the Center.

This collective myth created expectations that did not correspond to Syrian refugees' needs and realities.[26] When Wael was struggling, he went to the Refugee Center for help. But he was told that there was no money because "they only give financial support to the most vulnerable." As Wael recollects: "They said, 'There's no way for us to help you.'" Wael com-plains, "They always say, 'Ah, there's priority. Pregnant women, women with children, elderly, and minors.' That doesn't make sense." "We're com-ing from a war," "we did not choose to come here." He continues, "Our money was there . . . maybe they gave it to another person."

Wael was disoriented by the Center's evaluation that his family was not needy enough because, following that logic of vulnerability on its face, they should receive support. Wael's father is ailing and elderly. "My father is 81 years old, so there should be preference for him," Wael retorts, "but there wasn't." Wael's warm experiences with the public broadly con-trasted with his interactions at the Center.

In years prior, all asylum seekers received financial support—$300 Bra-zilian *reais* ($154 US dollars in 2012) a month for three months—from the Refugee Center.[27] As the number of refugees grew, the funds the Center received did not keep pace. Social workers started enacting vulnerability criteria to determine who would receive assistance. According to UNHCR guidelines, which provides much of the funds distributed, those under-stood as in situations of extreme vulnerability—women, children, the el-derly, those with mental and physical disabilities—are to be prioritized. Such criteria construct aid as a paternalistic form of protection. Rather than a right, humanitarian aid is charity. Provided on an ad hoc basis, its amount and duration are determined by evaluations of need. Those at the Center explained prioritization through the imperative to follow official vulnerability guidelines in the face of ever-limited funds. Yet such vocabularies of motive belie the racialized notions of capacity that con-figure assistance.

A racial logic of vulnerability undercuts how those decisions were made in practice, leaving Syrians unlikely to receive support—regardless of whether they qualified. Amira, a female Syrian asylum seeker, lives with and cares for her mother in Rio. Amira couldn't find work and quickly became destitute. "I was in a terrible situation," she tells me. "I had some money when I was working in Turkey and I brought some money with me. But after six months I was without anything because I had my mom as well, and I had to pay rent, had to pay food, transportation, and then I was broke." Nonetheless, Amira and her mother did not receive a financial subsidy from the Center. Though formal guidelines could make them a priority—both are women, and Amira's mother has health problems—they received no support.

Racial myths of Arab prowess also impacted how asylum officials made sense of Syrian refugees. When I ask Alicia what she most liked about her work, she lauds Syrians for their enterprising habits. "They're very entrepreneurial," Alicia tells me. "Generally, Syrians, Lebanese . . . they always arrive in Brazil and already they've opened a shop, a business, a restaurant. There are a lot of Lebanese restaurants here in Brasília started by refugees. They are people who are proactive." Alicia extols Syrians and Lebanese as entrepreneurs, and it positively informed how she understood her work. But go-getters are not seen as needing charity.

When Wael and his brother could no longer afford where they were living, and feared ending up on the street, Wael decided not to return to the Refugee Center. He thought to himself: "I'm not going to humiliate myself again." Wael reflects: "Unfortunately, when I am in a bad situation, I don't think of [the Refugee Center] as a solution. I don't have the expectation that they will save me." He continues: "I'm not going to humiliate myself to ask them for money, I'm going to work and earn my money. Not that it would be a humiliation to ask for my rights . . . but I can't fight with these people because they are going to decide my destiny, right?" In the end, he decides, "I'm going to depend on myself, and I will manage." Wael learns he needs to become what he does not feel he is, nor should have to be: already self-sufficient. Wael spent the next six months sleeping in a tent in an occupied building.

In their encounters with the social arm of the Refugee Center, Syrians learn they will not receive the support they ask for and that to seek aid can entail a political humiliation of the self. When Hamid asks for money to help his food street-vending business, he does not get it. The Center instead posts about Hamid's Arab fare on its Facebook. "They used my picture and said, 'refugee, refugee, refugee,'" Hamid tells me. "I didn't like it. When they used my picture, I felt I lost myself." Hamid did not seek financial support from the Center again. In their failed attempts to obtain assistance, Syrians learn racial lessons about who they are and where they stand in Brazil—in relation to other refugees, before the government, and in society.

Among those who worked and volunteered at the Center, it was often understood that Middle Eastern and Afghan refugees could and should manage on their own—even when they openly declared that they were struggling. Maria, a white volunteer at the Center, vents that a newly arrived Afghan couple—who speak no Portuguese and know nothing of Brazil—asked her to accompany them to the Federal Police Office and to find an apartment to rent. As we chat, she is visibly flustered and frustrated by the things she's being asked to do. When Frederic asks her if she can accompany them as an interpreter to the hospital—the man has head and stomach pains, and he suffers from high cholesterol—she says she won't. Frederic is taken aback by her uncharacteristic response. Maria had gone out of her way for many Francophone Africans—organizing a network of Brazilians to give them private one-on-one Portuguese lessons, daytrip excursions to parks and museums, and accompanying them to sites like the Children's Welfare Office. Confronted with Frederic's surprise, Maria backtracks to explain herself. "I have already gone many times to do many things with them," she responds. "They need to become more independent, to do things on their own—find their own way." I never heard Maria have expectations that any African develop such quick independence.

Aiding and Patronizing Africans

In the face of the unprecedented wave of donations, the Center hired Yornella to orchestrate distribution. Yornella speaks French, Lingala, and Portuguese, and she knows a few words of English from a course she took back in Kinshasa. She does not speak Arabic. With Yornella in charge, given her language skills and social ties, the people she calls when there are donations and who then, she tells me, "call amongst themselves," are Congolese, other Francophone Africans, and Angolans.

Brazilians often donated what they wanted to purge themselves of— old clothes and other textiles—what they imagined refugees wanted, and what gave them pleasure to give. These were rarely what refugees said they most needed. When bags of donations were coming in, volunteers at the Center would go through and sort them. "You have to look at the clothes, those things: Are they good to wear? Would I wear it?" Yornella explains. "I have to see if it's good. If it's not good, I throw it out . . . Food, milk, personal hygiene things . . . out of date? Throw it out." Donated clothing could be tattered and worn out. While some "bring good things," Yornella reflects, others donate "just trash." "He should throw it out, he can't use it anymore," she notes, "but he comes, gives it to others, just to say, 'I went, I donated.'" Though Brazilians often donated shoes and clothing, and imagined it would be greeted with gratitude, I never saw a refugee unclothed or request attire. What people donated often had little to do with what refugees clamored for.

Refugees at the Center asked for funds, justice, and their time to be respected—to no longer have to wait—and food. Outside on the patio at the Center, a boy approaches me to ask if there are any cookies. His request goes unheeded. There are no cookies today. Later, a school group arrives with presents wrapped for the refugee children present, all African. As they open the gifts, they find toys. Photos are taken and posted to social media to celebrate the generosity. The boy wanted food—instead, he gets a toy race car. What refugees receive often does not correspond to what they ask for. Acts of charity do not require horizontal solidarity.

While donated goods came from the public, the bulk of funds for financial assistance came from national government entities, like the Ministry of Justice and varied state committees; the UNHCR; and other partners.[28] According to an internal report, Congolese received half of the funds distributed, while Sub-Saharan Africans received 76 percent overall. On the other hand, those from the Middle East and North Africa (MENA) account for 4 percent, with Syrians receiving less than 2 percent. On average, Congolese received almost four times the monetary subsidies that Syrians did. Among those who sought assistance at the Center during that time, more than double the percentage of Congolese as Syrians received financial aid.[29] Taking gender into account, a formal criterion for assistance, demonstrates how a racialized sense of vulnerability configures criteria in practice; Congolese women were 2.5 times more likely to receive a subsidy than Syrian women, while Congolese men were 3 times more likely compared to Syrian men.

Funds can also be liberated for short-term housing in local hostels. A local church runs a shelter for refugees, and there are public shelters in the city, but the spaces available do not meet the need. While few receive hostel stays, I never saw Syrians receive such support—even when it was what they needed, like Wael and his brother. Though formal procedures would suggest women and children, the elderly, and those with disabilities would be prioritized, allocation was inflected by a racialized logic that saw black Africans as acutely vulnerable in Rio. Gabrielle, a social worker, comes into the legal office to tell us she is assisting a Francophone African man who has been living on the street. She liberated funds for him to stay at a hostel and asks if one of us can take him to the subway and show him where to get off. In doing so, she breaks from official priorities by providing support for a single, able-bodied man.

Aiding Africans was often a racial justice–minded praxis. Many at the Center recognized how pernicious anti-black racism stifled Africans' desires and pursuits, uniquely hindering their lives in Brazil. The Congolese who arrive in Rio are qualified, educated people, Adriana notes. "But, here," she says, "they discover a racist country."[30] Through such comments, Adriana and others signaled their awareness of race as deeply meaningful in organizing the unequal world around them.[31] Adriana's support and advocacy for Congolese refugees, particularly women and children, was driven by a longing for Brazil to do better by them than it had.

Nonetheless, aid is a discretionary concession. While Congolese and other Africans receive most of the social assistance available at the Center, they are not legally entitled to it. Humanitarian aid is inherently not a formal right, but charity determined by those who dispense it. The discourse of aid—the need to prioritize in the face of scarcity—disempowers refugees' claims to assistance. At an event to mark World Refugee Day, during the Q&A session, Mimi, an Ivory Coast refugee, stands up and decries the end of her financial assistance before the panel and audience. "The question of assistance is limited, and the situation is getting worse," the UNHCR representative calmly responds. "There's no way to continue assistance forever, so we have to give to those most vulnerable and not for forever." Despite Mimi's claims that she needs and deserves continued support, aid is fundamentally limited, discretionary, and finite. He moves to the next question, denying her further clamor. As Michel Agier writes, "There is no care without control," as "every policy of assistance is simultaneously an instruction of control over its beneficiaries."[32]

Requesting and intermittently obtaining such assistance uniquely exposed Africans to racial political domination. To receive support from the Center, they must wait outside in discomfort for hours in heat and hunger. According to internal reports, the majority of those who come to the Center—again and again—for social and economic assistance are from the Congo (54%) and Sub-Saharan Africa broadly (83%). In contrast, Syria and MENA represent 4 and 5 percent, respectively. Congolese were 2.6 times more likely than Syrians to meet with social workers three times or more. Unlikely to receive support, as Heitor, the communications coordinator, notes as we chat during lunch, "Syrians come less and less."

Asking for assistance can lead to patronizing interactions. I sit at a round table in the back room of the Refugee Center, alongside Absame, a Somalian refugee, and three white officials—Lucas, a social worker from the Center, and Geralda, a social worker from the public shelter where Absame is staying. Absame has come to ask for support to make his own economic way in Brazil. The officials discuss providing him support through the Social Fund Project, launched by the UNHCR in 2010, which afforded subsidies for refugees who want to start a small business.[33] As they do, they talk in front of him about him—about his life, what type of person he is, and what support he merits. Though my role is to translate for Absame, I am rarely given the opportunity to do so. The conversation swirls around him without him. Absame is denied the right to participate in matters that impact his livelihood and to which he has much to contribute. He is visibly upset and frustrated. His attempts to interject are ignored. Geralda belittles him to the rest of us in Portuguese, exclaiming his request as folly—exasperatedly declaring he does not have the wherewithal to be in control of his own economic fate. As refugees like Absame seek aid, they are subject to the judgment of people that do not look like them, and that can patronize them as they do. Even as white Brazilian bureaucrats attempt to empathize, anthropologist Jaime Amparo Alves writes, they can normalize and reproduce black suffering.[34]

That Congolese and other Africans receive the majority of aid is not to say they receive all they need. For Yornella, the assistance at the Refugee Center "for us is very important, but it is also difficult for [the Center] to get the money to help." Only 15 and 13 percent, respectively, of Congolese and Sub-Saharan African refugees who sought assistance received stipends. Syrians are not alone in protesting that the support they receive is insufficient. One afternoon at the Center, in a heated exchange between Guilherme and Lumbay, a Francophone African refugee, the tensions between the discretion of aid and the refugee desire to claim rights to it come to a head. Lumbay seeks financial and food support from the Center, and has heard "no" too many times.

Guilherme starts: "You need to hear this, because you . . ."

Lumbay cuts Guilherme off. "I understand, but you have to let me . . ."

Guilherme interrupts. "There are criteria that the UNHCR, you can call them. Listen to me, before you argue. Call the UNHCR and ask them if the money they give to the [Center] is sufficient for the whole world. They will say no. And then ask what the criteria are, who is going to receive or not. And they will explain to you exactly what I am saying now: women who arrive alone, with children, pregnant, elderly."

Lumbay retorts. "Okay, but you are supposed to receive a bag of foodstuffs [cesta básica], they never gave me the bag."

"Call the UNHCR!" Guilherme agitates. "There is no money."

"But when there is money, do you tell us that there is??" Lumbay declaims. "We have a right to something here!" Lumbay pulls out his phone and starts recording.

"I can speak even closer to the microphone if you want."

"Yes, yes! Go on."

Guilherme goes on. "The UNHCR cut [the budget by] 30 percent . . ." He grows more agitatedly flustered by Lumbay's reactions. "Do not point at me, do not point at me!"

"No, this is how I speak. I am going to speak." Lumbay circles back.

"But when there is money, you never tell me when there is money—it is *absurd*!"

"You do not know," Guilherme answers angrily. "You are imagining things. Do you think we do nothing?"

Lumbay signals to his adolescent son, sitting beside him. "Does he have a right or not to have the money?"

"I just explained this to you. There are criteria established by the UNHCR, and so there is no money." Guilherme starts to repeat the criteria: "Women that have children . . ."

"Men cannot receive money here then??"

"It doesn't help your cause to come here like this [*não adianta você chegar aqui com esta postura*]." Guilherme continues: "Do you know what the problem is: You do not know what the reality is here . . . Do you think we do nothing?"

"You are helping," Lumbay answers, "otherwise I wouldn't have this protocol . . . You are here. But you are here for us, to be our lawyer . . . yet we realized you are *not* on our side."

"What do you want me to do?"

"You have never said to me that there was money here. They only say that there is no money, that there is no money."

"You always come here . . ." As Lumbay continues to talk, Guilherme asks him rapid-fire until he responds: "How many years have you been in Brazil? How many years have you been in Brazil? How many years have you been in Brazil? How many years have you been in Brazil? . . ."

"EIGHT YEARS, and so what?"

"So you should know how things work." He continues: "Let's go speak to Adriana."

"No, I will not speak to her. Adriana doesn't even say good-day to me."

"What do you want then?"

Lumbay asks again about money, and Guilherme answers: "There's none."

"It is absurd."

"I agree with you, it is absurd!"

Lumbay signals again to his son. "He doesn't have a right? Why not?"

"Again??" Flustered from going in circles without recourse, Guilherme starts to speak directly to Lumbay's son in French. Lumbay joins in as they continue to debate in French. The heated conversation continues for roughly half an hour. It goes around in circles, between French and Portuguese.

Guilherme exclaims: "You can say it is racist, but that's the reality."

While Guilherme disagrees that racism underlies how support is allocated, he agrees the system is ridiculous. He shares Lumbay's frustration that he wishes it were otherwise, and feels his own sense of powerlessness. He agrees the situation is absurd, but it is the unfortunate reality that support does not match refugees' needs. Guilherme expects that after eight years Lumbay should understand—and acquiesce to—how things work in Brazil.

What angers Lumbay, and what he affirms as racist, is not only that his struggles are disregarded by a logic outside his control, but that, confronted with a logic that erases his vulnerability, he becomes powerless to claim the material entitlements he feels he and his family deserve. While he speaks of rights, Guilherme speaks of criteria. While social workers and others unevenly follow UNHCR guidelines, they can be readily mobilized in the face of recalcitrant refugees claiming something more— materially and politically. From the perspective of those like Mimi and Lumbay, refugees should receive assistance from the state that granted them asylum as long as necessary to establish a stable and dignified life. After many years in Brazil, both still struggled to meet their basic needs. Legal inclusion did not resolve the socioeconomic precarity and food insecurity they experience.

Refugees are not bystander victims of reality. Their decisions to flee mark their active attempts to determine their own lives and what they may be. They struggle to make their own way, laying claim to what they need and deserve—something more and different from the assistance that some may expect them to be grateful for. To see refugees as subjects of their own fate—producers of their own reality—entails a very different logic than seeing them as objects of aid. "Those who are fleeing, they have voices," Lucas observes. "This is not to remove the trauma, the scars, the tragedy—but life does not shrink because of tragedy. Life is *amplified* by the escape. The state says the *victim* is incapable, so the state has control; but they want what they want, they know what they want, and they are saying that, doing that."

"The refugees here are courageous," Frederic exclaims. "When we escape, the largest preoccupation is to *advance* life—we want dignified work, decent housing, a bank account . . . We want a better future." The next chapter turns to what happens after asylum claims are decided. After recognition, as refugees seek the formal rights now due to them and to advance their lives and futures in Rio—a city marked by socioeconomic inequality, housing insecurity, and racial discrimination—they learn vital racial lessons about what asylum means in Brazil.

So when I say that I am a refugee, you must
understand that there is no refuge.

CHRIS CLEAVE, *Little Bee*

All freedom is relative—you know too well—
and sometimes it's no freedom at all.

OCEAN VUONG, *On Earth We're Briefly Gorgeous*

7

After

Lionel, in his twenties, came to Brazil from the Democratic Republic of the Congo through family reunification. His wide smile is infectious. An adolescent when he arrived, Lionel picked up Portuguese quickly, and he speaks easily and fluently. But beneath his jokes lie much continued fear and hardship. When I ask him if there's anything difficult about his life, he responds, "the gunshots [*o tiro*]." I repeat the word, "The gunshots?" He explains:

> Where I am living now, it is in the favela . . . There, there are gunshots. If one day goes by without gunshots, the people are like . . . like, a little . . . I think there is something that's not normal, there has to be one shot or two, at least, for it to be normal. [I think to myself,] all's good, there were two shots . . .

> In Africa, there's conflict zones, and there will be a lot of gunshots, then after a moment it stops, and it's done. But here it is not a conflict zone, it is a place of residence, the people are there. But [there are] gunshots. Always there is death. And the majority are innocent . . . I always go out looking for work, and I come back late at night. And I always look for a friend's house to sleep, to not enter where I live at night. Because of fear.

Almost ten years after obtaining refugee status in Brazil, Lionel is unemployed and sometimes goes without food. He has lived in that favela, Vigário Geral, notorious for police killings, for two years.[1] For Lionel, finding a purported safe haven has meant anything but.

Hamid, also in his twenties, was born and raised in a Palestinian refugee camp in Syria. As the Syrian conflict escalated, Hamid's family decided he had to flee. He had already lost one brother to the war. The Brazilian consulate offered Hamid a humanitarian visa, and he flew to Rio. A few months after filing an asylum claim, he was recognized as a refugee in Brazil.

Two years later, Hamid and I sit out on an apartment balcony, smoking double apple hookah, his favorite, in between sips of coffee as he reflects on the trials and journeys of his life. Between drags on the hookah, I ask how his life has changed since receiving refugee status. He folds one hand in the other and clears his throat. "Nothing changed." Whether he has refugee status or not, Hamid says, "It's the same." Hamid has still been unable to return to university, his studies interrupted when he fled. And he continues to live in a church shelter and work reluctantly as a street vendor, just as he did before he was recognized. "We escaped war," Hamid reflects, "but here it's another war."

This chapter turns to the period after recognition, examining what refugee status does and does not do in Brazil. Refugee status is often imagined as a holy grail, demonstrating that the individual belongs to the most vulnerable and deserving category of migrants—"those who need our protection most."[2] Taken as a "privileged immigration status," saved for only the few deemed most worthy of exceptional protection, obtaining asylum is expected to be a defining point in a refugee's life.[3]

But asylum is how it is experienced. After recognition, the refugee regime continues to impart racial lessons, and it offers scarce protection from the harsh realities of Brazil. To understand why refugee status does not feel positively transformative for those like Lionel and Hamid requires turning to how they experience the rights, supports, and precarities it entails in practice.[4]

Racialized differences in treatment and experience do not stop after recognition. As Congolese refugees seek to claim the rights they now purportedly have—to a formal identity document, a path to citizenship, the right to family reunification, to travel internationally—they experience roadblocks, delays, and bureaucratic neglect. They continue to be subject to politically deflating entanglements with the state. As the state makes them wait for what the law says they are due, as it misrecognizes them and misrepresents their claims, as it imposes shifting and increasing demands, it stifles their autonomy. For Congolese, formal inclusion is underwritten by a racial political order that denies them full personhood.

Syrian refugees, on the other hand, long for freedoms that would only come with citizenship, feeling acutely the protracted wait to become citizens. And they are disenchanted by the divergence between the ease of their arrival and the lack of support once in Brazil. Congolese and Syrian refugees alike learn they cannot rely on the government to help them build the lives they long for.

While Brazil offers most asylum, it comes with little support. Refugees continue to variably encounter labor informality and economic exploitation, material deprivation, social exclusion, and racial marginalization in daily life. For Lionel and Hamid alike, asylum has meant downward mobility, housing insecurity, and economic precarity. For Lionel, it has also meant hunger, unemployment, and violence. Asylum does not ameliorate the social and racial hierarchies refugees navigate in Brazil. In the words of Heitor, who works at the Center: "Brazil's public institutions are not welcoming. The institutional racism is the worst that exists."

Altogether, these experiences imbue how refugees understand asylum in Brazil. Syrians feel what they have accomplished is because of themselves and the Brazilian people, not the state. In the face of racialized struggles to claim their formal rights, and continued material suffering, Congolese refugees can feel apathetic about asylum. When I ask Michele what changed in her life after recognition, she responds: "It is the same . . . for me, it is the same."

While asylum may not radically transform how refugees understand their daily lives or futures in Brazil, it is politically consequential. Asylum makes racialized political subjects, as refugees learn what they can expect from the state and their position in the national racial order where they have sought safe haven. That it does do.

Legal Rights in Practice

The rights, benefits, and limitations of refugee status matter for how those who seek asylum envision it. Internationally, refugee status protects someone from being forced to return to their country. At its most basic, it simply entails the right to stay. Beyond this, its relative entitlements vary dramatically across national contexts. Brazil diverges starkly from the draconian regimes seen throughout the Global North. Brazil's 1997 Refugee Act provides—for both asylum seekers and refugees—the right to reside, work, and move freely within the national territory, as well as access to public health, education, and social assistance programs. Moreover, Brazil does not detain or deport immigrants. Winning an asylum claim, in countries like the United States, can save you from deportation proceedings. Brazil, in contrast, does not have a deportation regime. If denied, a rejected asylum seeker falls into an irregular migratory status, but they are not forced to leave the country.[5] Asylum seekers and refugees noted a formal identity document, a pathway to citizenship, and the right to family reunification as meaningful entitlements of asylum (see table 4). Yet, the rights most salient are not necessarily expediently obtained. After recognition, African refugees continue to encounter a state that does not concertedly care for or about them.

IDENTITY DOCUMENTS: MORE THAN PRINTER PAPER

Asylum seekers and refugees alike see access to a proper identity document as a key concession of refugee status. In Brazil, refugees are entitled to different identity documents than asylum seekers. While refugees receive an RNE, a standard hard-plastic wallet-sized ID card, the asylum seeker document is instead the protocol, a physically precarious piece of printer paper. When Rosine, a Congolese woman in her late forties, found out she was recognized, she was excited about the RNE. "I said to my friends: 'I'm going to get the RNE,' and I was very happy." When "you aren't recognized, you don't have an RNE," Yornella reflects, and "you have some limits in some places. When you go [to those places], you don't have much will [*vontade*] like other people do." I ask Yornella what places she means, and she explains: "Some jobs, they don't accept those without the RNE. They don't accept people with the protocol . . . Some banks, you can't open a bank account. You can get work, go to open an account, and they don't accept it. And you go somewhere, and they say they don't know it: 'This is what?' It's ridiculous."

Obtaining asylum means the individual is included in the RNE (*Registro Nacional de Estrangeiros*, or the National Foreigner Registry), and they receive an identification number necessary for opening a bank account and requesting access to certain services. Even though the protocol legally guarantees the right to work, obtaining an RNE can ease the process of seeking employment, given employer hesitancy due to the lack of public familiarity with the protocol and its precarious nature. "Many Brazilians have never seen this protocol," Rosine reflects. "You say, 'This is my ID from the Federal Police.' 'No, this here, I don't know it.' I interviewed three places [for work] where I lost the opportunity just because I had the protocol." But, with the RNE, "they know they are looking at an ID card. With the protocol, nobody [knows]."

To get an RNE, refugees must take their CONARE notification letters of recognition to the Federal Police Office. But errors in those letters were frustratingly common. Recognition notices introduced errors by misspelling names or inaccurately noting birth dates. In those cases, refugees must request a new certificate before they can apply for an RNE, an issue often not quickly resolved. Such mishaps delayed getting the RNE and rights that came with it, and further tethered refugees to the Refugee Center to try to resolve them. Obtaining asylum—and claiming the right to formal identification to which refugees are legally entitled—can be undercut by bureaucratic misrecognition, imbuing the experience with frustration rather than empowerment.

Such bureaucratic slights appeared as a glaring pattern with black Africans. During one day at the Refugee Center, I worked with two African refugee women who experienced that same issue. Kadie, from Sierra Leone, had been recognized as a refugee in October, but only received her notification letter six months later when she came to the Center. Nonetheless, because the letter introduced an error in her mother's name, she had to request a new one. Kadie returned to the Center a week later, but CONARE had not emitted another notification letter. As I walk through the patio, Edward, also a refugee from Sierra Leone who accompanies her, grabs my attention. He is frustrated. "We've been here since 9 a.m. She missed work for this." Kadie and Edward wasted hours waiting at the Center, losing much-needed earnings, only to learn there was no update. Kadie did not feel the state cared enough to quickly rectify its mistake.

Bureaucratic neglect is a question of limited infrastructural capacity, but also a racialized sense of who among refugees matters. The following month, Yousef, from Syria, comes to the Center because his birth date is wrong on his notification letter. Rather than just send an email, as is standard practice, one of the lawyers calls CONARE directly to address the issue. Concerted care and attention when Syrians experienced bureaucratic mishaps appeared among CONARE representatives as well. When CONARE discovers a Syrian man never received his notification letter, great effort goes toward rectifying the issue, and as quickly as possible. In a CONARE meeting, the Justice Ministry representative describes the painstakingly "large archeological job" they underwent to locate his case. "We weren't able to locate the file that the official sent to the police," she says, "but we located the plenary file, the notes for that meeting, the agenda for that meeting, everything physical." She continues, "We looked for all physical files of everything and we were able to get the information I just shared, but believe me, it was not an easy process."[6] While such errors and mishaps were most common with Africans, they were not the only ones to experience them. But the attention and speed with which such mistakes are addressed can be markedly different—signaling whose rights and entitlements to redress matter.

CITIZENSHIP AND PERMANENCY: ASYLUM AS A STEPPING STONE

While most refugees want Brazilian citizenship, many asylum seekers and refugees were frustrated by the elongated timeline to obtain it.[7] For refugees, naturalization was only possible eight years after recognition. On the other hand, migrants who regularized their status through familial channels, for example, could become citizens in just one year—a seven-year difference. At the Center, when asylum seekers asked about different status options in Brazil, they often expressed disappointment when they learned the timelines for permanency and citizenship for refugees. "I know for us it's about eight years to become a citizen," Syrian refugee Adnan says, and that "sounds too long."

Such moments of disenchantment figured prominently for Syrians. They perceived asylum as a mere stepping stone on the way to something meaningful. "I just want to have refugee status," Amira shares, "to be able to apply for citizenship." She had spent over a year with her case pending, unusual for Syrians at the time. Because her time as an asylum seeker does not count toward the clock for citizenship, she tells me: "I'm not really *angry* about it or anything, but . . . I'm wasting my time." Even after she is recognized, she explains, "I will have to wait." Syrians lamented that the right of asylum they most sought—citizenship—felt long delayed.

Many wanted citizenship because they wanted a passport. From Hamid's point of view, though asylum changes nothing, he ascribes magical virtues to a Brazilian passport. "A passport equals freedom," he tells me. Born in a refugee camp in Syria, Hamid's inability to travel freely has deeply marked his life. "I am Palestinian," he affirms, "we are refugees there too." What Hamid wants is international freedom of movement, and neither his Syrian travel document nor refugee status provides that. "I need a passport from Brazil," Hamid affirms, "so I can travel to another country." Adnan, a pharmacist who travels internationally working with an NGO, feels similarly. "To me, it's important to become a citizen to facilitate my life," he reflects, because of "all this visa process, all that comes with having a Syrian passport, all the countries I can't go." According to the 2019 Henley Passport Index, which ranks passports according to travel access, Syria is tied with Somalia for the second most restricted passport in the world.

Refugees do not have access to the same passports as Brazilian citizens. They instead apply for a yellow passport, a single-use international travel document. Travel with the yellow passport is not easy, as many countries in the Global North flatly deny entry to those who carry it. It is for this reason that Hamid declares "refugee is one thing, a passport is another." Hamid had saved his money working as a street vendor to travel to London, where his uncle lives. He got the yellow passport and bought a plane ticket. But the UK denied his visa. While his Syrian travel document failed to provide Hamid the freedom of movement he desperately seeks, neither does the yellow passport offer relief. Refugee status does not grant the mobility that those like Hamid and Adnan dream of. Without a proper passport, Hamid feels he remains an "unknown person," because "the refugee does not have a right to a nationality." Hamid believes that only once he becomes a citizen will he find the freedom he clamors for.

While Syrians were disappointed about the wait between asylum and citizenship, such waits were not unique to them. They were driven by the law on the books, experienced by refugees broadly. On the other hand, even the formal rights of asylum coveted by African refugees fail to readily materialize for them in practice. For Rosine, her eyes have been set on permanent residency, possible four years after recognition. "It's a dream," she tells me, "permanency. Sometimes it feels like you are not secure [*certo*] . . . but after permanency—the name says it all." But the process of acquiring permanency was anything but a dream.

> I went to the Federal Police six times. You go . . . [and] the police officer who attends you says, "No, you have to bring this." But, since I'm smart, the thing I say is "No, give me a paper with what you need. And next time I'll bring it." That first day, they gave it to me. I came to the Refugee Center. "He's asking for this, this, and this." They gave me everything. I went back [to the Federal Police, but it was] someone else. "No! That's not it. You have to bring this, this, and this." . . . I went six times . . . it wasn't easy . . . People should not have to go back and forth six times. It's the cost of the trip and everything. It wastes time, and transit fare too.

The Federal Police worked against, rather than with, Rosine as she sought the legal firm ground that was formally hers. Though she tried to clarify what she needed to apply for permanency, the benchmark was ever shifting, forcing her to go over and over, back and forth, to the Federal Police Office and Refugee Center. While permanency was deeply meaningful for Rosine, the state made it exceedingly difficult—wasting her time, energy, and limited funds—for her to access it. And Rosine knew it shouldn't be that way.

Sima, a light-skinned refugee from Afghanistan, was the only one from that region I met who experienced issues seeking permanency. She applied for permanency based on having a child in Brazil, as the law provides, rather than asylum. This entailed different documents and fees. Sima was infamous at the Center for her obstinance. "Part of it is her fault, because of her demeanor," Guilherme posited. "She insists, insists, insists, and that closes doors and complicates things even more." When Guilherme says this, I am surprised. It is the first time someone at the Center explains issues at the Federal Police as the migrant's fault rather than the officers'. Sima's particular demeanor uniquely chafed those at the Police, and they produced roadblocks in her accessing her rights as a result. But her troubles were exceptional. Others from the Middle East and Afghanistan were instead often surprised by the positive treatment they experienced there.

FAMILY REUNIFICATION

Recognized refugees have the right to family reunification—to bring their immediate family to Brazil.[8] Legally, Brazil guarantees that right for partners, parents, children, and relatives who economically depend on the refugee.[9] Being able to reunite with their families was among the most salient rights for many, and essentially all refugees want to bring their family to Brazil.[10] In practice, for Congolese and other Africans, that right is acutely deferred. From 2014 to 2020, the average time to extend their refugee status to relatives was 0.8 year for Syrians, while for Congolese it was 11.1 years—an over ten-year difference.[11] The hurdles Congolese face—getting the visa, passing through the embassy, and extending their status to loved ones—produce a sense of powerlessness as they struggle to be together with their families again.

Family reunification is a very meaningful right. When I call Idumba, a sports coach and refugee from the Congo, to tell him the visas for his family have been issued, I can hear the elation in his voice. "Thank you very, very much." He repeats those words: "Thank you very, very much! Thank you very, very, very much!" He asks me if it was emitted just today because "today is my birthday." He is overwhelmed with joy. "So, so much thanks."

Another day at the Center, I work with Munir, a middle-aged Syrian refugee, to fill out the family reunification visa form for his wife, two sons, and daughter. His children are nine, eleven, and fourteen years old. As I complete the information for his daughter, he points to the screen. "My daughter," he smiles. "*Saudade, muita saudade*"—I miss them, I miss them so much.

"I can only imagine," I respond. "How long has it been since you last saw them?"

"One year and three months," he answers, and then corrects himself. I imagine the wheels in his head, counting the days that are so very present for him. "One year and two months."

As I fill out the form, he emphatically thanks me—*muito obrigado*. I write notes on the photocopies of his family's documents, to make clear who is who. As I do, he smiles and says his wife is also lefthanded. When we finish, I go to shake his hand, and he kisses the top of it in gratitude. Like Idumba, Munir is overwhelmed with joy and thanks at the thought of reuniting with family he deeply loves and misses.

While the right to family reunification is profoundly significant, it is delayed and curtailed for Congolese and other African refugees. Once the family member is in Brazil, they apply at the Federal Police Office to have their relative's refugee status extended to them at a CONARE plenary. But first, they must be in the country. For Congolese and other black Africans, this made family reunification a two-step process. First, they apply for a family reunification visa, providing documentary proof establishing the family tie. For requests based on economic dependence, this also involved receipts from money transfers. Then a visa would be emitted at the closest consulate so the family member could travel to Brazil.[12] For other nationalities, who do not need a visa for Brazil, they can arrive directly and apply for the status extension. Much of North Africa and Latin America, for example, does not need visas. While some, like Munir, chose to file for family reunification visas, Syrian families can come straight through the humanitarian visas available to them.

Throughout the family reunification process, Congolese and other Africans experienced manifold problems—unexplained delays, bureaucratic errors, other procedural mishaps—that impeded seeing their families again. The same morning I assist Kadie, I meet Divine, from the DRC, who comes to the Center to apply to bring her brother. But she cannot yet file an application because, like Kadie, there is an error in her notification letter. Though CONARE properly spells her name on one line, on another her last name is misspelled—though it is an easy six letters long. As I talk with the lawyers about her case, one frustratingly exclaims: "They can't even get that right!" Both Ana and Guilherme suggest she risk it and apply for family reunification, rather than wait for an updated notification letter to be emitted. It is a reasonable assessment. Antonio, the receptionist, told me earlier that day of refugees who had thus far been waiting for three months to have their notification letters corrected.

I go back to the patio and explain to Divine her two options. She can wait for a new notification letter, which could mean an indeterminate delay in bringing her brother. Or she could go to the Federal Police to apply for family reunification now, and try to explain the error, pointing out that her name is correctly bolded in the body of the letter and on her protocol. But she resists the idea. "No, no," she says, "they complicate things." She would rather wait. Though she has the right to bring her family to Brazil, her knowledge of the Federal Police stifles her into continuing to wait to be reunited with them.

Though Yornella is likewise formally entitled to this right, for her it had yet to materialize. "I knew that being recognized means that I can bring my family," Yornella tells me. "Now I can live together with my family, and that is very good." But "even here that I have been recognized," Yornella says, "as of now I have not been able to bring my family since I did the family reunification application. Still I have no response." At the time, applying for a family reunification visa was an administrative process suggested to take roughly three months, though no timeline had been formalized. Yornella had been waiting five months. She followed up with me multiple times to see what was happening with her application. But her frequent prodding was to no avail. There was no explanation provided by CONARE for the delay.

In this she was not alone. At the Refugee Center, my fieldwork was filled with instances of Congolese following up to see the status of their family reunification visa applications, which were often long delayed. Many hours were spent emailing CONARE about such requests. While I also helped Syrians apply, I have no documentation of Syrians having this right so hindered. In a review of national applications, political scientist Patrícia Nabuco Martuscelli found that "only the Congolese had a high number of visa denials without further information."[13]

At the Center I saw such hindrances most acutely with Congolese, but also with other African refugees. Mustafa, from East Africa, applied in January to bring his wife and children. Despite consistent prodding from the Refugee Center on his behalf, the visas were not emitted until eight months later. The Center tracks pending family reunification visa applications, and marks in red those delayed without cause or explanation. On a typical day at the Center, 33 of the 36 blocked out in red were from Africa, mainly from the DRC but also from Angola, Cameroon, Liberia, Nigeria, and Sierra Leone. While family reunification is a meaningful entitlement of asylum, black African refugees experience substantial hurdles in enacting that right.

Such delays can have devastating impacts for families. "To engage in politics in the Congo," as Wilson, a Congolese lawyer and organizer seeking asylum in Brazil, attests, "is also to expose your family." Beatriz, a lawyer at the Refugee Center in São Paulo, recounts a family reunification visa request by Patrice, a Congolese refugee, that Patrice pressed was exceedingly urgent. "We took that urgency to CONARE," Beatriz tells me, but they were paid no heed. In the wait, Patrice's brother was murdered. "Precisely what we were asking was that he come to Brazil," Beatriz deplores. "If he had come, he wouldn't have been assassinated." Patrice's brother has not been the only family member assassinated while the refugee waited for CONARE to process a visa request.

Delays were exacerbated by bureaucratic inattention and negligence, where officials created issues for Congolese refugees where there were none. Marcus, from the DRC, requested reunification visas for his partner and daughters three years after receiving asylum in Brazil. The next month, Frederic followed up with me to see its status. CONARE responded confirming receipt of the reunification form but contested that it did not include a marriage certificate. As I read this aloud to Frederic, he starts laughing. With his characteristic smile and wispy laugh, he retorts, "But it says civil union!" Marcus applied based not on marriage but civil union, as is his legal right. His application form states this and attached are the necessary documents. But the official gave little care to the claim, leading them to mischaracterize it and delay its processing. Understaffing and an overextended bureaucracy make this exceedingly possible. "It is a small team," official Isabela notes. "And we really do more than we can handle."

Dikembe, also from the DRC, applied for visas for six family members in March. CONARE responded requesting more documents, which he returned to the Center the following month to provide. As he goes to leave, he asks how long it will take.

"A few months," Ana says. "You don't have to come back. When there is a decision, we will contact you."

"Okay," he responds. "I will come back in two weeks."

Dikembe was right not to trust that the process would proceed without his prodding. The following day, CONARE responded that they could not open the attached documents. But someone in the legal office at the Center accidentally marked the email as read without responding. I only discover this a few weeks later when Frederic asks me to check Dikembe's application. If Frederic had not, I do not know how long it would have taken to have the attachments re-sent. It was a common issue that when CONARE did respond, no one would notice until the refugee returned to the Center to check the application's status. In the overwhelming flurry of the legal office's inbox, emails were quickly buried and lost track of.

The following week, Dikembe comes back to the Center to see about the visas. I send another follow-up email to CONARE on his behalf but receive no response. Frederic checks with me again a few weeks later, now three months since Dikembe filed. CONARE only responds that it is under analysis—the same as saying nothing.

Not trusting that the system will move forward in their best interest, Congolese refugees like Dikembe find they must persistently put pressure to try to get what is purportedly rightfully theirs. Congolese refugees would come to the Refugee Center weekly to monthly to follow up on family reunification visa requests. They would send weekly emails to the Center, and Dikembe sent emails to CONARE as well. Frederic would pester lawyers and volunteers alike on their behalf to check the status and get in touch again with CONARE. Even after recognition, these delays tethered Congolese refugees to the Center, bringing them back again and again, subject to the heat and hunger entailed in waiting there.

Brazilian law grants refugees the right to reunite with family that financially depend on them. Yet, documenting economic dependence proved a procedural hurdle that hindered access to that right. Two years after she got asylum, Jeanette, from the DRC, applied to bring her two sisters to Brazil in November. Jeanette provided her sisters' birth certificates to prove the familial relation. By April, the Center has sent two follow-up emails. Finally, in response, CONARE requests Jeanette provide parental authorization for her 17-year-old sister to travel to Brazil and proof of financial dependence. Guilherme sends the parental authorization, as well as a Western Union money transfer receipt in each's name to confirm Jeanette's financial support. Later that month, CONARE responds: "The applicant must submit one more proof of financial dependence, the form contains two and both are not in the brothers' names. She has to submit three vouchers in the brothers' names."

While some of the second first names are in different orders on the money transfers, the receipts appear clearly destined for her sisters. Though the passports and application confirm they are Jeanette's sisters, not her brothers, CONARE misgenders and misrecognizes them, suggesting the lack of care and attention given the claim. While CONARE had initially failed to declare how many monetary transfers would be needed, an official now affirmed only three—for each—would suffice.

Upon reading the email, I am livid. I ask Lucas, "Can they do that?"

"That is something they invented," he responds. CONARE Resolution 16, though extending the right to family reunification to economically dependent relatives, did not clarify what would count as proving a refugee's financial responsibility. In the absence of any standard, officials invented them arbitrarily. Left unformalized, refugees had no legal recourse or ability to know what the state would or could want from them. Each time Jeanette sought to acquiesce, she was met with new bureaucratic hurdles.

Rather than push back, Lucas tells me to get in touch with Jeanette to see if she has more receipts "to not fight with CONARE if there's no need to." Because there's no formalization, Lucas knows there's no room to fight. Jeanette returns to the Center in September, when she has finally gathered the requested transfer receipts from Western Union. Given the financial struggles Congolese refugees experience in Brazil, remitting money to family abroad is no small feat. Two weeks later, Frederic asks me if there's any response since sending the proof of economic dependence. Though she provided the documentation asked for, and it had been 10 months since she filed, Jeanette had received no response.

Delaying visas based on economic dependence led to other Congolese visas being delayed. Mbo applied for his mother, two brothers, and two other family members in March. Two months later, Mbo followed up again and Guilherme emailed CONARE on his behalf. The subsequent week, Frederic asks me to check again. In response, CONARE answers: "requests involving economic dependence . . . must wait." At the time, CONARE had paused processing visas based on financial responsibility, but the request for his mother had no reason for the delay. A week later, Mbo comes again to the Center and talks with Ana to see what is happening with the visas. She follows up with CONARE and affirms in her email that "there's no reason for the mother to be waiting."

We check again a month later, in June, and still there is no response.

By mid-July, Frederic has Sofia, a volunteer at the Center, send another email. CONARE responds only that the application is under evaluation. There is no recognition of the inordinate delay for Mbo's mother. By the end of August, Frederic again asks Sofia to email about Mbo's application. Finally, in September—seven months later—the visas are emitted for Mbo's family to come to Brazil.

Naomie, from the Congo, applied in May for her mother alone. The following month, with CONARE yet to respond, Ana sends a follow-up email imploring: "Please, this person comes here all the time wanting to know; she applied for her mother, it does not have to be judged based on economic dependence. Please, they need to leave the DRC urgently." Despite Naomie's consistent pleading and prodding, others like Frederic pressing about her case (Sofia noted how, by October, every week Frederic asked her to send another email—to the frustration of CONARE), and frequent follow-up emails sent by Ana, myself, and others, CONARE did not approve the emission of her mother's visa until seven months after she applied. And, another two months later, the consulate had yet to confirm receipt of the visa approval. For those like Naomie and Mbo, their purported right to be reunited with their mothers was deferred without recourse.

As Naomie's experience suggests, even once CONARE approves the visa, issues continue for Congolese refugees. Challenges at the Brazilian embassy in Kinshasa became more insidious in 2017, when consular authorities began interviewing family members and rejecting visas previously approved by CONARE without explanation. As political scientist Martuscelli found: "After that, refugees' family members, mostly in the DRC, began having their family reunification visas denied . . . Refugees described how their relatives had to pass through excruciating interviews, which could last 2 [hours], often asking the same things over and over and with questions designed to trick them." Even as Congolese refugees attested to presenting all requested documentation, racialized suspicions of fraud and corruption led to interrogative interviews, visa denials, and excessive wait times.[14]

Congolese experiences of bureaucratic neglect did not stop once relatives made it to Brazil. The familial extension of refugee status is an administrative process, not an adjudicative one. The relative does not have to prove they qualify for asylum. Once an application is filed at the Federal Police Office, such cases go before a CONARE plenary to be formalized. Then too, Congolese relatives are subject to delays.

Rosine comes to the Refugee Center with many issues she wants to address. Among them, she wants to check the status of her permanent residency application, her travel authorization request, and the extension of her refugee status to her daughter. For the latter, I check her daughter's case in SEI, the national asylum database, and see it is in red. "It's still pending," I tell Rosine, "there has not been a decision yet."

"It is *a very long* time!" She exclaims, "It has been a year!"

I try to assuage her, but it makes no difference. She and her daughter have no choice but to continue waiting. In the meantime, her daughter must endure life with the precarious protocol, and she cannot start her clock to citizenship. A different day at the Center, Rosine reflects about life in Brazil. "You have to wait for this here, these things." "When you are waiting," she tells me, "it is really frustrating." Though she admits experiencing "the very feeling of anxiety," she tries for "patience in everything. Just patience."

TRAVEL AUTHORIZATION

Refugee international mobility is contingent and subject to authorization in Brazil. To obtain a yellow passport, refugees must request travel authorization from CONARE, detailing their travel information, including location, dates, and length of travel; reasons for traveling; and contact information while, in Hamid's words, "away from this home." While the state provides the international protection of asylum, it also determines the mode of that protection. It does not allow the refugee to act autonomously in deciding if, when, and why he wants or needs to leave the country. Asylum actors understood the power underlying such control. Isabela, an official in Brasília, referred to travel authorizations as the state "wanting to show that it's the state and you are at its mercy." Requiring refugees to seek approval to leave Brazil provided a means for the state, as Lucas puts it, "to control the life of the refugee." Here too, black refugees experienced bureaucratic slights and delays that Hamid, for example, did not.

Aimee, from the DRC, was recognized in 2013. She submitted a travel authorization request for her and her daughter Micheline in February 2016. She wants to travel to Belgium for two months in late April. CONARE responds that "each travel applicant must complete a form separately." In his reply, Guilherme signals the absurdity of the demand and asks for comprehension: "As shown by the RNE attached, Micheline is only 11 years old. Her mother (legal guardian) made the request on her behalf. Furthermore, the child attends school (and cannot appear at the Refugee Center during its opening hours), and the mother is not able to send the travel request on her own. The journey from her home to the Refugee Center is, in addition to being long, financially costly for the applicant. We count on your understanding." The following week, the CONARE official responds, declaring only: "Could you send us the forms again? For some reason I can't open it again."

No one from the legal office responds. A month later Aimee comes to the Center, two weeks before her family plans to travel, to see if the authorization has arrived. When I go out to the patio to assist someone else, Aimee stands up, walks over, and stands close to me. She is much taller than I am, and looks down at my eyes with a straight face. "Did you forget about me?" Aimee had already been waiting an hour and a half, and I had yet to speak with her.

"No, no, I didn't forget about you," I emphatically answer, trying to appease her. Indeed, I hadn't. I had been trying to speak with Lucas to see if there was any way to expedite her request, but the two times I tried he was occupied. "The government said they couldn't open the document for your travel authorization," I tell her. "So, it hasn't come through yet." She repeats my words. "It hasn't come through?" I explain I have been trying to see what we could do. But everything else I say seems to fade into nothing. Her tone signals disappointment and a reserved indignance, and her face makes no indication that my attempts to assuage her work. Whatever I say now seems beside the point. As I continue to speak, she turns her head, looking away from me. She does not respond as I try to say we will find a way. She does not nod in agreement, there is no light in her eyes. All that has stuck, all that matters, is that she is not authorized to leave the country.

By the time Lucas and I can chat about her case, Aimee had already found and spoken with him, and Lucas had begun working on it. "So, you saw what happened?" I ask with fuming indignance. "CONARE responded over a month ago to have the travel authorization sent again—but no one responded?" I am livid about the blunder.

Instead, Lucas's tone is of defeated disappointment. He nods, and softly repeats with resignation, "No one responded." Given overburden at the Center, failing the refugees seeking assistance, and even causing problems for them, is not unusual. Remorse for not doing right by them, as he wishes he could, is not a new feeling for Lucas. He submits a new travel authorization for Aimee, her original travel dates no longer possible. Though Aimee followed protocol and requested authorization with ample time, she and her daughter are not able to travel to Belgium as they had hoped and planned because of multiple acts of neglect by those from whom she sought assistance.

Obtaining the travel authorization does not necessarily mark the end of issues for Congolese refugees. As I fill out a travel authorization for Rosine, she tells me about the last time she got authorization to leave the country. "At the airport," the Federal Police, she recounts, "kept me for an hour because they wanted to know if I was fleeing Brazil." She continues, "I was the last person on the plane." She was deeply embarrassed. "Now I know for next time," she tells me, "I have to arrive well in advance because they do this." Though she had the government's approval to leave the country, as she did, she was humiliated.

Material Continuities

Refugees do not experience asylum in isolation. How they feel about asylum is configured by the broader realities in which their attempts to build a place in the world unfold. While most who apply for asylum obtain it in Brazil, it does not ameliorate their daily struggles. It does not take someone out of economic precarity, allow them to continue their education, provide safe and secure housing, or improve the quality of the public services to which they have access. "There is a tension," Lucas notes, "between the policies for refugees and the realities of poverty in Rio."

About asylum, official Bianca reflects: "In the end, what does this resolve? I think it doesn't resolve much." She continues:

> Let's take a refugee that was recognized ... [asylum] is not going to, automatically, take her out of the precarious work situation in which she finds herself, it is not going to make it so that she can immediately validate her diploma. It is not going to incorporate her into the labor market. It is not going to make her integrated into society in the way that I would like to be included if I were a refugee ... Yesterday, an asylum seeker called us saying that he was seven days without light, and that [the light company] didn't come ... If he gets [asylum], will it improve the public service that he is going to have? ... I don't know if a document can provide anything [*suprir qualquer coisa*].

Sabrina, a lawyer at the Refugee Center, similarly muses: "What protection does a refugee receive relative to a migrant, for example, in reality? It doesn't make much difference." Elaborating, she notes: "Refugee protection in Brazil doesn't add hardly anything."[15]

After recognition, refugees continue to face economic precarity and labor informality, social exclusion, and stifling bureaucracies. For example, it is estimated that less than 10 percent of refugees have been able to have their degrees recognized.[16] For Yornella, still "nothing is easy." She continues: "In my country, I do not have the limits that I have here. Here there are many limits. It is difficult . . . It is difficult for us to do anything."

Asylum does not change refugees' housing issues in Rio. It does not guarantee a physical safe haven. Wael was unhoused, and Hamid lives in a church shelter. Yornella has still not been able to realize a deep desire: to have a space of her own. "You can't rent a home, an apartment on your own." She continues, "I rent with my sister and another refugee. We are three." "We share a room. It's difficult, isn't it?" Somalian refugee Absame continued to experience long stints of unemployment and had to rely on the abysmal public shelter system for housing. When I met him, he had bounced around between three such shelters, yet to find a permanent home. Like Lionel, other Congolese and black African refugees likewise lived in the most marginalized and peripheral zones of Rio, often favela communities.[17]

For Syrian refugees, the disparity between the ease of arrival and the lack of government integration programs once in Brazil was disenchanting. In the words of Nizar: "The thing about the Brazilian process is that it was very, very inviting. Because it was the only country that welcomes Syrians in a way. You can come legit, get a visa, you fly safely. But there's not much support after you arrive here, government wise. There's no systematic program for those people that are coming, they just invite people to come in and there's nothing on the ground." He continues: "On a certain level I am very thankful and grateful for this process, [but] . . . it's not really effective, there's no real program to integrate these people that you want in." How easy it was to come and obtain asylum in Brazil gave the expectation that things would be different. "You come here," Adnan reflects, and "you have to do it on your own."

Similarly, while Hamid appreciates what Brazil has done for him, he finds it deeply unsatisfactory because its objective consequences feel meager. His daily life looks the same. "Refugee status [did] not make anything for me," he tells me. "What I have, I have for myself." Hamid is disinclined to think of asylum in positively transformative terms. "The government doesn't help," Hamid says. "I depend on myself."

While Syrians can feel ambivalently welcomed and abandoned by the state, they do not experience the discrimination they felt elsewhere. Nizar had been living in Turkey prior. There, he told me, "I just felt unwelcomed," but in Rio, the people are "very easygoing and friendly." Before the Syrian war, Adnan traveled to and lived in many other countries, including studying abroad in the United States. He feels welcomed in Brazil in ways he wouldn't expect to find in other countries. "People are nice, honestly . . . Brazilians don't talk at you like an underling, like you're second or third class because you are not Brazilian. They don't have that kind of behavior . . . To live here a long time, this is important . . . otherwise you are under too much stress . . . Here in Brazil, I can go to a restaurant, I can sit anywhere I want, and nobody looks at me, like 'What the fuck do you want?' . . . This is something nice . . ." While Adnan experiences difficulties in Brazil, and is particularly frustrated by "their bureaucracy, which is too much for any small thing," he doesn't experience it as a form of discrimination. It's "not applied to us because we are refugees, but every Brazilian . . . it's general Brazilian culture."

While Adnan feels it would not be like this elsewhere, neither is it like that for other refugees in Brazil. According to a 2019 UNHCR Brazil study, less than two in ten Syrian refugees expressed suffering discrimination, compared to seven out of ten Congolese, "confirming," the report concludes, "that discrimination has a clear racial basis."[18] Congolese—for the fact of being black, and the second largest group of refugees in Brazil at that time—were those who most suffer obstacles to integration.[19]

Asylum does not resolve refugees' daily struggles, and anti-black racism exacerbates the harsh realities unresolved by recognition. For African refugees, it overdetermines the material deprivations they continue to experience. Refugee status does not protect Congolese and other African refugees from the racial order as they navigate the country where they sought safe haven. "Brazil has a lot of great things," Frederic shares, "but it also has bad things, like racism, primarily against Africans."

After recognition, black African refugees still experience racialized forms of economic exclusion and marginalization. Congolese refugees have higher levels of educational attainment than the average Brazilian.[20] But in Brazil, as Adriana, the coordinator of the Refugee Center, notes: "Unfortunately, a difference between black and white refugees exists. Syrians find work much more easily."[21]

Though applying for asylum grants the right to work, it does not guarantee employment or what that looks like. According to a national study, while the majority of Syrians are employed, the majority of Congolese are not; Congolese are over five times more likely than Syrians to live on less than $200 USD a month, roughly the Brazilian minimum wage.[22] In Rio, researchers found that 50 percent of Syrian respondents worked in their area of professionalization, whereas only 25 percent of Congolese did.[23]

Adnan was one of those Syrians who was able to get a job in his area. Getting that job had a substantial impact. While being recognized "feels more stable," he says: "What helped me is finding the job. I think if I didn't find the job, my life would be miserable . . . To me, when I found a job, it was really like . . . it changed a lot in my life. And I started to think about things in a more positive way, to use the opportunity of having a job. I have a salary, I can plan, I can think. I look at it like 'Okay, I'm alive again.'" "Because when you arrive, you don't have a salary from the government," he continues, "finding a job made like 90 percent of things easy for me. Because if you have a job, you have a salary and you can organize your life." Before that, Adnan explains, "every week I was thinking I need to pack my bag and go back to Turkey, because I was so very depressed. At that time, it was hard."

In his Portuguese course at a local university, Wael had class with a chemist who invited him to work in her lab. Three years later, he was still working there. For Wael, it wasn't the government that did it—but "because I got contacts."

For Africans, life in Rio can mean a descent into labor informality, economic precarity, and poverty unresolved by recognition. In the Congo, Frederic was a nurse. After almost 10 years in Rio, and fluent in Portuguese, he works in hotels as a messenger and doorman. Though Rosine has a bachelor's degree in information technology and speaks Portuguese comfortably, four years after recognition she finds herself unemployed. In Nigeria, Kemi was a human rights journalist. Years after recognition, Kemi still has days where she goes hungry, working when she can as a hairdresser.[24]

"A German trained in accounting, when he comes here, he works in his field," Andre, himself an accountant from the Congo, reflects. "If you're Congolese, they send you to wash the floors." Andre, like Kemi and others, struggles to make ends meet by cutting hair. "I've sent out over 50 resumés, I've done 12 interviews, but no one calls me."[25] Many recounted being denied jobs for being refugees, African, and Congolese. "Many of us fled here looking for peace and freedom," Frederic reflects. "But there is no freedom or peace without work. Only with work can we have a better future. But the work we want is dignified work."

Nor does asylum change the difficult work conditions to which black Africans are subjected. According to Adriana, many employers want Africans for the heaviest work because they believe they can withstand more. "I never expected the life of a telenovela," Congolese refugee Chadrack laments, "but here they only offer us manual labor."[26] "Because we are foreigners, because we are refugees and because we are Africans," Frederic says, "we are left with the toughest, most difficult jobs [*mais duros, os mais pesados*]. They give us the worst jobs and the worst working conditions. They think we have no intelligence and no training. Even with better resumés than the rest." Black African refugee women note that most options available to them were as cleaning ladies, cooks, or housemaids.[27]

"We need . . . decent jobs [*trabalhos dignos*]," Frederic continues, "so we aren't treated like slaves, so we aren't exploited."

There is a circulating assumption that Africans are without professions. At the opening of a refugee art exhibit at a cultural center in Rio, there is a panel with the artists whose work is on display—forced migrants from Syria, the Democratic Republic of the Congo, and Colombia. Following their introductory remarks, an audience member asks: "Those who started doing art now—Serge, Keto—do they plan to continue?" The only novices who participated in the exhibit were the two Syrians. Yet, that question was asked of the Congolese who were not. Serge is a sculptor, while Keto is a ceramicist.

"There must have been some confusion," Priscila, a staff member from the Center on the panel, answers. "Serge and Keto are artists."

"They have degrees in fine arts from the University of Kinshasa," the curator adds.

"Unfortunately, refugees usually can't work in what they did before they came," Priscila continues. "Serge and Keto have no workshop here."

This racialization of professional competence is not unique to Rio. In São Paulo, a local church began holding meetings three times a week with employers wanting to contract immigrants, principally Haitians and Africans, for which the church had become a conduit. During one such workshop, the social worker explains to the employers: "I know we aren't accustomed to seeing a warehouse full of black folk [*negões*[28]] with higher education, but leave any prejudice aside."[29] "Just because we are African," Frederic reflects, "we are considered illiterate . . . that we have no education, that we are ignorant."

I sit with Laurent, from the DRC, at the volunteer computer in the reception office at the Refugee Center. He's been having trouble finding work, and he's come to put together a resumé. As we fill out the Center's template, he chats fluently with me in English. He likes the practice. Laurent has a bachelor's degree in political science from the University of Kinshasa, but he tells me not to put that on his resumé. He worries people won't want to hire him because of his degree. He wants it to only say he completed high school. Laurent feels finding employment means downplaying his education.

These economic difficulties also impede refugees' ability to access in practice rights of asylum most salient to them. Edward, from Sierra Leone, wants to bring over his two brothers, but he doesn't know when he will have the money. Kemi, who yearns to reunite with her mother, does not have the financial capacity to access that right. I run into Marcus at the Federal Police Office, two months after the visas for his partner and daughters had been approved. I ask if his family is here yet. "No," Marcus answers, "tickets are very expensive."

Nor does asylum mean the threat of death is behind them. Economic exploitation, anti-black discrimination, and violence devastatingly intertwine in Brazil. Twenty-four-year-old Congolese refugee Moïse Mugenyi Kabagambe worked at a beach kiosk in Rio, in the elite neighborhood of Barra da Tijuca. He fled the Democratic Republic of the Congo with his mother and siblings when he was an adolescent. On January 24, 2022, he went to the kiosk to request two days of back wages due to him—totaling $38. An employee and two other men tied him up with a cord, and brutally beat him to death with a piece of wood and a baseball bat.

Moïse's murder is a tragic example of how violence and alienation shape the lives of Congolese refugees long after they obtain asylum. Continued struggles coalesce to produce a sense that they are not fully at home in the country that provided them asylum; it does not make them feel like they belong. "I am a foreigner, this is not my country," Yornella reflects. "I am a refugee, black, and don't speak Portuguese . . . I am never going to be Brazilian like them."

The experiences of refugees like Lionel, Hamid, Yornella, Moïse, and others push us to reconsider what asylum means and provides for those who receive it. Refugee status does not necessarily produce a positive rupture in their lives. Forced migrants can experience asylum ambivalently, as its salient rights are deferred in practice, and it does not resolve pertinent issues of daily life. Foregrounding refugee perceptions and experiences illustrates how and why asylum, even in the face of formally progressive policies, can fail to be transformative. While Syrians and Congolese alike expressed ambivalence about asylum, different practical and experiential dynamics produced that meaning.

The meaning of refugee status does not exist outside of society; it is dependent upon it. Whether refugee status is transformative depends on both the refugee regime and the broader social world where the refugee finds asylum. In Brazil, both are inflected by a hierarchical racial order. What matters is not refugee status, but what it does—and does not—do. Refugee status is neither universal, nor a panacea.

Encounters across the legal and socioeconomic milieu coalesce to give a feeling of who among refugees is and is not welcome, and what that welcome means in Brazil. How such policies are enacted and experienced in practice, and with what consequences in their daily lives, proves decisive for the racial production of refugee (non)belonging.

That's how it is when your oppressor is your liberator . . .
. . . your asylum has got you in a different war

DAVE, "Three Rivers"

CONCLUSION

Racial Domination through Inclusion

Who is a refugee is not a given. It is a state production. Following the asylum seeker through that process, this book exposes how the state racializes those seeking safe haven, the racial lessons it imparts, and the inequalities that result. As forced migrants encounter the refugee regime, they are incorporated into the national racial order. Though refugees can be offered a legal place in the nation, racial ideologies shape what asylum means and how it is experienced. For black African refugees, it is a recognition of a different kind.

Such modalities of racism are missed through interrogations of legal status as a primary axis of difference, or as racially othering in and of itself. Sociologists often investigate racism through divergences in particular outcomes—who is hired, who is incarcerated, who goes to college, who is made "illegal," and who obtains asylum. Such perspectives discipline us into a narrow vision of inequality, yet such mechanisms are not the only way racisms manifest. Racial political domination also occurs through processes of inclusion, producing racialized hierarchies within legal statuses rather than only between them.

The racial project of asylum in Brazil underscores how racial states take different permutations, and the importance of not presuming migrant racial domination always or only works through selection and exclusion as seen in the Global North. Brazil signals the need to analyze the bureaucratic operations of racial states to capture how race and racial hierarchies are produced. Racial domination occurs in the everyday workings of the refugee regime, while being mystified through the smoke screen of formally inclusive policies.

Asylum in Brazil is refracted through the racial order in which it unfolds, and racial logics shape the quotidian operations of refugee governance and assistance. Race works in asylum as, what Pierre Bourdieu would call, a principle of vision and division.[1] Race-making is fundamen-

tal in how asylum actors envision those seeking safe haven, how they attribute meaning, and how they manifest order and hierarchy. State bureaucracies not only mirror a racial social world, but also produce it. As
those working in the refugee regime perceive, interact with, and evaluate
those seeking safe haven, they racialize them, with trenchant sociopolitical consequences for the meaning of legal inclusion. Racial meanings are
ascribed to newcomers, and those imbue interactions and influence how
rights and resources are distributed. Racialized cognition, action, and interaction are intertwined.

Examining the diverging treatment that Syrians and Congolese find in
the process of obtaining asylum illuminates racial hierarchies produced
and enacted through the Brazilian refugee regime, even in the face of formal recognition and progressive policies. Though Syrian and Congolese
asylum seekers generally find the same legal outcome, their experiences
before, during, and after that decision are quite different. And those racialized divergences are, in the words of Robert Stam and Ella Shohat,
"intimately interconnected, sharing intersecting impulses and logics."[2]

Syrians are positioned within the Brazilian body politic. The state actively works to produce an imagined community based on ethnic ties said
to unite Brazil and Syria.[3] While historical and ethnic connections are
the mechanism of fabrication, inclusion in whiteness configures the possibilities of that welcome and how the boundaries of national community
are expanded.[4] "Asylum depends on the government," Frederic tells me.
"Brazil gives the message that it is opening its arms for all Syrians, that is
a political act." That the government has opened its doors to Syrians, and
more recently Afghans and Ukrainians, signals the power and capacity of
the state to do so. It is not outside the realm of the politically possible. Yet
if and how that prospect emerges has been shaped by racialized notions
of worth and belonging in Brazil.

Positioned inside that imagined community, Syrians are perceived and
treated as credible, legitimate, trustworthy—easily sped along. They are
not made to wait, not made to confess, not marginalized by the state in
the ways that Congolese are. If to wait is to suffer, such forms of political
domination are attenuated for Syrians in Brazil. In the face of the mass
displacement of refugees racialized as white in that country, the Brazilian refugee regime reconfigured from top to bottom, providing multiple
concessions that expedited and facilitated their immigration. But once in
Brazil, Syrian refugees discovered that, while the state made obtaining
refugee status easy, it would do little else. Imagined as self-starters, they
were expected to make their own way.

In contrast, shared historical and ethnic ties between Brazil and the
Congo are disregarded. The state does not imagine Congolese refugees

as members of the Brazilian nation. Congolese are ascribed with a dubious morality, and officials treat Congolese asylum claims with skepticism and suspicion. They are perceived as suspect, subject to close inspection and increased scrutiny, but also treated with disregard and neglect. After obtaining refugee status, they continue to be deferred access to the rights to which they are formally entitled. In their encounters and entanglements with the refugee regime, Congolese learn what it means to be black in Brazil.

Such patterns manifested across the heterogeneous backgrounds found among Syrians and Congolese, and extended beyond them. Frederic and Pierre came from opposite ends of the Democratic Republic of the Congo, and they had distinct occupational and educational backgrounds. Frederic applied for refugee status based on political persecution, while Pierre applied based on ethnic group. Both had their credibility questioned as they sought asylum, and in ways that neither Syrians nor others from the Middle East may experience. Frederic and Pierre were both recognized as refugees, but in the process they faced a state that did not readily believe them.

Racism is not relegated to the historical past of Brazil's immigration policies. Examining how the Brazilian refugee regime orients toward different forced migrants, and with what consequences, exposes how racial ideologies configure asylum today. Race and migration continue to be mutually constituted, as the treatment and experiences of forced migrants are formatively shaped by racial meanings of nation and political subjecthood in contemporary Brazil. At the same time, fully grasping the racial logics of asylum in Brazil requires situating them in the historical legacies of racist anti-racialism that continue to underlie the national polity. How asylum officials perceive, evaluate, and interact with asylum seekers cannot be understood through those perceptions, actions, and interactions alone.[5] That asylum officials see Syrians as proactive entrepreneurs, or suspect Africans of lying, is not idiosyncratic. It is set within the *longue durée* of racial ideologies of differential inclusion in the nation and its immigration policies.

The experiences of Congolese refugees like Frederic, Pierre, and Lionel expose the limits of legal inclusion and the promise of safe haven. The consequences of legal membership for Congolese refugees in Brazil trouble the premise of asylum as providing reprieve from political exclusion. Asylum does not necessitate full political personhood before the state. Not only is inclusion not enough for racial and refugee justice, it can be a mode through which racial domination is accomplished. Antiblack marginalization can emerge by way of, rather than despite, formal protection. Brazil has one of the most lauded refugee regimes in the world.

Yet, as Lilian Lourenço Basto, then secretary general of the Brazilian Red Cross of the State of Rio de Janeiro, reflected at a panel on refugees, there is a "question of inclusion: We receive them, but how? What is the quality of that reception?" Inclusion—even in a country seen as a model of refugee protection—can also be cruel.

Hierarchies of need and vulnerability are increasingly the logic by which the world is being governed.[6] Because the global landscape restricts the rights of migrants to move and belong, they are ever more subject to asylum-screening processes. Even in the face of seemingly humane policies, that process variably forces migrants to suffer heat, hunger, and time, and to expose their lives to the state's judgment, among other indignities and precarities.

Racial domination through inclusion is made possible by the subjective, discretionary nature of asylum. In the process of filtering the seemingly worthy from the unworthy, the state has ample room to racialize and incorporate forced migrants into a highly unequal national racial order. This discretion allows the refugee regime in Brazil to discriminate while being championed abroad, and even as it grants what is understood as the most exceptional of migratory statuses and legal recognition offered by the state. Asylum allows Brazil to present itself as compassionate, while concomitantly producing racialized subjects in practice. The lauded nature of asylum as an international human right provides particular purchase for that mission.

Asylum, as the humanitarian arm of immigration governance, expands rather than diminishes state power. Migrants have the human right to seek asylum—but not to obtain it. That power lies not with migrants but with the state. Through its processes of screening and categorizing, the sovereign power to determine the meaning of migrant mobility remains intact. In the words of Frederic at a meeting with the legal unit at the Refugee Center:

> Two people come from the Kivu region [in the Democratic Republic of the Congo]: Let's say two women—one was raped, the other wasn't. They arrive here, and you ask them, "What do you think will happen if you returned to your country of origin?" They will both have the exact same fear . . . I don't know why they are going to make a difference between those who are in the same conditions, come from the same conditions, who have the same thinking, the same fears, even those who didn't yet have anything happen to them . . . They still have the same objective: to work, to reorganize their lives, to help their family that is there. We

shouldn't discriminate, one versus the other. That's why I say this is political, because it depends on the government . . .

Frederic believes there is no meaningful difference. But he knows it is ultimately the government that will decide who is and is not a refugee.

Societal investment in asylum makes the politics of whether the state should have the power to decide largely unrecognizable. Citizens, scholars, politicians, and media pundits alike are invested in contesting the boundaries and consequences of refugee status—who should and should not have access to that protection, and the supports and entitlements extended to asylum seekers and refugees. Rarely do we interrogate asylum itself. Questioning the necessity and efficacy of refuge—whether and why it is imperative, what it fundamentally does and does not do, what it can and cannot do—does not arise.

The refugee regime is a taken-for-granted, naturalized apparatus of classification, regulation, and exclusion. After spending the day assisting Senegalese asylum seekers who had empty stomachs and no hopes for asylum, Refugee Center volunteer Sofia's heart went out to them. She laments their characterization as economic migrants without legitimate claims for refugee status. As we go for a walk, she unloads her frustrations. She cries: "There has to be a filter, but . . . !" and trails off. She questions the form of the filter, but not its existence.

Scholars demonstrate their investment in the refugee regime as they map its inconsistencies. Much research charts inequities found in the system rather than interrogating injustices inherently of it. Documenting when the state fails to determine who among asylum seekers are legitimate presumes the refugee status distinction is a genuine one. Struggles for reform and due process, and critiques of biased treatment, denied access, or the circumscribed parameters of the refugee definition, reaffirm the obviousness of the refugee regime. "Sometimes I wonder, do I believe in refugee status determination? Is this necessary?" Bianca, an asylum official, answers her own question. "I've been thinking not." It is a question few of us ask.

The point of dispute begins at who should count, not whether the refugee—as a way of categorizing and stratifying migrants—should exist in the first place. Our adherence to the seemingly self-evident categories of immigration—economic migrant or refugee—presumes the ontological preexistence of such distinctions, normalizing the categories of the state. In doing so, we reproduce the logic of the refugee regime, rather than seeing such "categories as governmental contrivances."[7] That the world's migrants should be classified and divided as such—understanding refugees as fundamentally different from other migrants—goes unquestioned.[8]

If we are so invested in refuge—to find and fix its flaws, to expand who counts—what is it we are invested in? *The Color of Asylum* pushes us to rethink the meanings and consequences of that filter. Asylum generates racialized political violence, veiling the domination entailed for both those included and excluded, while presenting the state as benevolent. By assuming few migrants deserve such protection, we make unrecognizable the suffering produced among those who receive it (by presuming it is, indeed, a protection), and normalize that to which those migrants excluded, deemed unworthy and undeserving of asylum, are subjected. We live in a world deeply invested in the notion that asylum has the power to resolve the suffering migrants experience. Rather than only reducing social suffering, asylum also induces and sanctions it. True migrant justice entails upending that selection and differentiation itself.

Asylum is rooted in exceptionalism.[9] As Jasbir Puar writes in *Terrorist Assemblages*, "Exceptionalism paradoxically signals *distinction from* (to be unlike, dissimilar) as well as *excellence* (imminence, superiority)." In this, "the double play of exception," she continues, "the deferred death of one population recedes as the securitization and valorization of the life of another population triumphs in its shadow."[10] What deferred deaths recede, as the purportedly securitized lives of (some) refugees triumph in the migrant shadows of the socially dead and ignored? Irrespective of what refuge accomplishes—whether this valorization is a cutting fiction—refugees are understood as separate from the rest, fundamentally different from other migrants.

"Refugee," as a universal value of recognition, is meant to uniquely arouse our sympathy. By seeking to capitalize on the refugee frame as the most deserving and worthy migrant, we reproduce rather than upend the stratifying logic of worth and belonging embedded. The categorical difference ascribed suggests those who are not refugees are not worth compassion and do not deserve our solidarity.[11] Refuge, as exception and exceptional, produces a hierarchy of suffering that allows most misery to fall outside its limited boundaries. To have asylum as a mechanism for inclusion provides for legitimizing and normalizing the exclusion of everyone else.

The refugee—as exemplary victim, deserving of concessions and of special treatment, as a universal good, to be valued and cherished—mystifies the state power served by its existence. Asylum does more for the state than for those seeking its protection. As sociologist Liza Schuster writes: "[The] principle of 'asylum' is in fact safe in the hands of . . . governments, because it is an instrument of the state . . . and because *it serves to legitimate the state in moral terms* . . . While it may not be a reliable instrument for the protection of individuals, its (unreliable) benefits will remain so long as it retains some utility for the state."[12]

The humanitarian safety valve of asylum makes a world of immigrant exclusions morally defensible. Its existence legitimates the global migration landscape that fails to see and treat migrants as humans, as it softens the moral and political pressure points that would provide for the whole system's undoing.[13] The exception to the rule allows the rule to continue.

The possibility of refuge, and our investment in it, makes open borders politically unthinkable.[14] It forecloses that the desire for mobility would be sufficient for the freedom to do so. To think and enact "refugee" as a category is to have already acquiesced to a hierarchical differentiation of human movement—to say refugee is to not say migrant—and legitimated the state's sovereign right to make the distinction. And, as long as it does so, it is likely to continue—regardless of the consequences for those who seek and obtain asylum.

Acknowledgments

To say this book benefited from the many who engaged it would be the grossest of understatements. It would not have been possible without them. Thank you to Javier Auyero for your care and brilliance. Your unwavering presence and intellectual support throughout this journey cannot be expressed in words. It is more than I ever could have imagined in an advisor, and I have been so lucky to know and learn from you. I cannot picture how these pages would look without your mentorship. Thank you, Javier, for teaching me, among so many innumerable things, the meaning of waiting.

This book began in the Sociology Department at the University of Texas at Austin. My sincerest thanks to Ben Carrington, Denise Gilman, Lorraine Leu, Néstor Rodríguez, and Harel Shapira for supporting this research. Their sage words and thought-provoking guidance during my time at UT-Austin, which I carried with me in the field and beyond, left indelible marks on what the book would become. Special gratitude to Ben Carrington, whose teaching continues to shape how I think, teach, and mentor. Thank you for always greeting my nascent ideas with encouragement and kindness.

The Urban Ethnography Lab at the University of Texas at Austin was the intellectual home that sustained me through my graduate school years, and a community I have always come back to. All the love to its inaugural fellows and those who continue to make the UEL the special place that it is.

Before joining the University of Wisconsin–Madison, I had the opportunity to spend a year at the Center for Inter-American Policy & Research at Tulane University. Thanks to the support and camaraderie of director Ludovico Feoli and the rest of those at the Center during my time there. Thanks to those of the Sociology Department's Culture Workshop, for welcoming me as a fellow sociologist: Robin Bartram, Mariana Craciun, Amalia Leguizamón, Camilo Leslie, and David Smilde.

At the University of Wisconsin–Madison, I am thankful to colleagues in Sociology and International Studies for their mentorship: Mustafa Emirbayer, Ted Gerber, Jenna Nobles, Erica Simmons, and Scott Straus. Thanks also to Chad Alan Goldberg and Pam Oliver for providing helpful feedback on the book's introduction. Max Besbris, Jordan Conwell, Edna Ely-Ledesma, Mosi Ifatunji, James McMaster, Karen Oberhauser, Eunsil Oh, Marla Ramírez, and Kelly Ward have helped make Wisconsin feel like home. Three cheers to the folks of the Wisconsin Collective for Ethnographic Research, and to Sadie Dempsey and Kristina Fullerton, who provided feedback on chapter three. Thanks to Lisa M. Sousa Dias and Benny Witkovsky for research support.

My interest in Latin America was concretized during my undergraduate years at Vassar College. Katie Hite, Joe Nevins, and Leslie Offutt fundamentally shaped how I see the world, and the types of research I pursue, and that left a lasting impression. If it had not been for advice from Katie Hite, I do not know if I would have pursued a PhD. Thank you.

I am grateful for many other kind, brilliant, and generous humans whom I have been lucky enough to call friends, mentors, teachers, supporters, inspirators, and intellectual interlocutors: Maria Akchurin, Rawan Arar, Riad Azar, Sarah Ball, Nino Bariola, Robin Bartram, Claudio Benzecry, Lucy Blumberg, Gabriel Chouhy, Caitlyn Collins, David Cook-Martín, Jacinto Cuvi, Kevin Dupzyk, Sefira Fialkoff, Brodwyn Fischer, David FitzGerald, Andrea Gómez Cervantes, Heba Gowayed, Monika Krause, Natasha Merklein, Samantha Plummer, Dennis Rodgers, Mary Ellen Stitt, Dani Swaiman, João H. Costa Vargas, and Jake Watson, among them. Special shout-out to my dear friend Sarah Ball, who read a full draft from cover to cover, and whose words buoyed me during revisions. And love to all the humans I've organized with along the way, who keep me believing.

Special thanks—above all, most of all—to all those whom I met during fieldwork, whose generosity of heart and mind made this work possible. I have endeavored to treat with thoughtful care and attention the words and experiences you shared with me.

To my editor at the University of Chicago Press, Elizabeth Branch Dyson: You have been this book's unwavering champion and shepherd. Your clarity, care, and sharp mind are more than I ever could have asked for in an editor. I am grateful to the three anonymous reviewers who read the manuscript with close attention and offered valuable feedback. Thanks to Mollie McFee, and the rest of the editorial team at the University of Chicago Press, for making this book more than a Microsoft Word document.

To my family, thank you for accompanying me on this unknown journey. Thank you for supporting me and caring enough to ask questions about what I research and write about. To Mom and Grandma for always believing in my potential. To John, for being my rock.

I developed ideas for chapter four in my article "The Epistemic Logic of Asylum Screening: (Dis)embodiment and the Production of Asylum Knowledge in Brazil," in *Ethnic and Racial Studies*, and portions of chapter seven emerged from "Contexts of Reception Seen and Constituted from Below: The Production of Refugee Status Apathy," in *Qualitative Sociology*. I am grateful to special-issue editors and anonymous reviewers for their constructive and insightful comments on those versions of my work.

Parts of what would become this book benefited from the engagement of colleagues at various talks and conferences, including the American Sociological Association Annual Meetings; ASA Development in Dialogue Conference; ASA Junior Theorist Symposium; Boston Migration Area Workshop Series; Latin American Studies Association Conference; Politics of Race, Immigration, and Ethnicity Consortium; Social Science History Association Annual Meeting; Society for the Study of Social Problems Annual Meeting; and the Sociology Department and the Center for Latin American Studies at the University of Chicago.

Funding support for this research was provided by the U.S.–Brazil Fulbright Commission; P.E.O. International; the University of Wisconsin–Madison's Office of the Vice Chancellor for Research and Graduate Education, with funding from the Wisconsin Alumni Research Foundation; and the Teresa Lozano Long Institute of Latin American Studies and the Urban Ethnography Lab of the University of Texas at Austin. Without this support, this book would not have been possible. And I am grateful to have had the opportunity to finish it while a fellow at the Institute for Research in the Humanities at the University of Wisconsin–Madison.

I dedicate these pages to all those who struggle for a different world—with their feet, with their minds, and with their hearts.

Until Liberation.

APPENDIX A

On Data and Methods

After college, long before I started the research in Brazil that would become *The Color of Asylum*, I moved to Argentina. I lived there for two years conducting field research, working, and studying at the University of Buenos Aires. I also struggled to obtain legal residency. I shuffled from one office to another to request the required Argentine paperwork, translate my US documents, and notarize and authenticate all papers. By the time my US criminal background check arrived, many other documents had expired. Back I went to offices throughout the city. When I had my state interview, the official told me I had been misinformed. I did not need most of the documents I had accumulated. Regardless, I was elated to finally be a resident.

My experiences obtaining residency in Argentina, navigating misleading bureaucratic labyrinths, as a college-educated white woman from the United States and fluent in Spanish—someone not disposed to fear the state, adept at interfacing with bureaucracies and organizations of power, and whom such institutions are often quite disposed to care about—gave me the slightest glimpse into the role of legal structures and state bureaucracies in determining the lived experiences of migrants as they navigate them and the world beyond. If it were like this for me, someone with extreme advantage in the global landscape, what for the vast majority not positioned with such confluence of capitals?

Meanwhile, I was becoming increasingly interested in racial politics in Brazil, which seemed to contrast greatly with what I knew of both the United States and Argentina. I began taking Portuguese classes at the University of Buenos Aires, and I traveled to Brazil before returning to the United States for graduate school. The following year, I returned to Rio de Janeiro for an academic program on African Diaspora in the Americas at Rio de Janeiro State University (UERJ), through which I began fieldwork at the Refugee Center.

I had sought out fieldwork at the Center with very different research in mind. I had imagined it as a site of encounter between Afro-Brazilians and Africans, apt for investigating the politics, tensions, and possibilities of transatlantic black identity formations. But the world of asylum I found was very different from what I expected. Black Brazilians were notably absent from that space. I had to change my research plan. Precisely where ethnography can be most useful is in such moments of surprise: when what we discover does not align with what we imagined from afar. I was not expecting black migrants coming to Brazil to encounter a white apparatus of governance. Few working in asylum were black, and no one was black like them.

As I walked toward the subway after my first visit to the Refugee Center, I passed two police officers who had stopped a black adolescent boy. They had him spread-eagled, with his hands against the police car. They frisked him and turned his shorts pockets inside out. It appeared they found nothing. He had no bag, and wore a tank top, board shorts, and flipflops. The police officers put him, not in the backseat, but in the hatchback of the patrol car.

Over time, as I reflected on my experiences at the Center and the racial violences of the city around it, I thought about blackness and the state, as well as my previous experiences with state contact in Argentina, and I began to reimagine what such a site could speak to, what it could be a case of. Under the mentorship of political ethnographer Javier Auyero during graduate school at the University of Texas at Austin, I pulled my attention from the state as a formal structure of policies, to how those policies manifested in implementation, as officials acted and interacted with black migrant communities, and with what consequences for our understandings of the state and racial political belonging in Brazil. I turned the ethnographic gaze back on the state—in a drive to decipher state practices of support, governance, and subjugation. I wanted to know how forms of racial domination may happen not only through the punitive arms of the state in Brazil, but also through formally inclusive policies like its refugee regime in the face of the African newcomers who sought safe haven there.

Brazil's highly lauded refugee policies differed greatly from what I had ever imagined possible. Coming from the United States, and full of ethnocentric assumptions of how racial exclusion worked through immigration policies, I could not readily understand how an asylum regime might function when infused with human rights and without a looming threat of deportation. How might the racial politics of such regimes differ in practice? Racism in Brazil has often played out in the everyday milieu without being underwritten by law. And, based on my experiences in Argentina, I knew there could be important gaps between policy on the books and their everyday operations, vitally important for how migrants experience such legal processes. What if such sites and policies in Brazil, rather than producing the possibilities of racial ties, as I had originally wondered, instead entailed racial political marginalization?

In the following years of my fieldwork at the Refugee Center, and through research on the refugee regime broadly, I came to see not only how the state responded to the African newcomers who originally predominated, but also how differently those encounters, and the relations produced, played out in the face of Syrian forced displacement. My research shifted again, as I turned to take seriously the whiteness of the state, and to attend to how both blackness and whiteness configured the everyday racial politics of the refugee regime.

Methods and Data Collection

I investigated the racial politics of the refugee regime relationally and processually, from many different angles to form as comprehensive a picture as possible. Over the course of my research, I carried out 15 months of fieldwork from 2012 to 2016, with the bulk of my research occurring in the final year. Research also involved interviews with asylum officials and forced migrants; analysis of documents produced by state and civil society actors, primarily asylum case opinions; and the construction and analysis of a national individual-level dataset of asylum decisions. In total, the research design sought to exhaust internal variation—in terms of asylum seekers, officials, case treatment, institutional epochs, and final outcomes—to bolster the external validity of conclusions.[1]

Different types of data show things others may not. My dataset, for example, allowed me to know how long asylum seekers waited to receive a decision and to compare variations in wait time across applicants. But that data cannot tell me what happens during those days. It cannot address the relations produced between the state and forced migrants during that wait. Qualitative data, both interviews and participant observation, on the other hand, captured how officials and forced migrants alike perceived and experienced those days of waiting.

The research process was an iterative one. As I went in and out of the field, what I looked for developed over time. What I thought this was a case of, and what I pursued, were intertwined rather than separate and sequential.[2] In between field visits, through removed reflection and analysis, I reformulated the questions that drove observations during the following visit. While in the field, I also produced initial and integrative memos, making sense of data as I produced it. Those analytical jottings helped clarify what I found most salient and surprising, which then inspired what I further followed. During and after field research, I pursued and analyzed the variation captured, looking for structural and interpretive patterns of similarity and difference.

FIELDWORK

The bulk of fieldwork took place at the Refugee Center in Rio de Janeiro. Because the Center participates in the asylum process and provides various forms of assistance, it presented a strategic research site to access the operations of the refugee regime, and to investigate how asylum seekers and refugees were treated in and experienced that process. During fieldwork, I focused on capturing the perceptions, actions, and interactions entailed in the everyday workings of asylum. I witnessed interactions between migrants and asylum actors, and I followed actions and conversations regarding cases and the process broadly to understand what meanings people attributed to them.

At the Refugee Center, my fieldwork consisted primarily of participant observation with the legal unit. I participated in intake interviews of applicants, usually as translator, note taker, or co-interviewer; I also conducted research for and produced civil society case recommendations. I assisted asylum seekers and refugees in all aspects of the process. I oriented asylum seekers as they filled out the application and prepared them for their eligibility interviews; reviewed officials' case opinions in preparation for GEP meetings; worked on case appeals; and processed requests for travel authorization and family reunification, for example. I also served as a translator between Portuguese, Spanish, and English throughout the Center, which provided insight into the meaning-making practices of the reception and social assistance sectors of the Center.

During my fieldwork in 2012 and 2013, I spent most of my time in the legal unit's cramped cubicle, from which I could hear much of what happened in the Center. Before CONARE opened its own office in Rio, this included the eligibility interviews conducted by asylum officials. During that time, the legal "unit" was a single cubicle among the social workers. In later years, the legal sector would expand to the second wing of the building, physically separating the legal and social assistance sectors.

In 2016 alone, I observed cases from 47 countries from five continents, in alphabetical order: Afghanistan, Angola, Argentina, Benin, Cameroon, Cape Verde, China, Colombia, Cuba, the Democratic Republic of the Congo, Dominican Republic, Egypt, Eritrea, Ethiopia, Gambia, Ghana, Guinea, Guinea-Bissau, Haiti, India, Iran, Iraq, Israel, Ivory Coast, Kenya, Liberia, Mali, Mexico, Morocco, Namibia, Nigeria, Pakistan, Palestine, Peru, Romania, Russia, Sao Tome and Principe, Senegal, Sierra Leone,

Somalia, South Africa, Syria, Togo, Uganda, Ukraine, Uruguay, and Venezuela (see fig. 7).

Because I focused my analysis on those refugees racialized as white and black in Brazil, this book leaves under-addressed questions of color and racial mixture, and how those perceived between those racial poles experienced the process, though they were captured in the study. Many Latin Americans, for example, were likely understood as racially mixed. While attending to the experiences of disparately racialized migrants from a single country would have been a worthwhile way to investigate the racial politics of asylum, I did not encounter sufficient variation by nationality to follow this line of inquiry. As I argue in the introduction, focusing on the poles of a color continuum brings into stark relief the racial order manifest in the refugee regime. At the same time, I had intended to return to Brazil in summer 2020 to examine the screening and experiences of Venezuelan refugees. However, the COVID pandemic that ensued made this impossible. In other work I discuss how Venezuelans have been racialized in the media in Brazil.[3] Investigating the racial project of asylum in the face of other nationalities is an apt avenue for future research, particularly given how refugee demographics in Brazil have shifted since my research.

Gaining entrée at the Center was surprisingly easy. At the time there was limited local interest in refugees, as discussed in chapter six, and Lucas was happy to have a volunteer help and accompany him in the work. I was the first volunteer the legal sector received. Lucas's only concern was where to fit me in the small cubicle. My language skills—fluent in English and Spanish, increasingly comfortable in Portuguese—made me a useful asset. Rapport was deepened by coming back, year after year. When I return in 2016, Lucas introduces me to those in the legal sector's office; "she was here long ago," he explains, as he looks over and points to a black-and-white photograph of us still pinned to the bulletin board from years ago.

That rapport was furthered still by taking seriously the work by coming in all day, day after day. I was a constant presence. In the hope to not only take but also be of use, I sought to be more participant than observer. I was not a fly on the wall. I learned and did the work to the extent I became responsible for orienting and teaching other volunteers how to carry out the various procedures and forms of assistance provided at the Center.

When I first returned in 2016, Guilherme was nervous that I would just take up space. He was apprehensive, even annoyed, about my intention to come "every day." On my first day back, Ana and Guilherme debated and struggled over what to do with me. By the following month, the meaning of my presence had radically shifted. When I tell Ana that I've been asked to translate in the social service sector on Thursdays, she makes a sad face. "I dislike it," she responds in English. Months later, Guilherme reflects on that first day. With relief, he tells me it's instead been "like having another lawyer."

Pursuing an ethic of solidarity in the field also meant doing things that did not figure into my research. It meant staying after hours to help a refugee apply for a visa to the United States (which was, despite our best efforts, denied), or building a Facebook page for Hamid's Arab food business. I accompanied asylum seekers to the other side of the city to the church where they would stay when they had nowhere else to turn. Politically conscious and ethically sound ethnography demands—but does not end at—a consideration for the requests of others, those who give you their time, those who share their stories with you.

I also conducted field observations at the Federal Police Office in Rio de Janeiro, located in the International Airport, where asylum seekers initiate the process and renew their documents, and at the state and civil society organizational offices in Brasília and São Paulo. I attended relevant activities like the annual World Refugee Day events and related symposiums. Generally, over the course of my research, I took care to follow asylum claims and field observations that elicited surprise and contrasted with what existing theory and initial analyses suggested.

Unfortunately, despite my attempts, I was not able to observe GEP meetings or CONARE plenaries. As such, I relied on others' accounts of those meetings and confirmed details from multiple actors as feasible. However, this was not always possible, as at times only one representative from the Refugee Center in Rio was present at such reunions. At the same time, as noted in chapter three, decisions rarely deviated from the opinion of the adjudicating asylum official, signaling that I captured much of the determinative perceptions and actions. I also collected and analyzed the case decisions and formal resolutions that resulted from those meetings. Nonetheless, I had restricted access to the meaning-making practices manifest in the upper-echelon workings of asylum. This is a limitation of the data. Since concluding my research, CONARE has made its plenary meeting minutes digitally available, and I have triangulated my ethnographic findings with those archives.

FIELD NOTES

At the Refugee Center, I produced field notes on the computer with which I worked. At the Federal Police, and other sites, I used a field notebook or my phone. I did not record. As such, quotations, when not from document sources or interviews, are close approximations. I also removed grammatical errors in quotes when refugees spoke in a language they did not navigate fluently.

I spent the working day at the Refugee Center. Usually and when possible, I took notes contemporaneously and made jottings as the day went, which I further developed in detail that night and sometimes the next day. Jottings were at times quite lengthy themselves, five single-spaced pages, for example, as I took advantage of breaks in the workflow, and usually had my computer in front of me or easily in reach. Either during or shortly after, depending on my participation in the occurrence, and the workload in the office, I would document as many details, phrases, and key elements about an interaction or observation as I could, to form the basis of my field notes and as strategic mnemonic devices for recall. Occasionally, I also audio-recorded notes if I was unable to get right to the computer that night. I produced roughly seven to ten pages of single-spaced field notes per day of fieldwork.

Because I molded myself to the routines of the Center, I invariably spent more hours doing fieldwork than writing field notes. On many days, more time was spent participating as a member of the social world than documenting its workings. This is not what some consider the ethnographic gold standard. Certainly, things did not get written into field notes. But, in other ways, it improved the research. To be there, from the day's start to its end, whenever that might be, was crucial to understanding the rhythm of work at the Refugee Center. The way it tires the body, the way it tires the nerves. It helped me appreciate—in ways nothing other than embeddedness could, to *feel* the exhaustion of such work through my own body—how the structural conditions could produce a lack of attention, curtness, or disdain; and understand tactics to avoid those seeking assistance, as discussed in chapter two. It also meant, for those at the Center, I was not in the way. I was appreciated as part of the team because I put in the hours and did as they did. While I became primarily responsible for orienting new asylum seekers, on a particularly busy day, Guilherme shares the workload and orients two Angolans. When I thank him, he responds, "*é nós.*" Literally translating to "it's us," the expression means "I'm with you, we got this"—we were in it together.

Nonetheless, these are post hoc explanations. I didn't step away to write my field notes because there were always people waiting hours outside to be assisted; someone needing translating; someone appearing at the end of operating hours, just arrived in the country, suitcase in hand, with nowhere to go. To step away was to look away. My field notes could wait. That was my decision, and for me, it is "good enough."[4]

INTERVIEWS

I triangulated fieldwork with three other bodies of data. I conducted 42 semi-structured interviews with those disparately positioned in the refugee regime in Brazil. Given their varied vantage points and experiences, differently positioned actors can have distinct ways of interpreting the social worlds they traverse. All interviews were guided by "how" rather than "why" questions, audio-recorded and subsequently transcribed.[5] After interviews, I wrote up observations documenting the scenes, feelings, bodily expressions, and demeanor entailed in those encounters.

I interviewed 26 officials and participating civil society actors, including employees and volunteers, in Rio, São Paulo, and Brasília.[6] At the time, these were the only cities with refugee centers and where asylum officials worked and processed claims. All asylum officials had worked as eligibility officials, responsible for interviewing applicants and evaluating claims, during the fieldwork period. I interviewed the majority of the eligibility officials working in that position at the time the interviews were conducted. On reflection, I wish I had tried to interview federal police officers, social workers, and CONARE representatives, beyond a participating UNHCR representative that I did. My failure to do so limited my understanding of how they perceived this work. At the time, my focus on the everyday encounters of asylum screening produced this blindness.

I employed the same interview guide with state and civil society actors, which I followed up with additional questions. These interviews addressed life trajectories, and their everyday work practices and how they made sense of them—what they thought and felt about those experiences—to document the meanings asylum actors gave this work. I interviewed asylum actors and civil society staff in São Paulo and Brasília to better understand to what extent the processes and practices I observed in Rio related to dynamics elsewhere.

To conduct interviews, I mobilized my association with and networks through the Refugee Center, which opened doors with the asylum offices and other refugee centers. Others reached out on my behalf, and often after interviewing one official, they would vouch for me and the experience to others. I met individuals wherever they wanted to conduct the interview. This took me to asylum offices and refugee centers across those cities, to coffee shops and bars, and to the beaches of Rio. Another entailed a hike.

I also interviewed 16 asylum seekers and refugees in Rio de Janeiro. This was purposively a sample of "inconvenience," to capture the perceptions and experiences of forced migrants who did not frequent the Center.[7] I did so to increase the internal variation of the study, and to search for negative cases—to see if perceptions and experiences fundamentally differed among those I did not encounter during fieldwork. Exceptions were made for two refugees because of their unique practical knowledge of the Center and refugee regime broadly.

Within that parameter, I focused on major applicant nationalities as well as those with whom I interacted less frequently at the Center. Among those interviews there was rough gender parity (ten male, six female), and interviewees hailed from the DRC (6), Syria (5), Venezuela (3), Colombia, Guinea, and Togo. The average age was 37, ranging from 18 to 58. Interviews were geared toward understanding how they experienced the asylum process. Given the trauma entailed in forced displacement, as discussed in chapter four, I did not ask about why or how they fled. I did not ask forced migrants directly whether they would be interested in being interviewed, but had others introduce the opportunity on my behalf via email, to which those willing to participate could respond or decline. Though difficult to ascertain, I did not note any patterns in who decided to pursue an interview.

Interviews were conducted in Portuguese, English, and Spanish, as preferred by the interviewee. Interviews were mostly conducted in a dominant language of the interviewee—Portuguese, Spanish, or English—except for those from Syria, whose interviews were conducted in English or Portuguese, and of those from Francophone Africa, which were conducted in Portuguese. Interview excerpts have been translated and edited for clarity if they were not conducted in the interviewee's first language, as appropriate. This meant that my interviews with Francophone Africans were with those more established in Rio, not recently arrived. By happenstance, interviews with Spanish speakers, on the other hand, were more likely to be asylum seekers. This lack of similarity is a drawback of the interview sample.

Because I was embedded within the power structure that has much say over their lives, I largely did not and could not establish rapport with asylum seekers and refugees to the degree I did with officials. As sociologist Matthew Desmond suggests, this is one of the pitfalls of relational ethnographic work, where it can be difficult to obtain equivalent ethnographic proximity to all groups, especially when stark power differentials organize the social world under investigation.[8] I worked to combat this by conducting interviews with asylum seekers and refugees who did not frequent the Refugee Center, and thus were less likely to read me as an insider with authority—though this was an attenuation rather than eradication of this limitation.

CASE DOCUMENTS AND FILES

My participant observation provided access to the national case database, including ongoing and adjudicated claims. This included case documents (e.g., application forms, declarations taken at the Federal Police, eligibility interview audio recordings, interview summary reports, case recommendations, official decision letters) produced by all participating actors. I analyzed such documents to understand how asylum seeker claims, and how they were made sense of, materialized in the files that culminated in decisions. I also reviewed documents meant to guide the process, produced by the UNHCR and CONARE, as well as formal legislation. This provided for detailing how, and the extent to which, state practice followed, reconfigured, or deviated from mandated and recommended procedure.

ASYLUM CASE DATASETS

I analyzed asylum datasets and reports produced by local, national, and international entities. The book includes descriptive statistics of application data publicly available from the Brazilian government (2013–2021), the UN Refugee Agency (1996–2020), and a national report (1998–2014).[9]

I also constructed a comprehensive individual-level dataset of the roughly 1,300 claims decided nationally in Brazil between September 2015 and April 2016. Because this data was disaggregated, I could analyze cases at the individual level, holding constant other factors to evaluate the role of nationality and region of origin. That dataset includes information on the year, date, and locality of application; country of origin; gender; age; family versus single application; asylum official case recommendation; and final decision from CONARE. This dataset allowed me to see national patterns in recognition and wait times, investigate the relationship between asylum seeker characteristics and case outcomes, and situate my qualitative research in national trends.

Seeing and Being Seen

Reflexivity includes being cognizant of the relations of power in which the researcher and researched exist. As sociologists Rebecca Hanson and Patricia Richards write, disembodying ethnographic work—and failing to engage in embodied reflexivity—is both "ethically and epistemologically problematic."[10] Axes of social difference meaningfully manifest through interactions, themselves structured by social relations of inequality, that reflect and give insights into them—with pertinent ethical, methodological, and epistemological ramifications. Positionality impacts what the ethnographer perceives and is privy to, and thus the form and nature data collection takes, in ways that can differ from what we imagine from afar.

Reflecting upon how and why I both fit into and disrupted the social world I examined provided powerful signals to the power structures and social dynamics in which I had embedded myself, that I was drawn into and through which I was made sense of. What matters is not researcher positionality on its own, but self-awareness and intellectual reflection regarding how social location impacts the data and can illuminate interpretive structures of the social universe under investigation. Interlocutors respond as members of their social worlds, highlighting what sense-making prisms are salient for them, and the cleavages that exist. When attended to reflexively, such encounters provide insights into the cognitive and interpretive structures of social commonality and difference in production and contestation, how they appear and operate, and the meanings individuals attribute to them.

During fieldwork, aspects of my social identity shifted in salience for how others interacted with and perceived me. Who I was, and how I behaved, had different ramifications for different people. I was not read uniformly. Varied levels of insider and outsider statuses can have distinct benefits and drawbacks for research.[11] A lack of closeness, for example, can ease a researcher's ability to trouble the everyday, taken-for-granted aspects of the social universe, what can otherwise appear hidden in plain sight.[12] While never working in isolation—instead constituted in and through each other—social axes of race, class, gender, sexuality, and nationality variably came to the fore.

The ease with which I got close to lawyers and asylum officials was facilitated by our similar age, race, class, and educational backgrounds. Like myself, they had traveled, studied, or lived abroad; lived in the more affluent neighborhoods in Rio's Southern zone; spoke multiple languages; and were pursuing or planned to pursue graduate degrees focused on refugees. On the other hand, social chasms emerged between lawyers and the social workers at the Center, who did not share such classed experiences. This likewise manifested between the social workers and myself. The class tensions that played out between the legal and social sectors of the Center impacted my interactions with some in the social wing and dampened the rapport I was able to accrue with them. While the lawyers, legal volunteers, and I spent significant time socializing outside of the Center, my interactions with those in other sectors were largely limited to the Center. Nonetheless, interactions were cordial, and I had access to the social sector because of my language skills and the need for translation. While those in the legal sector often spoke three languages, those who worked in the reception and social sector mainly knew Portuguese, itself further signaling the diverging class backgrounds between the two wings.

As the pages of this book show, whiteness was rarely explicitly addressed. My own whiteness was no different. It was always present but never named. Though I was not the only fair-skinned white blond woman at the Center, what seemingly distinguished me from most who worked and volunteered at the Refugee Center was not my whiteness but its degree—not my race but my color. Nonetheless, it went largely unmentioned.[13] While my race and color certainly impacted how others perceived and interacted with me, they remained implicit during fieldwork. But that doesn't mean they went unnoticed. While conversing after our interview, official Isabela tells me that "in the South [of Brazil], there, they are all like you: blond with blue eyes, German descent." As I chat with Yornella, a Congolese refugee, in the multipurpose room at the Refugee Center, she holds a child's doll in her arms as if it were a baby. It is a blond girl doll with green eyes. As Antonio and then Adriana pass through the room, each makes comments about how the "baby" looks like it's mine. One jokes it should be in my arms, not Yornella's.

My gender and physicality made it variably harder and easier to build rapport. During the early years of fieldwork, the legal unit of the Refugee Center was led by Lucas and included only women volunteers; all the social workers were women, coordinated by women. One of the social workers called us "Lucas and his girls." At the time, I felt some viewed me as just one of "Lucas's girls." While other aspects of social difference contributed to social distance between myself and those in the social sector, neither did our shared gender necessarily produce social ties.

Sometimes rapport garnered was shaped by my sexual objectification by others, structuring the possibilities for ethnographic proximity established through disquieting forms of intimacy, across social divides and power differentials, as gendered hierarchies were produced through sexualized interactions. I was flirted with, received WhatsApp messages that made me uncomfortable, and had to deal with sexual advances. I received a marriage proposal. Sometimes men refugees would prefer to wait to speak with one of the men lawyers, rather than be attended by a woman.

As I assist Naem, reviewing his asylum application, he wants to take a picture with me, and he tries to expand my limited vocabulary in Arabic. "Inti heyluway qatir," he makes me repeat after him. "In English, it means you are very beautiful," he says. It feels out of place and makes me uncomfortable. My physical appearance was irrelevant to the work. I heard and felt things like that intermittently, and other women had similar experiences. A few days later, when Naem returns with his completed application, he sees me greet Frederic with the characteristic Brazilian kiss on the check. He pointedly asks me where his kisses are. Later, when I tell the receptionist Antonio this, his own response is gendered, performing the role of protector for the mostly women who work and volunteer there. He quickly retorts: "Next time, if he wants kisses from you, he can get punches from me."

While sexist microaggressions from migrants were fleeting, and relatively innocuous, I experienced more pointed sexual harassment by a colleague at the Center, who professed his desire for me—telling me that he "found it difficult not to grab me." As *Harassed* details, such experiences are part of what women ethnographers often navigate in the field, though we rarely write about them because of androcentric standards embedded in the ethnographic craft. While I fear reproducing racialized notions of male threat, I mention them to break a culture of ethnographic silence around sexual harassment, and the threats, risk, and danger to which bodies can be subject—themselves shaped by the social relations of power and domination in the everyday milieu ethnographers traverse.[14]

My nationality deeply shaped my experiences at the Center and in Brazil. Because I was also a foreigner, like the refugees I assisted, I had to navigate the Federal Police Office to regularize my status and obtain my identity document, the RNE. As I text Guilherme from the Office as I await processing, he responds: "Hahaha, you're like a refugee in the Federal Police." Guilherme's joke marked the absurdity of the difference. Through my own few experiences there, amicable rather than demeaning, I saw acutely how race and nationality inflected what that encounter felt like, and provided for the ease of my arrival and stay in Brazil. I had no problems obtaining visas, and while I received an RNE—a proper identity card—asylum seekers instead receive the protocol, a precarious piece of printer paper. At the end of each bout of fieldwork, I flew home—a right denied refugees in Brazil. Unlike those who shared their stories with me, I did not have to ask permission to leave.

In contrast to the implicit undercurrent of my whiteness, my nationality was often marked. The salience of my Americanness, as a noted aspect for those with whom I interacted, signals the importance of national origin as a prism of meaning-making for those in the refugee regime. With the staff at the Refugee Center, this manifested in conversations about language, food, and politics. In my first conversation with Lucas, as we discuss how I can assist, I offer to help with Spanish speakers. "How funny to have an American translating," he responds. Some would speak to me briefly in English to practice, or ask me questions about how to say something in my language. I was associated with Thanksgiving turkey, gingerbread, and chocolate chip cookies. Emanuelle, responsible for organizing the Portuguese language classes, loved to ask me about what we eat in the

United States. While I do not have a talent for baking, those at the Center were emphatic about my chocolate chip cookies. In 2016, questions posed turned from food to the US presidential election. The day after Trump's election, people wanted me to explain what had happened. Yornella was deeply sad. "The president of the United States is the president of the whole world," she tells me. "We should all vote."

My nationality also played a recurring role in how asylum seekers and refugees interacted with me. As the only person from the United States, I was a surprising object of curiosity to the extent that it interrupted the work I did there.

"Excuse me, are you American?" is the first thing Naem says as he comes in.

"Yes."

"Which state?"

"Can we get on with the assistance?"

"Yes, of course, sorry."

The questions continue. He asks if I really am American because I speak Portuguese so well. As I try to explain how the process works, he asks me about whether I took language classes in the United States.

While I and others prodded into the lives of refugees daily, I felt unease when they responded in kind. I preferred to be unknown and unknowable. The discomfort I felt in such moments proved generative for findings presented in chapters two and four, pushing me to reflect on the dynamics of unequal visibility and the power relations embedded in asylum.

At times, refugees didn't know how to make sense of me, and in ways I did not experience with Brazilians. I was frequently asked where I was from. As I would meet with and assist asylum seekers and refugees at the Center, they would become perplexed, not knowing how to read me. Whether I was speaking in English, Spanish, or Portuguese, there was always something not quite right. Those I interacted with in English, predominantly Anglophone Africans and Middle Easterners, wondered why my English was so clear and perfect. Angolans and refugees long established in Brazil heard my Portuguese, and asked with a tone of doubt— "Are you Brazilian?" Colombians, Dominicans, Venezuelans, and Cubans furrowed their brows perplexingly: "Are you Argentinian?" I was confusing to many—almost passing as Brazilian, possibly Argentinian, confusion about why my English was fluent. I did not make sense; I was not easily placed in that space. Other times, my foreignness provided a source of comfort. As I walk out to the patio to attend a family from the Dominican Republic, I begin to speak in Spanish. One of them quickly smiles at me with a face of relief. "You're not from here."

Being from the United States was not innocuous. Lucas tells me about a conversation he had with someone from the Public Defender's Office, who said the United States was responsible for most conflicts in the world. "Don't say that!" Lucas tells me he thought. "My friend Katie is from the United States!" I laugh at Lucas wanting to support me by defending the United States. But an unshakable truth existed as an ever-present undercurrent during my research: my country produced refugees, sometimes the very ones I interacted with.

I sit in the backseat of a taxi with Graciela, a young Colombian asylum seeker, to accompany her to the church shelter. It is pouring rain; the traffic feels never-ending. We have much time to talk. She asks me where I am from: "Argentina?" "No," I respond, "the United States."

"The United States dropped the bomb that killed my father," Graciela responds.

My research in Brazil was shaped by and took place in the broader context of US empire, militarism, and meddling interventions throughout the world. Such violence precipitated the forced displacement of refugees I met. Mohammad had served as an interpreter for the US forces in Afghanistan. But the United States denied resettling him, so he fled to Brazil where he obtained asylum. Altogether, my multiple positionalities had different meanings for those I interacted with during my research, providing varied experiences of proximity and difference, rapport and distance.

Figures and Tables

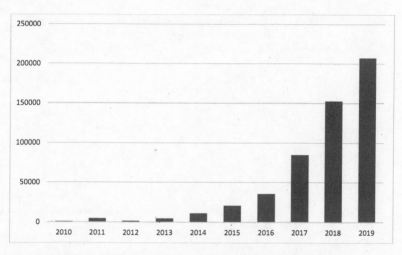

FIGURE 6 Pending asylum applications in Brazil. Data Source: UNHCR.

FIGURE 7 Asylum cases observed during fieldwork. Countries of origin of asylum cases observed during fieldwork marked in dark gray, country of study in white.

TABLE 1 *Asylum case decisions*

Country of origin	Recognition rate	Percentage of total	N
Syria	100%	19%	245
DRC	86%	9%	124
Pakistan	75%	9%	118
Ghana	18%	6%	78
Guinea-Bissau	3%	5%	70
Nigeria	18%	5%	67
Other	39%	46%	598

Note: Other includes 62 countries of origin and stateless. This table shows the top countries of origin for the 1,300 asylum claims decided nationally in Brazil between September 2015 and April 2016. It presents, for each country, the percentage of cases that were recognized as refugees, the percentage of total decisions, and the raw number of decisions during that time.

TABLE 2 Estimated likelihood of recognition

Variable	Odds ratio (Z score)
Country of origin	
Guinea-Bissau	0.115**
	(−2.78)
Nigeria	0.626
	(−1.03)
Pakistan	12.956***
	(6.95)
Other	2.053*
	(2.30)
Other characteristics	
Woman	1.219
	(1.05)
Age	0.999
	(−0.21)
With family	3.844***
	(−12.29)
Constant	0.236
	(−3.75)

Note: Ghana as reference group; Syria and DRC removed. $N = 924$.
*** $p < 0.001$, ** $p < 0.01$, * $p < 0.05$.
This table shows the odds ratios and Z scores from a logistic regression estimating likelihood of recognition for the top four asylum-seeking countries in my decision dataset (September 2015 to April 2016), excluding Syria and the Congo, with Ghana as the reference group. Controlling for gender, age, and single versus family application, Guinea-Bissau is 90 percent less likely to receive asylum than Ghana; Nigeria is 35 percent less likely (the latter is not statistically significant). Pakistan is 1,200 percent more likely to be awarded asylum than Ghana.

TABLE 3 Time to decision

Variable	B coefficients (SE)
Country of origin	
Ghana	−56.423
	(75.87)
Guinea-Bissau	−98.782
	(67.55)
Nigeria	124.047+
	(69.57)
Pakistan	−292.546***
	(71.79)
Syria	−349.899***
	(57.96)
Other	−78.312
	(52.82)
Other characteristics	
Woman	−60.377+
	(31.77)
Age	1.574
	(1.17)
With family	79.597*
	(39.108)
Constant	582.699
	(59.42)
R^2	0.26

Note: DRC as reference group. $N =314$.

*** $p < 0.001$, * $p < 0.05$, + $p < 0.10$.

This table presents the results of a regression model for days until decision, relative to the Democratic Republic of the Congo (DRC), for claims adjudicated in February and March 2016, for which I had exact date of application. The variations between African countries are not statistically significant. However, Syria and Pakistan waited an average of 12 and 10 months less, respectively, than the DRC, while controlling for gender, age, and single versus family application.

TABLE 4 Rights and restrictions by migratory status in Brazil, 2016

	Identity documents		Cumulative time to status			Right to travel		Other	
Status	ID	Yellow passport	Residency	Permanency	Citizenship	Domestic	International	Family reunion	App fees
Asylum seeker	Protocol	✗	✗	✗	✗	✓	✗	✗	$0
Refugee	RNE	✓	✓	4 yrs	8 yrs	✓	Restricted	✓	$0
Familial ties	RNE	✗	N/A	✓	1 yr	✓	✓	✗	$150
Mercosur	RNE	✗	✓	2 yrs	6 yrs	✓	✓	✗	$150

Notes

Introduction

1: In its 2009 World Refugee Survey, the US Committee for Refugees and Immigrants (USCRI) assigned countries Refugee Rights Report Cards. Brazil received a perfect 4.0 across their rubric, the only country in the world to do so (Forster 2011). See also Andrade and Marcolini 2002; Jubilut 2006; White 2012.

2: Nogueira and Marques 2008:57.

3: On how the normalization and naturalization of law and immigration regimes produces social suffering and legal violence, see Menjívar and Abrego 2012.

4: On Brazil as a "humanitarian superpower," see Amar 2013. As an example of the political discourse of Brazilian exceptionalism, in the words of a UNHCR Brazil official at a 2016 event for World Refugee Day: "Unfortunately [refugees] are all the time finding more closed doors, closed borders . . . our country has been an example of another type of reception."

5: FitzGerald and Cook-Martín 2014:296.

6: On how the shifting, contested constitution of whiteness has played out similarly and differently given the dynamism of immigration, geopolitics, and racial orders in Brazil, the United States, Europe, and Latin America, and the complex role of Arab and Iranian populations in those race-making processes, see Jensen and Sousa Dias 2022; Karam 2021; Lesser 1999; Maghbouleh 2017, 2020; Said 1978. As Shohat and Stam (2014) write, Brazil is marked by a "Tropical Orientalism," an ambivalent Orientalist exoticism that contrasts with the Islamophobia that imbues Arab racialization in the United States and Europe.

7: The term "Middle East" has been rightly critiqued for its colonialist origins, with calls to refer to the subregion as Southwest Asia. I ultimately opted to use Middle East due to its greater familiarity, and because it was the term used by those in this study.

8: Karam 2007:143; Najar 2012.

9: Karam 2007; Lesser 1996.

10: Amar 2014:4; Karam 2021.

11: Karam 2007:15.

12: *Prima facie* recognition entails the extension of refugee status on a group basis, thus eliminating the adjudication of individual claims.

13:   CONARE Resolution 28, March 3, 2022. CONARE had never so delimited who qualified; prior, humanitarian travel visas were extended to all people affected. This restriction occurred in a context where African and other black migrants had encountered racial discrimination as they struggled to flee, which received coverage in Brazilian media (Conectas 2022; Mantovani 2022).

14:   CONARE 2022.

15:   As political scientist Juliet Hooker (2017) observes, engaging in juxtaposition entails placing experiences within a single frame for "simultaneous reading," rather than a comparative "exercise in ranking" which invariably leads to aspects being misread, downplayed, and glossed over. Comparison, on the other hand, involves reading experiences separately, and can reify the very categories we purport to analyze, as it "compares and contrasts" rather than "connects" (Goldberg 2009b:1276).

16:   This number also includes Venezuelans displaced abroad, which the UNHCR has categorized separately (UNHCR 2022c). On the sociopolitically constructed nature of these numbers, see FitzGerald and Arar 2018; Mayblin 2017.

17:   UNHCR 2022a. This percentage was largely consistent in recent years, until Russia's invasion of Ukraine in 2022.

18:   UNHCR 2019a.

19:   Arendt 1951.

20:   In doing so, Agamben crosspollinates Arendt's theory with Foucault's biopolitics (2008).

21:   Agamben 1997:14.

22:   Agamben 1998; Agier 2011:148–49; Arendt 1951; Nyers 2005; Soguk 1999.

23:   Malkki 1995; see also Hamlin 2021.

24:   In immigration scholarship, see De Genova 2002; Donato and Armenta 2011; Kim 2019; Menjívar and Kanstroom 2014; Menjívar and Lakhani 2016. In refugee studies, see Brown 2011; Gowayed 2020.

25:   De León 2015:28.

26:   Mezzadra and Neilson 2013:159. Emphasis in original.

27:   On the racial othering of asylum seekers and its consequences, see Garner 2013; Hirsch 2019; Hubbard 2005; Mayblin 2017.

28:   Schuster 2003:245.

29:   Morgan and Orloff 2017; Maghbouleh 2017.

30:   See also "predatory inclusion" (Taylor 2019). On differential citizenship and inclusion, see Caldwell 2007; De Genova 2013; Espiritu 2003; Holston 2008; Lowe 1996. For empirical examples of differential inclusion among resettled refugees in the Global North, see Ong 2003; Ramsay 2017; Tang 2015.

31:   Mezzadra and Neilson 2013:7.

32:   Mezzadra and Neilson 2013:7, 159; Fourcade 2021; Gowayed 2022.

33:   At Arendt's writing, to be a refugee often required whiteness; the 1951 Refugee Convention allowed countries to circumscribe inclusion in the refugee category and its attendant rights to the boundaries of Europe.

34: Haney López 1996; Jung, Vargas, and Bonilla-Silva 2011; Loveman 2014; Nobles 2000; Omi and Winant 1994.

35: Goldberg 2002; Mills 1997. Racialization refers to "the processes by which ideas about race are constructed, come to be regarded as meaningful, and are acted upon" (Murji and Solomos 2005:1). Addressing the practices of racialization provides for capturing the modalities of racism in specific contexts, what Stuart Hall (1980) refers to as "historically-specific racisms" (336). As Bonilla-Silva (1997:475) argues, "racism should be studied from the viewpoint of racialization" (see also Miles and Brown 2003). On the theoretical imperative and utility of racialization, see also Gans 2017; Omi and Winant 1994; Walker 2016. For critiques of racialization, see Feagin 2006; Goldberg 2002.

36: Balibar 2011; Goldberg 2002; Lentin and Lentin 2006; Miles and Brown 2003; Nobles 2000.

37: Bracey 2015; Goldberg 2002; Jung and Kwon 2013.

38: FitzGerald and Cook-Martín 2014; Haney López 1996; Ngai 2004.

39: Racial ideologies refer to collections of ideas, beliefs, and understandings about race. On the relationship between racial ideologies, social structures, and racism, as Omi and Winant (1994) write: "ideological beliefs have structural consequences and . . . social structures give rise to beliefs. Racial ideology and social structure, therefore, mutually shape the nature of racism in a complex, dialectical, and overdetermined manner" (74–75).

40: Omi and Winant 1994:5.

41: Omi and Winant 1994:56, 60; Brown 2020. As Jones and Brown (2019:531) note, most research on race and the state "envisions the state as a uniform entity, with race-making occurring at a single level of political action."

42: Lipsky 1980.

43: Ray, Herd, and Moynihan 2022:2; Ray 2019. On racialized social systems, see Bonilla-Silva 1997.

44: Paschel 2017.

45: Fox 2012. Valentino (2021:2) defines logics as "shared, internalized, cognitive structures which are fundamentally evaluative in nature." On the analytical purchase of logics, see DiMaggio 1997; Zuberi and Bonilla-Silva 2008.

46: Auyero 2012; Gupta 2012.

47: On such political lessons generally, see Gupta 1995, 2005; Haney 1996; Jensen 2021a; Soss 1999. Legalization processes can be formative and transformative, and experiences with immigration bureaucracies have long-term effects for migrant subjectivities, claims-making, legal consciousness, and belonging (Galli 2020; Menjívar and Lakhani 2016).

48: Holston 2008:15.

49: Auyero 2012:7; see also Lipsky 1980:4.

50: The law in operation is frequently absent in migration literature. As Zatz and Rodriguez (2014:668) attest, "immigration scholars are more apt to write about . . . the law on the books—than about . . . the law in action." For important exceptions, see Calavita 1992; Heyman 1995; Nevins 2002; Mountz 2010; Jubany 2011, 2017; Shiff 2022.

51: De Genova 2002; Jones and Brown 2019. See Castles 2004; Massey 1999; Ngai 2004; Zolberg 2008.

52: Bohmer and Shuman 2008:48; Pachirat 2011; Sjoberg and Miller 1973.

53: FitzGerald and Cook-Martín 2014:25.

54: Bourdieu 1994; Ferguson and Gupta 2002; Gupta 1995, 2005; Haney 1996; Morgan and Orloff 2017; Valverde 2012; Yang 2005. On immigration regulation, see Calavita 1992; Mountz 2010; Rodriguez and Paredes 2014.

55: On calls to conduct ethnographies of the state, see Auyero 2012; Gupta 2012; Mountz 2010.

56: Hernández 2013; Koifman 2012; Lesser 1999, 2013; Loveman 2014; Skidmore 1974.

57: Skidmore 1974. Such national discourses were prevalent throughout Latin America (De la Fuente and Andrews 2018).

58: FitzGerald and Cook-Martín 2014:260.

59: Hasenbalg 1979; Holston 2008; Nascimento 1979; Schwarcz 2012; Skidmore 1999; Telles 2004.

60: For a classic debate on racial hegemony and ideology in Brazil, see Bairros 1996; Bourdieu and Wacquant 1999; French 2000; Hanchard 1994, 2003; Telles 2003. See also Goldberg 2009a.

61: Caldwell 2007; Goldstein 2003; Paixão 2004; Silva and Paixão 2014; Telles 2004, 2012; Twine 1998. On treating race and color as analytically distinct, see Monk 2016. While Brazil is known for racial categorical ambiguity, it is lower than elsewhere in Latin America, and the ideology of racial mixture did not lead to the elision of racial categories in Brazil (Telles 2014). Numerous studies have shown brown and black Brazilians to be equivalently socioeconomically disadvantaged relative to whites (Silva and Paixão 2014).

62: On how Brazilians both recognize and deny race and racism, see Sheriff 2001; Twine 1998; Vargas 2004. Moreover, the state has come to embrace rigid racial categories through quota policies (Bailey, Fialho, and Loveman 2018; Lehmann 2018; Schwartzman 2009).

63: Paschel 2016; Silva and Paixão 2014.

64: In surveys since the 1980s, most Brazilians acknowledge racism and racial discrimination (Bailey 2009; Silva and Paixão 2014:215; Telles and Bailey 2013). Over 90 percent believe racial prejudice exists in Brazil (Silva 2016:800), and 80 percent of Brazilians support race-based affirmative action policies and anti-discrimination laws (Telles 2014:222, 234).

65: Paschel 2016.

66: Andrews 1991; Caldwell 2007; Guimarães 2005; Hanchard 1994; Sheriff 2001; Skidmore 1974; Vargas 2004.

67: Bailey 2009; Telles 2014:223, 234.

68: Alves 2014; Caldwell 2007; Ferreira da Silva 2007; Smith 2016; Vargas 2008; Vargas and Alves 2010.

69: CONARE Plenary No. 145, December 12, 2019.

70: For an exception, see FitzGerald and Cook-Martín 2014. There is little scholarship on racism and contemporary migration policies in the region broadly (Freier, Bird, and Castillo Jara 2020), and immigration is predominantly a historical object of inquiry in Afro-Latin American studies (Andrews 2004; Gates 2011).

71: Cintra de Oliveira Tavares 2022; Cogo 2018; Jensen and Sousa Dias 2022; Wejsa and Lesser 2018.

72: In the last national census in 2010, 47.5 percent self-identified as white, 43.4 percent as mixed, and 7.5 percent as black.

73: Telles 2014:222.

74: Contemporary studies of whiteness in Brazil have been rare (Winant 2001). On whiteness and its privileges for nationals in Brazil and Latin America, see Alves and Vargas 2017; Ribeiro Corossacz 2018; Roth-Gordon 2016; Sheriff 2001; Silva, Souza Leão, and Grillo 2020; Telles and Flores 2013. We know little about the perceptions of and attendant privileges for white migrants in contemporary Latin America broadly (Freier et al. 2020:148).

75: Hamlin 2012, 2014.

76: Bohmer and Shuman 2008:261; Hamlin 2021.

77: Kim 2019:360.

78: Freier et al. 2020:144, 146.

79: Ashutosh and Mountz 2012; Dev 2009; Mountz 2003, 2004; Schuster 2011.

80: Regarding immigration generally, see for example: Anderson, Gibney, and Paoletti 2011; Golash-Boza 2012. With asylum, see Bloch and Schuster 2005; Conlon and Gill 2013; FitzGerald 2019; Gibney 2008; Gill 2009; Hynes 2011; Malloch and Stanley 2005.

81: Freier and Gauci 2020; Hammoud-Gallego and Freier 2022; Nogueira and Marques 2008.

82: Auyero 2012:18.

83: Fratzke 2013.

84: Bezerra Lima et al. 2017.

85: A relational approach takes its object of inquiry as a social question for which a web of relations is constitutive (Desmond 2014; Emirbayer 1997).

86: Wacquant 2003:5.

87: On this methodological approach, see Katz 2001.

88: From 1998 to 2014, Rio was the principal city for recognized refugees after São Paulo (Bezerra Lima et al. 2017:130).

89: This conceptualization of refugee regime differs from that usually mobilized, which refers to the global complex of refugee governance and assistance, rather than the workings of refugee governance in a particular country (Betts 2010, 2015; Zolberg, Suhrke, and Aguayo 1992). On the utility of migration regimes as a concept, see Mezzadra and Neilson 2013:179.

90: FitzGerald and Cook-Martín 2014; Haney López 1996; Ngai 2004.

91: According to a national representative survey, most refugees who self-identify as white and black in Brazil are Syrian and Congolese, respectively. More-over, almost all Syrian and Congolese respondents self-identified as white and black, respectively; over 90 percent of Syrians self-identified as white, less than 10 percent identified as mixed (*pardo*), while over 90 percent of Congo-lese identified as black (Oliveira 2019a:10, 58–59). The survey used the race/color categories of the Brazilian Institute of Geography and Statistics (IBGE): white (*branco*), black (*preto*), brown (*pardo*), indigenous (*indígeno*), and yellow (*amarelo*).

92: Syrians and Congolese were also the top two nationalities recognized as refu-gees in Brazil each year from 2015 to 2018 (Silva et al. 2021:43).

93: On the similar educational and occupational backgrounds of Syrian and Con-golese refugees, see Bezerra Lima et al. 2017:118–22. A national survey similarly found analogous education between Syrians and Congolese, and that refugees' years of schooling broadly did not vary by race/color (Oliveira 2019a:60).

94: CONARE 2022.

95: Bezerra Lima et al. 2017:124.

96: Legal liminality—when migrants have in-between, "gray area" legal statuses— and the uncertainty and ambiguity it entails, has broad ramifications for im-migrants' belonging and incorporation (Menjívar 2006).

97: Molina 2014.

98: According to a national survey, 46 percent identified as black and 40 percent as white, totaling 86 percent of refugees surveyed (Oliveira 2019c:10).

Chapter 1

1: UNHCR 2014.

2: Based on applications from 1998 to 2014, maritime entry represented 12 per-cent of refugee arrivals overall. A third of refugees who declare arriving to Brazil by boat are from the Congo, and a third of Congolese refugees claim arriving by maritime routes (Bezerra Lima et al. 2017:126). Media reports similarly suggest this is common among Congolese (Briso 2016, 2017; Carta-Capital 2017; Mello 2016). Regarding travel authorization, roughly half (48%) of Congolese refugees declaring arrived irregularly from 1998 to 2014 (Bezerra Lima et al. 2017:129). A total of 24 percent of refugees declared irregular entry in applications during that period; of those, 25 percent were Congolese, the largest nationality represented (Bezerra Lima et al. 2017:129).

3: This is not to say that the past overdetermines the present but to highlight their constitutive connection. Goldberg 1993, 2009b:1279–80.

4: Schwarcz 1998:189.

5: Andrews 1991.

6: Cottrol 2013:4.

7: Cottrol 2013:143, 149; FitzGerald and Cook-Martín 2014:266; Skidmore 1999:55.

8: FitzGerald and Cook-Martín 2014:270.

9: Andrews 2004:118. This entailed a Brazilian reconfiguring of eugenics and scientific racism that saw racial mixture as driving racial improvement rather than degeneration, influenced by the French naturalist Jean-Baptiste Lamarck.

10: Loveman 2014; Telles and Flores 2013.

11: Loveman 2014:148.

12: On immigration policies regarding Black US citizens in the early twentieth century, see FitzGerald and Cook-Martín 2014:260–61; Lesser 1991.

13: FitzGerald and Cook-Martín 2014; Ngai 2004; Fischer 2018:397–98; see also Weinstein 2015:337.

14: Andrews 2004:136; Cottrol 2013:149; FitzGerald and Cook-Martín 2014:269; Loveman 2014:148.

15: Levy 1974; Silva and Paixão 2014:177.

16: Campos 2015:494.

17: Lesser 1994:24.

18: Lesser 1999.

19: Lesser 2013:159.

20: Karam 2007:10. For more on Middle Eastern immigration, see Lesser 1996, 1999, 2013.

21: Karam 2007:10; Lesser 1996:46; Najar 2012. With their own particularities, similar trends appeared with other Arab immigrants (see Lesser 1996).

22: Lesser 1996:50; Najar 2012.

23: Dávila 2005; Karam 2007.

24: Najar 2012.

25: Loveman 2014:150; Skidmore 1999:76.

26: Karam 2007.

27: Najar 2012. Similar debates regarding the whiteness of various immigrant groups, including Southern and Eastern Europeans, were happening in the United States (Fox and Guglielmo 2012; Haney López 1996; Maghbouleh 2017).

28: Najar 2012:7.

29: Lesser 1996:58; see also Karam 2007.

30: FitzGerald and Cook-Martín 2014:297; Lesser 1994.

31: Koifman 2012; Lesser 1996.

32: Andrews 2004:154.

33: FitzGerald and Cook-Martín 2014:260.

34: Andrews 2004:162; FitzGerald and Cook-Martín 2014:297.

35: Nascimento 1979.

36: FitzGerald and Cook-Martín 2014:269; Koifman 2012:30.

37: FitzGerald and Cook-Martín 2014:284, 289; Skidmore 1974.

38: Koifman 2012:32; Lesser 1994:24.

39: Lesser 1994:25.

40: FitzGerald and Cook-Martín 2014:261; Koifman 2012; Lesser 1994.

41: Koifman 2012:423, 424.

42: While principally associated with Gilberto Freyre, he did not coin the term and first used it in 1962.

43: Hanchard 1994; Winant 2001:220.

44: FitzGerald and Cook-Martín 2014:296, 278.

45: This was exemplified by UNESCO funding research in the 1950s to understand this purportedly racially harmonious society after the atrocities of the Holocaust and World War II. The resultant studies, however, showed the realities of racism, discrimination, and inequality (Fernandes 1965; Costa Pinto 1952; Nogueira and Cavalcanti 1998).

46: According to the OECD, only 18 percent of Brazilian adults had college degrees in 2019. As of 2010, 6 percent of black Brazilians had a secondary education, versus 20 percent of whites; a third of whites are in white-collar occupations, versus roughly a quarter for mixed and black Brazilians (Telles 2014:224).

47: During fieldwork, I met one black asylum official, one black lawyer, two volunteers who identified as Afro-Brazilian, and a few black social workers.

48: Bezerra Lima et al. 2017:3.

49: The right to asylum, for example, was included in the French Constitution of 1793. The first treaty provisions for asylum and refugee protection to emerge anywhere in the world appeared in Latin America, with the Montevideo Treaty on International Penal Law of 1889—signed and ratified by Argentina, Bolivia, Paraguay, Peru, and Uruguay (Johnsson 1989). Previous international instruments had also addressed specific refugee groups, such as the UN Relief and Works Agency (UNRWA) established in 1949 for Palestinian refugees forcibly displaced with Israel's founding.

50: Betts and Collier 2017:45.

51: Mayblin 2017.

52: Betts and Collier 2017.

53: Kobelinsky 2015:71; Mayblin 2017:129.

54: For an account of the anticolonial perspective in the drafting of the 1951 Convention, see Mayblin 2017; Hamlin 2021:96–99.

55: Andrade 2011; FitzGerald and Cook-Martín 2014:292.

56: In its 1961 ratification, Brazil also excluded articles 15 and 17, regarding rights of association and wage-earning employment, respectively (United Nations 1960:430).

57: FitzGerald and Arar 2018; Mayblin 2017.

58: Betts and Collier 2017:38–39.

59: Lawrance et al. 2015:8–9; Chimni 1998.

60: This is a source of debate. Jubilut (2006), for instance, argues that this is transformative.

61: Winant 2001:231.

62: Karam 2007:96, 106–7.

63: Exact estimates are difficult, but could be as high as 60,000 (Dávila 2010:180).

64: Dávila 2010.

65: Jubilut 2006.

66: Bezerra Lima et al. 2017:63.

67: Fischer 2018:401.

68: Green and Skidmore 2022:233.

69: Fischer 2018:401–2.

70: Silva and Paixão 2014:173.

71: Lesser 1999:168. For the political, economic, and cultural transformations that provided for this shift, see Karam 2007.

72: Magalhães 2016:138.

73: Brazil acceded to the 1967 Protocol in 1972, during the dictatorship. Andrade and Marcolini 2002; Bezerra Lima et al. 2017:56.

74: Andrade and Marcolini 2002; Bezerra Lima et al. 2017:56; Jubilut 2006:26. This was preceded by Brazil's introduction of a specific administrative process for granting refugee status which incorporated the UNHCR in 1991.

75: Magalhães 2016:138; Andrade and Marcolini 2002.

76: Jubilut 2006; White 2012.

77: FitzGerald and Cook-Martín 2014:294. Moreover, numbers of immigrants continue to be low. In 2021, there were 1.3 million immigrants residing in Brazil—less than 1 percent of the national population (Mantovani 2021b).

78: On the UNHCR response to the Venezuelan decision, see UNHCR 2019b.

79: The UNHCR, and later the DPU, participates but has no right to vote.

80: Jubilut 2006.

81: While the Refugee Act does not specify which refugee assistance organizations will serve as the participating civil society representatives, these have included Caritas-Rio de Janeiro, Caritas-São Paulo, and the IMDH from Brasília.

82: Based on asylum decisions from 2013 to 2021 (CONARE 2022; Godinho 2013).

83: Jubilut 2006:37–39; Menezes and Kostas 2017.

84: Schiocchet 2019:85.

85: Dávila 2010. Between 1996 and 2010, Africa was the largest sending region of asylum applicants to Brazil in all but four years (UNHCR 2022b).

86: Bezerra Lima et al. 2017:101. These numbers are for asylum, not including resettled refugees. Brazil was also the largest receiver of African forced migrants to the region at 38 percent, followed by Argentina at 17 percent (UNHCR 2012). During this time, Congolese came to be the largest asylum-seeking population and Angolans the largest refugee community in Brazil (Bezerra Lima et al. 2017:53).

87: Bezerra Lima et al. 2017:54, 193.

88: Bezerra Lima et al. 2017:31, 51.

89: Bezerra Lima et al. 2017:55.

90: Bezerra Lima et al. 2017:110–11, 113, 132.

91: Brumat 2022.

92: Zolberg 1999.

93: Bezerra Lima et al. 2017:55. CONARE renewed Resolution 17 by unanimous vote in 2015 for another two years (Ministry of Justice 2015), and again in 2017 for another two.

94: Following the 2010 earthquake, Haitians began to apply for asylum in Brazil in numbers that far surpassed anything CONARE had previously seen. CONARE declined to recognize them as refugees, and the National Immigration Council (CNIg) extended travel visas and residency on humanitarian grounds to resolve the asylum case backlog created. Haitian experiences of formal legal inclusion suggest similarities with what I documented with black African refugees. For example, the limited infrastructure for visa processing, and the bureaucracies entailed, have made these difficult to access in practice (Agência Brasil 2017; Mantovani 2021a). On racial discrimination in the possibilities and experiences of asylum, migration, and residency for Haitians, see Cogo 2018; Martínez and Dutra 2018; Schwartzman 2022. On how the humanitarian visas depoliticized Haitian migration and served Brazil's branding mission as a benevolent leader in the Global South, see Thomaz 2018.

95: CONARE meeting minutes, November 20, 2015.

96: CONARE meeting minutes, March 18, 2011.

97: These were through Brazilian diplomatic missions, primarily through consulates in Lebanon, Jordan, Turkey, and Iraq (Bezerra Lima et al. 2017:55; Portal Brasil 2015).

98: President Rousseff was not alone in constructing Arab-Brazilian solidarity through references to historical ethnic ties. Lula da Silva similarly foregrounded the "Arab presence in Brazil" during his presidency, framing his visits to the region as "the reencounter of South Americans with a civilization that first came to us by way of the Iberian heritage and, after, by way of immigration" (Karam 2007:174).

99: Such estimates are claimed by former presidents and state entities, including the Ministry of Foreign Affairs (see Karam 2007:10).

100: Bezerra Lima et al. 2017:126.

101: Briso 2016.

102: Roughly one in ten refugees declared not knowing Brazil was their destination. Among them, 85 percent were from Africa, with Congolese predominating at 30 percent; 23 percent of Congolese did not know they were heading to Brazil. Regarding maritime routes, 74 percent of those who did not know where they were going came by sea, and 84 percent of those who came by boat came from Africa (Bezerra Lima et al. 2017:129). On the trade routes between Africa and Brazil, see Pereira 2014:4.

103: In total, most forcibly enslaved Africans trafficked to Brazil originated from what are now Angola and the DRC (Ramos 1939). Those sent in large scale to Northeastern Brazil originated from West Africa, in greatest number from what are now Guinea, Nigeria, Ghana, Benin, and Guinea-Bissau. Those forcibly brought to Southeastern Brazil came predominantly from what are now Angola, the Democratic Republic of the Congo, and Mozambique (Andrews 2004; Araujo 2015; Geipel 1997). Rio de Janeiro was directly connected to the Congo and Angola on transatlantic trade routes (Andrews 2004:20).

104: Dávila 2010:245.

105: Lesser 1999:49–50.

106: On the social construction of ethnic affinity migrations, see Brubaker 1998; Joppke 2005; Kim 2019.

107: Malkki 1995:1.

108: Ministry of Foreign Relations 2021.

Chapter 2

1: On the domination embedded in the logics and practices of humanitarianism seen in the face of refugees and other politically vulnerable subjects, see Fassin 2011a; Harrell-Bond 2002.

2: Goffman 1951:297.

3: Goffman 1961:21.

4: On the political meanings and ramifications of asylum seeker physical deprivation, see Mayblin 2020.

5: Bourdieu 1989:17; Emirbayer and Desmond 2015:237.

6: On time, power, and waiting, see Auyero 2012; Bourdieu 2000:228; Herzfeld 1992; Reid 2013; Schwartz 1974. While scholarship has focused on the temporal dynamics of political domination in state encounters, it has paid the body little analytical heed. On the politics of waiting and asylum specifically, see Griffiths 2014; Haas 2017; Rotter 2016. However, asylum scholarship has focused on the legal condition of waiting, rather than the sites where waiting occurs.

7: Fassin and d'Halluin 2005:597.

8: Brown 2017.

9: On biopolitics and refugees, see Agamben 1998. For a critique of the inability of Agamben's theories to account for the ontological impossibility of black humanity or citizenship, see Alves 2014; Mbembe 2003.

10: This included five Syrians, two Afghans, two Iraqis, and one Iranian. As Syrians were one of the largest asylum-seeking populations in Rio and nationally, this far from corresponded to the size of that population.

11: Mauss 1925.

12: Goffman 1961:22.

13: Auyero 2012; Ong 2003; Ordóñez 2008.

14: Auyero 2012; Foucault 1977:23.

15: Auyero 2012:2.

16: Schwartz 1974; see also Auyero 2012.

17: Bourdieu 1989:18; Emirbayer and Desmond 2015.

18: For work on legal status as a fundamental axis in political, social, and economic incorporation and stratification in the United States, see, for example, Light, Massoglia, and King 2014; Menjívar 2006. For how race informs claims making by refugees from a different vantage point, see Brown 2011.

19: On the differences and relationships between domination, inclusion, and exclusion, see De Genova 2013; Wright 2015.

20: Cooper 2015.

21: Bourdieu et al. 1999:126; Sullivan 2018.

22: Schwartz 1974:847.

23: Bourdieu et al. 1999:101–5.

24: Goffman 1961:8.

25: Such dynamics of overburden and limited resources were diffuse across the refugee regime. CONARE eligibility officials in Brasília and São Paulo, for example, spoke frequently of structural constraints: running out of pens, having nowhere to sit, and not having enough rooms to conduct interviews.

26: Goffman 1961:46–47; Herzfeld 1992; Jensen and Auyero 2019; Mills 1940; Tilly 1998.

27: Bourdieu 1989:16.

28: Herzfeld 1992:49.

Chapter 3

1: On a sense of knowledge cultivated through the work but seemingly unnamable, see Jubany 2011, 2017.

2: For further examples of this in the United States, see Anker 1990, 1992; Ramji-Nogales, Schoenholtz, and Schrag 2009.

3: Goffman 1974:21.

4: This is different from seeing frames as coming to play only in instances of bias or prejudice. On biases, stereotypes, prejudices, and assumptions in asylum decisions, see Bohmer and Shuman 2007, 2008; Herlihy, Gleeson, and Turner 2010; Ordóñez 2008.

5: State classification, rather than merely describing the world, constitutes it as it orders social life and creates particular kinds of people, like refugees (Bourdieu 2014; Loveman 2005). "State legibility," as coined by James Scott (1998), refers to "a knowledge-based optic" through which states—using practices of measurement, classification, enumeration, and aggregation—turn the messiness of the social world into coherence. It captures how states obtain and exert symbolic and political power over subjects through practices of classification.

6: This refers to moving from things presumed in the world, such as treating race as a given and preconstructed discrete demographic variable, to processes of racialization in cognition. On ways of seeing, in racialization and beyond, see Brekhus et al. 2010; Brubaker, Loveman, and Stamatov 2004:45; Emirbayer and Desmond 2015; Durkheim 1915.

7: Research on racial cognition and immigration has focused on citizens rather than state actors (Maghbouleh 2020; Roth 2012). Cognitive approaches generally, and racialized cognition in particular, are largely absent from scholarly apprehensions of the state in immigration research (on cognitive processes, see Shiff 2021). Work on the racial state often misses its everyday functions, and this chapter builds on notable exceptions in other arenas (on prisons, see Walker 2016; on welfare, see Watkins-Hayes 2009).

8: Keith, Holmes, and Miller 2013; Ramji-Nogales et al. 2007, 2009; Schoenholtz, Schrag, and Ramji-Nogales 2014.

9: Bohmer and Shuman 2008; Jubany 2017; Magalhães 2016.

10: Thomson 2012:193. See, for example, Bohmer and Shuman 2008:121.

11: CONARE 155th plenary meeting minutes, July 17, 2021.

12: Human Rights Watch 2022.

13: On how the state and asylum process classifies and evaluates sexuality in the United States, see Vogler 2021. On how that is racialized, see McKinnon 2016.

14: Norman 2007.

15: Flahaux and Schoumaker 2016.

16: For more on this alternative framing, see Souter 2016.

17: Nigerian asylum decisions from 2011 to 2016; the recognition rate for Nigeria is 26 percent overall (CONARE 2022). Based on my September 2015 to April 2016 dataset, only 18 percent received asylum from September 2015 to April 2016.

18: UK Home Office 2015:18, 21.

19: Reuters 2015.

20: CONARE 2021. In 2022, CONARE shifted its online platform, which now suggests even starker percentages for that period.

21: UNHCR 2014.

22: For a partial account of these discussions, see CONARE Plenary No. 113 Meeting Minutes. Notably, to evaluate whether Mali qualified as a context of generalized violence, CONARE prepared a study explicitly comparing Mali to Syria and Colombia on a range of indicators. As such, it assesses the context of Mali relationally, with Syria and Colombia the purported benchmarks for GGHRV recognition, rather than evaluating Mali on its own terms based on a formal set of criteria.

23: In a longer view, this becomes starker. Between 2016 and 2020, almost five times as many Palestinians as Congolese were recognized under GGHRV (CONARE 2021).

24: Karam 2007:170.

25: This dovetails a broader racialization found with Syrians as well in the public sphere: that Arabs are ill suited for the violent context of Brazil (Jensen and Sousa Dias 2022).

26: Barnes 2016; Romero and Schmidt 2016.

27: As Karam (2007:170) writes, "the image of 'the Arab' as a security threat and a target of surveillance has been categorically associated with U.S. American power . . . the image of 'the Arab' as a security threat does not translate easily into Brazil."

28: CONARE 2022.

29: WHO 2014.

30: Serricella 2016:60.

31: Miraglia 2016.

32: Uebel 2018.

33: Existing asylum scholarship on Europe and the United States suggests that a racial cognitive approach could have broad applicability (for the United States, see Ordóñez 2008; Schoenholtz et al. 2014; for Europe, see Jubany 2011, 2017).

Chapter 4

1:   Fassin 2011b:284; Fassin and d'Halluin 2005; Oertli 2019; Ticktin 2011.
2:   Jensen 2018.
3:   Benzecry and Krause 2010:419.
4:   Zuberi and Bonilla-Silva 2008:17–18.
5:   Fassin 2011b; Fassin and d'Halluin 2005:597; Oertli 2019.
6:   Alcoff 1991; Fonow and Cook 1991; Haraway 1988; Harding 1986; Ticktin 2011.
7:   Fourcade 2010:570.
8:   Haraway 1988:575. Emphasis in the original.
9:   Haraway 1988:581.
10: Scheurich and Young 1997:8.
11: Ticktin 2011:175.
12: Oertli 2019:13.
13: Bezerra Lima et al. 2017:86.
14: This can be seen as a particular permutation of white ontological expansiveness broadly; see Emirbayer and Desmond 2015:253.
15: Goffman 1961:23.
16: Campbell 2013:676.
17: Taussig 1997:3.
18: Césaire 2000:69.
19: UNHCR 2012.
20: Good 2004:360.
21: Magalhães 2016:135.
22: Existing research signals that these epistemic practices are not unique to Brazil. In the United States, for example, judges expect applicants to provide "testimony regarding events . . . that they directly had experienced or visually observed" while contrastingly considering "printed corroborative proof" as "'objective' evidence" (Anker 1992:449, 478), while officials expunge questions from reports in Belgium (Gómez Díez 2011) and privilege medical certificates in France (Fassin and d'Halluin 2005). Moreover, "Googling judges" use informal and unvetted web sources—"not edited for accuracy or bias"—to come to conclusions about claims across the Global North (Byrne 2015:638–40; Dahlvik 2018:135).

Chapter 5

1:   CONARE 2022.
2:   These approval rates hold quite consistent across time and beyond my dataset. Based on the Ministry of Justice (MJ) database of 2014 to 2020 decisions: Syria (100%), Pakistan (77%), DRC (85%), Guinea-Bissau (3%), Ghana (11%),

and Nigeria (18%). Indeed, these rates suggest the preference for non-African claims as even starker (CONARE 2021).

3: CONARE 2022.

4: They are responsible for cases from states, including in the Northwest (Amazonas, Acre), Northeast (Ceará), Southeast (Rio de Janeiro, Minas Gerais), and South (Rio Grande do Sul, Paraná).

5: For anonymity, I do not individually specify year of application and removed specific locations. Given the small number of applicants from Mauritania, I do not clarify the state of application.

6: Seydou is indeed removed from the plenary; that is the last information I have. He also should have been added to the CNIg list that provided residency to those who had been waiting longer than three years for asylum decisions, but as of my last notes on the case, he had not been. I do not know the outcome of his case. However, it is likely he was ultimately denied, given the recognition rate for Mali at the time.

7: Immigration law provided for permanent residency for those who had a child in Brazil or married a citizen or other permanent resident.

8: This recounting is based on a civil society representative's meeting notes taken during the GEP.

9: Numbers of total officials varied. In 2012, there were only two asylum eligibility officials in all Brazil (CONARE Plenary No. 79 Meeting Minutes, April 19, 2012). A UNHCR Brazil report suggests that, in 2015, there were only five eligibility officials (Cruz Leo, Morand, and Feitosa 2015:21). I believe differing numbers in part result from whether "asylum official" is taken broadly or used to refer to those tasked with eligibility assessments specifically.

10: Godinho 2013; CONARE 2021.

11: According to a 2005 CONARE report (Bezerra Lima et al. 2017:97, 107, 134).

12: CONARE 2022.

13: CONARE 2022.

14: UNHCR 2022b.

15: In the July 2014 plenary, a total of 678 claims were decided: Syrian 534, Mali 57, DRC 28, Nigeria 19, Guinea 15, Cameroon 5, Pakistan 5, Angola 4, Togo 3, Colombia 2, Ivory Coast 2, Lebanon 1, Palestine 1, Serbia 1, Sudan 1.

16: CONARE 2022.

17: CONARE 2021.

18: CONARE 2022.

19: This model is restricted to observations from February and March 2016 because it is only for those claims that I have the exact date of asylum application in my dataset.

20: CONARE 2021.

21: CNIg is presided over by the Ministry of Labor, and composed of representatives from a range of ministries, as well as civil society and business sectors (for more on CNIg, see Bezerra Lima et al. 2017:26).

22: As of 2014, with CONARE Resolution 18, the protocol was changed from six months to a year of initial validity, to be successively renewed for equal periods until the decision, though this varied in practice. For example, based on the whims of the Federal Police, it was sometimes renewed for another six months instead of a year.

23: Bezerra Lima et al. 2017:68, 88. Problems of public and private entities not recognizing the protocol were discussed in CONARE Plenary No. 114 (August 26, 2016), following the sentencing of a public civil action filed by the Federal Public Defender's Office. Following the sentence orders, representatives discuss measures to strengthen the recognition of the protocol as a document of identification. Not discussed, however, is instead providing asylum seekers with a formal identity card.

24: This entails submitting the appeal to the Federal Police, which relays it to CONARE. Appeals are subject to administrative review, leading to either recognition or a reaffirmation of rejection. That decision is final.

25: On legal liminality, see Menjívar 2006; Del Real 2022.

26: This was the case until 2021, but that data was then removed in 2022 (CONARE 2021, 2022).

27: Schwartz 1975:7.

Chapter 6

1: Vis and Goriunova 2015.

2: BBC and ComRes 2015; Binder and Jaworsky 2018; Prøitz 2018; Slovic et al. 2017. For a nuance of the fleeting nature of empathy, see Sohlberg, Esaiasson, and Martinsson 2019.

3: See Campos 2015; Jensen and Sousa Dias 2022; Stuenkel 2015.

4: Morgan and Orloff 2017:20.

5: The relationship between race, worthiness, and assistance can take disparate forms. In other contexts, financial assistance marks who is seen as a deserving refugee (see Boeyink [2019], who finds that cash goes to Syrians but not Sub-Saharan African refugees).

6: The move to asylum as a regime of compassion, rather than admiration, as Fassin (2011a) describes it, has not been a universal transformation. To understand how need gets understood, and acted upon, also entails turning to the ways that logics of political and social vulnerability can be racially configured and configuring.

7: An analysis of the newspaper *Folha* showed that, relative to Kurdi's death, coverage of asylum seekers and refugees increased by 2.7 times in the three months after versus the three months prior; 1.9 times in the six months after versus the six months prior; and 1.6 times in the year after compared to the year prior.

8: Sousa Arruda 2012.

9: Pota 2017.

10: Stuenkel 2015.

11: Dávila 2005:193; Karam 2007.

12: On how ethnic entrepreneurs also invested in propagating these stereotypes, see Karam 2007.

13: Schiocchet 2019:86.

14: Schiocchet 2019:92.

15: *Folha* coverage from September 3, 2014, to September 3, 2016, of Syrian conflict/displacement versus Congolese conflict/displacement.

16: Sohlberg et al. 2019.

17: El-Enany 2016.

18: Butler 2009.

19: For examples, such as Angolan refugees as outlaws and drug traffickers, see Campos 2015:477–78.

20: Bezerra Lima et al. 2017:102, 106.

21: Jensen and Sousa Dias 2022.

22: According to the Brazilian Institute of Geography and Statistics (IBGE), in 2016, Brazil had a national average of 10.5 years of formal education.

23: Based on head applicants for successful asylum applications from 1998 to 2014, 76 and 67 percent of Syrians and Congolese, respectively, had completed at least high school, and 33 percent of both Syrians and Congolese had completed some education beyond high school, whether college or professional schools (Bezerra Lima et al. 2017:121–22; Oliveira 2019a:60).

24: Bezerra Lima et al. 2017:118–19.

25: Mello 2016.

26: This was likewise seen historically (Karam 2021).

27: According to Bezerra Lima et al. (2017:70, 71), since 2005, asylum seekers and refugees in Brazil have been granted up to R$300 a month for up to six months, and that support was up to R$370 a month in 2014. Nonetheless, in Rio I documented support to continue at R$300, usually for three months. They also highlight that aid also came as funds for attending classes or for finding work, the former being a common biweekly practice at the Rio Refugee Center while the latter I did not document.

28: Bezerra Lima et al. 2017:63, 65.

29: Some 37 percent of Congolese who sought assistance at the Center obtained at least one subsidy, versus 13 percent of Syrians.

30: See Martínez and Dutra 2018.

31: On how recognitions of racism and discrimination can likewise entail and constitute racialization, see Brown, Jones, and Becker 2018.

32: Agier 2011:4, 12.

33: Bezerra Lima et al. 2017.

34: Alves 2014.

Chapter 7

1: Vigario Geral has been marked by violence, including a massacre in 1993 where police killed twenty-one people.

2:   Bohmer and Shuman 2007:268.

3:   Betts and Collier 2017:43. Some have shown that refugee status has deep subjective meaning for resettled refugees (Brown 2011), while others note disenchantment or its lack of transformative powers (Ramsay 2017; Tang 2015).

4:   Jensen 2021a, 2021b.

5:   However, as discussed in chapter five, an asylum seeker has the right to appeal the first instance of rejection and, as of 2016, CONARE had not adjudicated an appeal in the previous three years. While awaiting their appeal decision, such applicants have the same rights as other asylum seekers, including the protocol identity document.

6:   CONARE meeting, July 17, 2021.

7:   In a national survey, 96 percent of refugees wanted to obtain Brazilian citizenship (Oliveira 2019a:50).

8:   At the time of my research, this right was specific to refugees. In 2017, the New Migration Law extended the right to family reunification to all permanent residents in Brazil.

9:   While Resolution 16 states this includes the right to bring family members who economically depend on the refugee, I only saw this option mobilized to reunite with siblings during fieldwork.

10:   Oliveira 2019a:55.

11:   CONARE 2022.

12:   This process became even more arduous in 2018 with Resolution 27, when the family member abroad, rather than the refugee in country, became the applicant for family reunification (Martuscelli 2021).

13:   Martuscelli 2021:3402.

14:   Martuscelli 2021:3409, 3414.

15:   Other studies have found similar perspectives among officials. As another official stated in 2021: "The status of asylum in Brazil is every day more and more of an equivalent of an authorisation for residence than a protective [legal] status. So this protective approach is not evident to me. Well, [asylum] is an empty concept, because today is one more form of regularization" (Brumat 2022).

16:   Oliveira 2019a:14.

17:   Carneiro, Souza, and Teixeira 2018.

18:   Oliveira 2019a:64; on the anti-black racism experienced in the public sphere by African and Haitian immigrants broadly in Brazil, see, for example, Kaly 2001; Martínez and Dutra 2018.

19:   Oliveira 2019c:15. Congolese were the second largest group of refugees.

20:   A national representative survey showed that all Congolese refugees had finished at least high school, compared to 2017 PNAD data that found that only 34 percent of the Brazilian population had completed elementary school and only 27 percent had finished high school (Martuscelli 2021; Oliveira 2019a).

21:   See Carneiro and Teixeira 2018; Oliveira 2019a.

22:   Some 41 percent of Congolese self-identified as employed, while 64 percent of Syrians did (Oliveira 2019a:61–62).

23: This study's researchers based in Rio found that the majority of refugees did not work in their area; 50 percent of Syrians versus 25 percent of Congolese worked in their area of professionalization (Oliveira 2019b). Nationally, 32 percent of refugees broadly attested to working in their professional fields in their current jobs (Oliveira 2019c:9).

24: This is a common occupational path for African asylum seekers and refugees in Rio. According to the Rio site of the national study, "the main profession mentioned was hairdresser, occupation exercised mainly by Congolese and Angolans" (Oliveira 2019b:133; see also Briso 2016).

25: Briso 2016.

26: Briso 2016.

27: Serricella 2016.

28: This can also be translated as the N-word.

29: Sanches 2014.

Conclusion

1: Bourdieu 1989.

2: Stam and Shohat 2012: xvii.

3: Anderson 1983.

4: Balibar 2011.

5: Fassin 2013:44.

6: Fassin 2011a; Krause 2014.

7: De Genova 2016; see also Bourdieu 1977:164; Magalhães 2014.

8: On such "silent self-evidence," see Bourdieu 2000:188. For a critique of the migrant/refugee binary, see Hamlin 2021.

9: For more on refugee exceptionalism, see Tang 2015.

10: Puar 2007:3. Emphasis added.

11: Taylor 2015.

12: Schuster 1998:16. Emphasis added.

13: Bhabha 2002:160, 161.

14: Bourdieu 1982:172; see also Lukes 1974.

Appendix A

1: Katz 1983.

2: Jensen and Auyero 2019.

3: Jensen and Sousa Dias 2022.

4: Scheper-Hughes 1993.

5: Katz 2001; Weiss 1995.

6: Due to the small number of eligibility officials, and explicit requests from those I interviewed, not providing the number of asylum officials interviewed at each location is crucial to maintaining the anonymity of said officials. For this reason as well, I do not provide a chart of interviewee demographics. Moreover, deciding to not declare what was or wasn't changed to protect those in this study more broadly is also crucial to maintaining anonymity (Reyes 2019). All names, though, have been changed except for public figures.

7:   See Stuart 2016.

8:   Desmond 2014.

9:   Bezerra Lima et al. 2017; CONARE 2022; UNHCR 2022b.

10: Hanson and Richards 2019:4.

11: Reyes 2020.

12: Desmond 2008.

13: This is in some ways surprising, given the findings that whites in Rio can make sense of and deny their own whiteness by pointing to those whiter than themselves, such as foreigners (Roth-Gordon 2017).

14: Hanson and Richards 2019.

References

Agamben, Giorgio. 1997. *Homo sacer*. Paris: Éd. du Seuil.

Agamben, Giorgio. 1998. *Homo Sacer: Sovereign Power and Bare Life*. Stanford, CA: Stanford University Press.

Agência Brasil. 2017. "Governo prorroga prazo para permanência de haitianos no Brasil." January 23. https://agenciabrasil.ebc.com.br/geral/noticia/2017-01/governo-prorroga-prazo-para-haitiano-tirarem-visto-permanente-no-brasil.

Agier, Michel. 2011. *Managing the Undesirables: Refugee Camps and Humanitarian Government*. Cambridge: Polity Press.

Alcoff, Linda. 1991. "The Problem of Speaking for Others." *Cultural Critique* 20(Winter):5–32.

Alves, Jaime Amparo. 2014. "Neither Humans Nor Rights: Some Notes on the Double Negation of Black Life in Brazil." *Journal of Black Studies* 45(2):143–62.

Alves, Jaime Amparo, and João Costa Vargas. 2017. "On Deaf Ears: Anti-Black Police Terror, Multiracial Protest and White Loyalty to the State." *Identities* 24(3):254–74.

Amar, Paul, ed. 2013. *Global South to the Rescue: Emerging Humanitarian Superpowers and Globalizing Rescue Industries*. New York: Routledge.

Amar, Paul, ed. 2014. *The Middle East and Brazil: Perspectives on the New Global South*. Bloomington: Indiana University Press.

Anderson, Benedict. 1983. *Imagined Communities: Reflections on the Origin and Spread of Nationalism*. New York: Verso.

Anderson, Bridget, Matthew J. Gibney, and Emanuela Paoletti. 2011. "Citizenship, Deportation and the Boundaries of Belonging." *Citizenship Studies* 15(5):547–63.

Andrade, José H. Fischel de. 2011. "Brazil and the International Refugee Organization (1946–1952)." *Refugee Survey Quarterly* 30(1):65–88.

Andrade, José H. Fischel de, and Adriana Marcolini. 2002. "Brazil's Refugee Act: Model Refugee Law for Latin America?" *Forced Migration Review* 12:37–39.

Andrews, George Reid. 1991. *Blacks & Whites in São Paulo, Brazil, 1888–1988*. Madison: University of Wisconsin Press.

Andrews, George Reid. 2004. *Afro-Latin America, 1800–2000*. New York: Oxford University Press.

Anker, Deborah E. 1990. "Determining Asylum Claims in the United States: Summary Report of an Empirical Study of the Adjudication of Asylum Claims before the Immigration Court." *International Journal of Refugee Law* 2(2):252–64.

Anker, Deborah E. 1992. "Determining Asylum Claims in the United States: A Case Study on the Implementation of Legal Norms in an Unstructured Adjudicatory Environment." *New York University Review of Law and Social Change* 19(3):433–528.

Araujo, Ana Lucia, ed. 2015. *African Heritage and Memories of Slavery in Brazil and the South Atlantic World*. New York: Cambria Press.

Arendt, Hannah. 1951. *The Origins of Totalitarianism*. New York: A Harvest Book.

Ashutosh, Ishan, and Alison Mountz. 2012. "The Geopolitics of Migrant Mobility: Tracing State Relations Through Refugee Claims, Boats, and Discourses." *Geopolitics* 17(2):335–54.

Auyero, Javier. 2012. *Patients of the State: The Politics of Waiting in Argentina*. Durham, NC: Duke University Press.

Bailey, Stanley R. 2009. *Legacies of Race: Identities, Attitudes, and Politics in Brazil*. Stanford, CA: Stanford University Press.

Bailey, Stanley R., Fabrício M. Fialho, and Mara Loveman. 2018. "How States Make Race: New Evidence from Brazil." *Sociological Science* 5:722–51.

Bairros, Luiza. 1996. "Orfeu e Poder: Uma perspetiva afro-americana sobre a política racial no Brasil." *Afro-Ásia* (17):173–86.

Balibar, Étienne. 2011. "Racism and Nationalism." In *Race, Nation, Class: Ambiguous Identities*, ed. I. Wallerstein and É. Balibar, 37–68. New York: Verso.

Barnes, Taylor. 2016. "Brazil Uses Collaborative Approach to Track Terror Threats during Olympics." *USA Today*. August 12. https://www.usatoday .com/story/sports/olympics/rio-2016/2016/08/12/brazil-uses-collaborative -approach-track-terror-threats-during-olympics/88613260/.

BBC and ComRes. 2015. "BBC Newsnight Migrant Crisis Survey." https:// 2sjjwunnql4lia7ki31qqubl-wpengine.netdna-ssl.com/wp-content/uploads/ 2015/09/BBC-Newsnight_Migrant-Crisis-Survey_September-2015.pdf.

Benzecry, Claudio, and Monika Krause. 2010. "How Do They Know? Practicing Knowledge in Comparative Perspective." *Qualitative Sociology* 33(4):415–22.

Betts, Alexander. 2010. "The Refugee Regime Complex." *Refugee Survey Quarterly* 29(1):12–37.

Betts, Alexander. 2015. "The Normative Terrain of the Global Refugee Regime." *Ethics & International Affairs* 29(4):363–75.

Betts, Alexander, and Paul Collier. 2017. *Refuge: Rethinking Refugee Policy in a Changing World*. New York: Oxford University Press.

Bezerra Lima, João Brígido, Fernanda Patrícia Fuentes Muñoz, Luísa de Azevedo Nazareno, and Nemo Amaral. 2017. *Refúgio no Brasil: Caracterização dos perfis sociodemográficos dos refugiados (1998–2014)*. Brasília: IPEA.

Bhabha, Jacqueline. 2002. "Internationalist Gatekeepers: The Tension between

Asylum Advocacy and Human Rights." *Harvard Human Rights Journal* 15:151–81.

Binder, Werner, and Bernadette Nadya Jaworsky. 2018. "Refugees as Icons: Culture and Iconic Representation." *Sociology Compass* 12(3):1–14.

Bloch, Alice, and Liza Schuster. 2005. "At the Extremes of Exclusion: Deportation, Detention and Dispersal." *Ethnic and Racial Studies* 28(3):491–512.

Boeyink, Clayton Todd. 2019. "A 'Worthy' Refugee: Cash as a Diagnostic of 'Xeno-Racism' and 'Bio-Legitimacy.'" *Refuge* 35(1):61–71.

Bohmer, Carol, and Amy Shuman. 2007. "Producing Epistemologies of Ignorance in the Political Asylum Application Process." *Identities* 14(5):603–29.

Bohmer, Carol, and Amy Shuman. 2008. *Rejecting Refugees: Political Asylum in the 21st Century*. New York: Routledge.

Bonilla-Silva, Eduardo. 1997. "Rethinking Racism: Toward a Structural Interpretation." *American Sociological Review* 62(3):465–80.

Bourdieu, Pierre. 1977. *Outline of a Theory of Practice*. New York: Cambridge University Press.

Bourdieu, Pierre. 1982. *Language and Symbolic Power*. Malden: Polity Press.

Bourdieu, Pierre. 1989. "Social Space and Symbolic Power." *Sociological Theory* 7(1):14–25.

Bourdieu, Pierre. 1994. "Rethinking the State: Genesis and Structure of the Bureaucratic Field." *Sociological Theory* 12(1):1–18.

Bourdieu, Pierre. 2000. *Pascalian Meditations*. Stanford, CA: Stanford University Press.

Bourdieu, Pierre. 2014. *On the State: Lectures at the Collège de France, 1989–1992*, ed. P. Champagne. Cambridge: Polity Press.

Bourdieu, Pierre, and Loïc Wacquant. 1999. "On the Cunning of Imperialist Reason." *Theory, Culture & Society* 16(1):41–58.

Bourdieu, Pierre, et al. 1999. *The Weight of the World: Social Suffering in Contemporary Society*. Stanford, CA: Stanford University Press.

Bracey, Glenn E. 2015. "Toward a Critical Race Theory of State." *Critical Sociology* 41(3):553–72.

Brekhus, Wayne H., David L. Brunsma, Todd Platts, and Priya Dua. 2010. "On the Contributions of Cognitive Sociology to the Sociological Study of Race." *Sociology Compass* 4(1):61–76.

Briso, Caio Barretto. 2016. "O sofrimento silencioso dos refugiados do Congo em Brás de Pina." *O Globo*. June 19. https://oglobo.globo.com/rio/o-sofrimento-silencioso-dos-refugiados-do-congo-em-bras-de-pina-19538015.

Briso, Caio Barretto. 2017. "Congoleses no Rio: Entre a fome, o desemprego, e o desejo de partir." *O Globo*. August 20. https://oglobo.globo.com/rio/congoleses-no-rio-entre-fome-desemprego-o-desejo-de-partir-21726113.

Brown, Hana E. 2011. "Refugees, Rights, and Race: How Legal Status Shapes Liberian Immigrants' Relationship with the State." *Social Problems* 58(1):144–63.

Brown, Hana E. 2017. "Immigrant Bodily Incorporation: How the Physical

Body Structures Identity, Mobility, and Transnationalism." *Social Problems* 64(1):14–29.

Brown, Hana E. 2020. "Who Is an Indian Child? Institutional Context, Tribal Sovereignty, and Race-Making in Fragmented States." *American Sociological Review* 85(5):776–805.

Brown, Hana E., Jennifer A. Jones, and Andrea Becker. 2018. "The Racialization of Latino Immigrants in New Destinations: Criminality, Ascription, and Countermobilization." *RSF: The Russell Sage Foundation Journal of the Social Sciences* 4(5):118.

Brubaker, Rogers. 1998. "Migrations of Ethnic Unmixing in the 'New Europe.'" *International Migration Review* 32(4):1047–65.

Brubaker, Rogers, Mara Loveman, and Peter Stamatov. 2004. "Ethnicity as Cognition." *Theory and Society* 33(1):31–64.

Brumat, Leiza. 2022. "Migrants or Refugees? 'Let's Do Both.' Brazil's Response to Venezuelan Displacement Challenges Legal Definitions." *Migration Policy Centre Blog.* January 11. https://blogs.eui.eu/migrationpolicycentre/migrants-or-refugees-lets-do-both-brazils-response-to-venezuelan-displacement-challenges-legal-definitions/.

Butler, Judith. 2009. *Frames of War: When Is Life Grievable?* New York: Verso.

Byrne, Rosemary. 2015. "The Protection Paradox: Why Hasn't the Arrival of New Media Transformed Refugee Status Determination?" *International Journal of Refugee Law* 27(4):625–48.

Calavita, Kitty. 1992. *Inside the State: The Bracero Program, Immigration, and the I.N.S.* New York: Routledge.

Caldwell, Kia Lilly. 2007. *Negras in Brazil: Re-Envisioning Black Women, Citizenship, and the Politics of Identity.* New Brunswick, NJ: Rutgers University Press.

Campbell, John. 2013. "Language Analysis in the United Kingdom's Refugee Status Determination System: Seeing through Policy Claims about 'Expert Knowledge.'" *Ethnic and Racial Studies* 36(4):670–90.

Campos, Gustavo Barreto de. 2015. "Dois Séculos de Imigração no Brasil: A construção da imagem e papel social dos estrangeiros pela imprensa entre 1808 e 2015." PhD diss., Federal University of Rio de Janeiro, Rio de Janeiro.

Carneiro, Júlia, Felipe Souza, and Fabio Teixeira. 2018. "Fugindo da guerra, congoleses enfrentam violência, racismo e desemprego para recomeçar no Brasil." *BBC News Brasil.* July 30. https://www.bbc.com/portuguese/internacional-44893024.

CartaCapital. 2017. "Sylvie, a advogada congolesa que viu seu amor ressuscitar no Brasil." June 29. https://www.cartacapital.com.br/sociedade/sylvie-a-advogada-que-viu-seu-amor-ressuscitar-no-brasil/.

Castles, Stephen. 2004. "The Factors That Make and Unmake Migration Policies." *International Migration Review* 38(3):852–84.

Césaire, Aimé. 2000. *Discourse on Colonialism.* New York: Monthly Review Press.

Chimni, B. S. 1998. "The Geopolitics of Refugee Studies: A View from the South." *Journal of Refugee Studies* 11(4):350–74.

Cintra de Oliveira Tavares, Natália. 2022. "A razão antinegra do refúgio e afromobilidades no Brasil." PhD diss., Pontifical Catholic University of Rio de Janeiro, Rio de Janeiro.

Cogo, Denise. 2018. "O Haiti é Aqui: Mídia, imigração haitiana e racismo no Brasil." *Revista Latinoamericana de Comunicación* 139:427–48.

CONARE. 2021. "Plataforma Interativa de Decisões Sobre Refúgio." *Ministério da Justiça e Segurança Pública*. Retrieved September 15, 2021. https://app.powerbi.com/view?r=eyJrIjoiNTQ4MTU0NGItYzNkMi00M2MwLWFhZWMtMDBiM2I1NWVjMTY5IiwidCI6ImU1YzM3OTgxLTY2NjQtNDEzNC04YTBjLTY1NDNkMmFmODBiZSIsImMiOjh9.

CONARE. 2022. "Refúgio em Números." *Ministério da Justiça e Segurança Pública*. https://www.gov.br/mj/pt-br/assuntos/seus-direitos/refugio/refugio-em-numeros-e-publicacoes/capa.

Conectas. 2022. "Federal Decree Mentions Only Ukrainians and Stateless Persons as Eligible for Humanitarian Visas." September 3. https://www.conectas.org/en/noticias/federal-decree-mentions-only-ukrainians-and-stateless-persons-as-eligible-for-humanitarian-visas/.

Conlon, Deirdre, and Nick Gill. 2013. "Gagging Orders: Asylum Seekers and Paradoxes of Freedom and Protest in Liberal Society." *Citizenship Studies* 17(2):241–59.

Cooper, Amy. 2015. "The Doctor's Political Body: Doctor–Patient Interactions and Sociopolitical Belonging in Venezuelan State Clinics." *American Ethnologist* 42(3):459–74.

Costa Pinto, Luiz de Aguiar. 1952. *O negro no Rio de Janeiro: relações de raças numa sociedade em mudança*. Rio de Janeiro: UFRJ.

Cottrol, Robert J. 2013. *The Long, Lingering Shadow: Slavery, Race, and Law in the American Hemisphere*. Athens: University of Georgia Press.

Cruz Leo, Claudia, MaryBeth Morand, and Vinicius Feitosa. 2015. "Building Communities of Practice for Urban Refugees: Brazil Roundtable Report." *UNHCR Policy Development and Evaluation Service*. https://www.unhcr.org/en-in/research/evalreports/5613d73c9/building-communities-practice-urban-refugees-brazil-roundtable-report.html.

Dahlvik, Julia. 2018. *Inside Asylum Bureaucracy: Organizing Refugee Status Determination in Austria*. New York: Springer Berlin Heidelberg.

Dávila, Jerry. 2005. "Ethnicity and the Shifting Margins of Brazilian Identity." *Diaspora: A Journal of Transnational Studies* 14(1):185–200.

Dávila, Jerry. 2010. *Hotel Trópico: Brazil and the Challenge of African Decolonization, 1950–1980*. Durham, NC: Duke University Press.

De Genova, Nicholas. 2002. "Migrant 'Illegality' and Deportability in Everyday Life." *Annual Review of Anthropology* 31(1):419–47.

De Genova, Nicholas. 2013. "Spectacles of Migrant 'Illegality': The Scene of Exclusion, the Obscene of Inclusion." *Ethnic and Racial Studies* 36(7):1180–98.

De Genova, Nicholas. 2016. "The 'Crisis' of the European Border Regime: Towards a Marxist Theory of Borders." *International Socialism* 150. http://isj.org

.uk/the-crisis-of-the-european-border-regime-towards-a-marxist-theory-of
-borders/.

De la Fuente, Alejandro, and George Reid Andrews, eds. 2018. *Afro-Latin American Studies: An Introduction*. Cambridge: Cambridge University Press.

De León, Jason. 2015. *The Land of Open Graves: Living and Dying on the Migrant Trail*. Oakland: University of California Press.

Del Real, Deisy. 2022. "Seemingly Inclusive Liminal Legality: The Fragility and Illegality Production of Colombia's Legalization Programmes for Venezuelan Migrants." *Journal of Ethnic and Migration Studies* 48(15):3580–601.

Desmond, Matthew. 2008. *On the Fireline: Living and Dying with Wildland Firefighters*. Chicago: University of Chicago Press.

Desmond, Matthew. 2014. "Relational Ethnography." *Theory and Society* 43(5):547–479.

Dev, Sanjugta Vas. 2009. "Accounting for State Approaches to Asylum Seekers in Australia and Malaysia: The Significance of 'National' Identity and 'Exclusive' Citizenship in the Struggle Against 'Irregular' Mobility." *Identities* 16(1):33–460.

DiMaggio, Paul. 1997. "Culture and Cognition." *Annual Review of Sociology* 23(1):263–87.

Donato, Katharine M., and Amada Armenta. 2011. "What We Know About Unauthorized Migration." *Annual Review of Sociology* 37(1):529–43.

Durkheim, Émile. 1915. *The Elementary Forms of the Religious Life*. New York: Free Press.

El-Enany, Nadine. 2016. "Aylan Kurdi: The Human Refugee." *Law and Critique* 27(1):13–15.

Emirbayer, Mustafa. 1997. "Manifesto for a Relational Sociology." *American Journal of Sociology* 103(2):281–317.

Emirbayer, Mustafa, and Matthew Desmond. 2015. *The Racial Order*. Chicago: University of Chicago Press.

Espiritu, Yên Lê. 2003. *Home Bound: Filipino American Lives across Cultures, Communities, and Countries*. Berkeley: University of California Press.

Fassin, Didier. 2011a. *Humanitarian Reason: A Moral History of the Present*. Berkeley: University of California Press.

Fassin, Didier. 2011b. "The Trace: Violence, Truth, and the Politics of the Body." *Social Research: An International Quarterly* 78(2):281–98.

Fassin, Didier. 2013. *Enforcing Order: An Ethnography of Urban Policing*. Cambridge: Polity Press.

Fassin, Didier, and Estelle d'Halluin. 2005. "The Truth from the Body: Medical Certificates as Ultimate Evidence for Asylum Seekers." *American Anthropologist* 107(4):597–608.

Feagin, Joe R. 2006. *Systemic Racism: A Theory of Oppression*. New York: Routledge.

Ferguson, James, and Akhil Gupta. 2002. "Spatializing States: Toward an Ethnography of Neoliberal Governmentality." *American Ethnologist* 29(4):981–1002.

Fernandes, Florestan. 1965. *A integração do negro na sociedade de classes*. São Paulo: Dominus Editora.

Ferreira da Silva, Denise. 2007. *Toward a Global Idea of Race*. Minneapolis: University of Minnesota Press.

Fischer, Brodwyn. 2018. "Ethos and Pathos in Millennial Brazil." *Latin American Research Review* 53(2):394–402.

FitzGerald, David. 2019. *Refuge beyond Reach: How Rich Democracies Repel Asylum Seekers*. New York: Oxford University Press.

FitzGerald, David Scott, and Rawan Arar. 2018. "The Sociology of Refugee Migration." *Annual Review of Sociology* 44(1):387–406.

FitzGerald, David, and David Cook-Martín. 2014. *Culling the Masses: The Democratic Origins of Racist Immigration Policy in the Americas*. Cambridge, MA: Harvard University Press.

Flahaux, Marie-Laurence, and Bruno Schoumaker. 2016. "Democratic Republic of the Congo: A Migration History Marked by Crises and Restrictions." *Migration Policy Institute*. April 20. https://www.migrationpolicy.org/article/democratic-republic-congo-migration-history-marked-crises-and-restrictions.

Fonow, Mary M., and Judith A. Cook, eds. 1991. *Beyond Methodology: Feminist Scholarship as Lived Research*. Bloomington: Indiana University Press.

Forster, Bruce. 2011. "Report Cards on Refugees' Rights." *Forced Migration Review* 37:57–58.

Foucault, Michel. 1977. *Discipline and Punish: The Birth of the Prison*. New York: Pantheon Books.

Foucault, Michel. 2008. *The Birth of Biopolitics*. London: Palgrave Macmillan.

Fourcade, Marion. 2010. "The Problem of Embodiment in the Sociology of Knowledge: Afterword to the Special Issue on Knowledge in Practice." *Qualitative Sociology* 33(4):569–74.

Fourcade, Marion. 2021. "Ordinal Citizenship." *British Journal of Sociology* 72:154–73.

Fox, Cybelle. 2012. *Three Worlds of Relief: Race, Immigration, and the American Welfare State from the Progressive Era to the New Deal*. Princeton, NJ: Princeton University Press.

Fox, Cybelle, and Thomas A. Guglielmo. 2012. "Defining America's Racial Boundaries: Blacks, Mexicans, and European Immigrants, 1890–1945." *American Journal of Sociology* 118(2):327–79.

Fratzke, Susan. 2013. "Recognizing Their Evolving Migration Roles, Emerging Economies Overhaul Their Immigration Systems." *Migration Policy Institute*. December 18. https://www.migrationpolicy.org/article/recognizing-their-evolving-migration-roles-emerging-economies-overhaul-their-immigration.

Freier, Luisa Feline, Matthew D. Bird, and Soledad Castillo Jara. 2020. "'Race,' Ethnicity, and Forced Displacement." In *The Handbook of Displacement*, ed. P. Adey, J. C. Bowstead, K. Brickell, V. Desai, M. Dolton, A. Pinkerton, and A. Siddiqi, 143–56. Cham: Springer International Publishing.

Freier, Luisa Feline, and Jean-Pierre Gauci. 2020. "Refugee Rights Across

Regions: A Comparative Overview of Legislative Good Practices in Latin America and the EU." *Refugee Survey Quarterly* 39(3):321–62.

French, John D. 2000. "The Missteps of Anti-Imperialist Reason: Bourdieu, Wacquant and Hanchard's Orpheus and Power." *Theory, Culture & Society* 17(1):107–28.

Galli, Chiara. 2020. "The Ambivalent U.S. Context of Reception and the Dichotomous Legal Consciousness of Unaccompanied Minors." *Social Problems* 67(4):763–81.

Gans, Herbert J. 2017. "Racialization and Racialization Research." *Ethnic and Racial Studies* 40(3):341–52.

Garner, Steve. 2013. "The Racialisation of Asylum in Provincial England: Class, Place and Whiteness." *Identities* 20(5):503–21.

Gates, Henry Louis. 2011. *Black in Latin America*. New York: New York University Press.

Geipel, John. 1997. "Brazil's African Legacy." *History Today* 47(8):18–24.

Gibney, Matthew J. 2008. "Asylum and the Expansion of Deportation in the United Kingdom." *Government and Opposition* 43(2):146–67.

Gill, Nicholas. 2009. "Governmental Mobility: The Power Effects of the Movement of Detained Asylum Seekers around Britain's Detention Estate." *Political Geography* 28(3):186–96.

Godinho, Luiz Fernando. 2013. "Acuerdo perfecciona el reconocimiento de la condición de refugiado en Brasil." *UNHCR*. October 8. https://www .acnur.org/noticias/noticia/2013/10/5b0c1b55a/acuerdo-perfecciona-el -reconocimiento-de-la-condicion-de-refugiado-en-brasil.html.

Goffman, Erving. 1951. "Symbols of Class Status." *British Journal of Sociology* 2(4):294–304.

Goffman, Erving. 1961. *Asylums: Essays on the Social Situation of Mental Patients and Other Inmates*. Garden City: Anchor Books.

Goffman, Erving. 1974. *Frame Analysis: An Essay on the Organization of Experience*. Cambridge, MA: Harvard University Press.

Golash-Boza, Tanya Maria. 2012. *Immigration Nation: Raids, Detentions, and Deportations in Post-9/11 America*. Boulder: Paradigm Publishers.

Goldberg, David Theo. 1993. *Racist Culture: Philosophy and the Politics of Meaning*. Oxford: Blackwell Publishers.

Goldberg, David Theo. 2002. *The Racial State*. Malden: Blackwell Publishers.

Goldberg, David Theo. 2009a. *The Threat of Race: Reflections on Racial Neoliberalism*. Malden: Wiley-Blackwell.

Goldberg, David Theo. 2009b. "Racial Comparisons, Relational Racisms: Some Thoughts on Method." *Ethnic and Racial Studies* 32(7):1271–82.

Goldstein, Donna M. 2003. *Laughter Out of Place: Race, Class, Violence, and Sexuality in a Rio Shantytown*. Berkeley: University of California Press.

Gómez Díez, Isabel. 2011. "How the Officials' Styles of Recording the Asylum Seekers' Statements in Reports Affect the Assessment of Applications: The Case of Belgian Asylum Agencies." *Text & Talk* 31(5):553–77.

Good, Anthony. 2004. "Expert Evidence in Asylum and Human Rights Appeals: An Expert's View." *International Journal of Refugee Law* 16(3):358–80.

Gowayed, Heba. 2020. "Resettled and Unsettled: Syrian Refugees and the Intersection of Race and Legal Status in the United States." *Ethnic and Racial Studies* 43(2):275–93.

Gowayed, Heba. 2022. *Refuge: How the State Shapes Human Potential.* Princeton, NJ: Princeton University Press.

Green, James Naylor, and Thomas E. Skidmore. 2022. *Brazil: Five Centuries of Change.* 3rd ed. New York: Oxford University Press.

Griffiths, Melanie B. E. 2014. "Out of Time: The Temporal Uncertainties of Refused Asylum Seekers and Immigration Detainees." *Journal of Ethnic and Migration Studies* 40(12):1991–2009.

Guimarães, Antônio Sérgio Alfredo. 2005. *Racismo e Anti-Racismo no Brasil.* São Paulo: FAPESP.

Gupta, Akhil. 1995. "Blurred Boundaries: The Discourse of Corruption, the Culture of Politics, and the Imagined State." *American Ethnologist* 22(2):375–402.

Gupta, Akhil. 2005. "Narratives of Corruption: Anthropological and Fictional Accounts of the Indian State." *Ethnography* 6(1):5–34.

Gupta, Akhil. 2012. *Red Tape: Bureaucracy, Structural Violence, and Poverty in India.* Durham, NC: Duke University Press.

Haas, Bridget M. 2017. "Citizens-in-Waiting, Deportees-in-Waiting: Power, Temporality, and Suffering in the U.S. Asylum System." *Ethos* 45(1):75–97.

Hall, Stuart. 1980. "Race, Articulation, and Societies Structured in Dominance." In *Sociological Theories: Race and Colonialism*, 305–45. Paris: UNESCO.

Hamlin, Rebecca. 2012. "International Law and Administrative Insulation: A Comparison of Refugee Status Determination Regimes in the United States, Canada, and Australia." *Law & Social Inquiry* 37(4):933–68.

Hamlin, Rebecca. 2014. *Let Me Be a Refugee: Administrative Justice and the Politics of Asylum in the United States, Canada, and Australia.* New York: Oxford University Press.

Hamlin, Rebecca. 2021. *Crossing: How We Label and React to People on the Move.* Stanford, CA: Stanford University Press.

Hammoud-Gallego, Omar, and Luisa Feline Freier. 2022. "Symbolic Refugee Protection: Explaining Latin America's Liberal Refugee Laws." *American Political Science Review*:1–20.

Hanchard, Michael. 1994. *Orpheus and Power: The Movimento Negro of Rio de Janeiro and São Paulo, Brazil, 1945–1988.* Princeton, NJ: Princeton University Press.

Hanchard, Michael. 2003. "Acts of Misrecognition: Transnational Black Politics, Anti-Imperialism and the Ethnocentrisms of Pierre Bourdieu and Loïc Wacquant." *Theory, Culture & Society* 20(4):5–29.

Haney, Lynne. 1996. "Homeboys, Babies, Men in Suits: The State and the Reproduction of Male Dominance." *American Sociological Review* 61(5):759.

Haney López, Ian. 1996. *White by Law: The Legal Construction of Race*. New York: New York University Press.

Hanson, Rebecca, and Patricia Richards. 2019. *Harassed: Gender, Bodies, and Ethnographic Research*. Oakland: University of California Press.

Haraway, Donna. 1988. "Situated Knowledges: The Science Question in Feminism and the Privilege of Partial Perspective." *Feminist Studies* 14(3):575–99.

Harding, Sandra G. 1986. *The Science Question in Feminism*. Ithaca, NY: Cornell University Press.

Harrell-Bond, Barbara E. 2002. "Can Humanitarian Work with Refugees Be Humane?" *Human Rights Quarterly* 24(1):51–85.

Hasenbalg, Carlos Alfredo. 1979. *Discriminação e desigualdades raciais no Brasil*. Rio de Janeiro: Graal.

Herlihy, Jane, Kate Gleeson, and Stuart Turner. 2010. "What Assumptions about Human Behaviour Underlie Asylum Judgments?" *International Journal of Refugee Law* 22(3):351–66.

Hernández, Tanya Katerí. 2013. *Racial Subordination in Latin America: The Role of the State, Customary Law, and the New Civil Rights Response*. Cambridge: Cambridge University Press.

Herzfeld, Michael. 1992. *The Social Production of Indifference: Exploring the Symbolic Roots of Western Bureaucracy*. New York: St. Martin's Press.

Heyman, Josiah. 1995. "Putting Power in the Anthropology of Bureaucracy: The Immigration and Naturalization Service at the Mexico-United States Border." *Current Anthropology* 36(2):261–87.

Hirsch, Shirin. 2019. "Racism, 'Second Generation' Refugees and the Asylum System." *Identities* 26(1):88–106.

Holston, James. 2008. *Insurgent Citizenship: Disjunctions of Democracy and Modernity in Brazil*. Princeton, NJ: Princeton University Press.

Hooker, Juliet. 2017. *Theorizing Race in the Americas: Douglass, Sarmiento, Du Bois, and Vasconcelos*. Oxford: Oxford University Press.

Hubbard, Phil. 2005. "Accommodating Otherness: Anti-Asylum Centre Protest and the Maintenance of White Privilege." *Transactions of the Institute of British Geographers* 30(1):52–65.

Human Rights Watch. 2022. "#Outlawed: 'The Love That Dare Not Speak Its Name.'" http://internap.hrw.org/features/features/lgbt_laws/?gclid=Cj0K CQiAgribBhDkARIsAASA5bvA23Mb5TqG1q8aRp4LTLKXXNbPb2gWy7E -8czqCdgMFPUY_zCUeP0aArUSEALw_wcB.

Hynes, Patricia. 2011. *The Dispersal and Social Exclusion of Asylum Seekers: Between Liminality and Belonging*. Bristol: Policy Press.

Jensen, Katherine. 2018. "The Epistemic Logic of Asylum Screening: (Dis)embodiment and the Production of Asylum Knowledge in Brazil." *Ethnic and Racial Studies* 41(15):2615–33.

Jensen, Katherine. 2021a. "Contexts of Reception Seen and Constituted from Below: The Production of Refugee Status Apathy." *Qualitative Sociology* 44(3):455–71.

Jensen, Katherine. 2021b. "The Meanings of Refugee Status." *Contexts*
    20(1):10–15.

Jensen, Katherine, and Javier Auyero. 2019. "Teaching and Learning the Craft:
    The Construction of Ethnographic Objects." In *Urban Ethnography: Legacies
    and Challenges, Research in Urban Sociology*, ed. R. E. Ocejo, 69–87. Bingley:
    Emerald Publishing.

Jensen, Katherine, and Lisa M. Sousa Dias. 2022. "Varied Racialization and Legal
    Inclusion: Haitian, Syrian, and Venezuelan Forced Migrants in Brazil." *American Behavioral Scientist* 66(13):1797–815.

Johnsson, Anders B. 1989. "Montevideo Treaty on International Penal Law:
    1889–1989—100 Years of Treaty Making on Asylum Issues." *International Journal of Refugee Law* 1(4):554–57.

Jones, Jennifer A., and Hana E. Brown. 2019. "American Federalism and Racial
    Formation in Contemporary Immigration Policy: A Processual Analysis of
    Alabama's HB56." *Ethnic and Racial Studies* 42(4):531–51.

Joppke, Christian. 2005. *Selecting by Origin: Ethnic Migration in the Liberal State.*
    Cambridge, MA: Harvard University Press.

Jubany, Olga. 2011. "Constructing Truths in a Culture of Disbelief: Under-
    standing Asylum Screening from Within." *International Sociology* 26(1):
    74–94.

Jubany, Olga. 2017. *Screening Asylum in a Culture of Disbelief: Truths, Denials and
    Skeptical Borders.* New York: Palgrave Macmillan.

Jubilut, Liliana Lyra. 2006. "Refugee Law and Protection in Brazil: A Model in
    South America?" *Journal of Refugee Studies* 19(1):22–44.

Jung, Moon-Kie, and Yaejoon Kwon. 2013. "Theorizing the US Racial State: Soci-
    ology Since Racial Formation." *Sociology Compass* 7(11):927–40.

Jung, Moon-Kie, João H. Costa Vargas, and Eduardo Bonilla-Silva, eds. 2011. *State
    of White Supremacy: Racism, Governance, and the United States.* Stanford, CA:
    Stanford University Press.

Kaly, Alain Pascal. 2001. "O Ser Preto africano no 'paraíso terrestre' brasileiro:
    Um sociólogo senegalês no Brasil." *Lusotopie* 8(1):105–21.

Karam, John Tofik. 2007. *Another Arabesque: Syrian-Lebanese Ethnicity in Neo-
    liberal Brazil.* Philadelphia: Temple University Press.

Karam, John Tofik. 2021. "The Levant in Latin America." In *Global Middle East:
    Into the Twenty-First Century*, ed. A. Bayat and L. Herrera, 253–66. Berkeley:
    University of California Press.

Katz, Jack. 1983. "A Theory of Qualitative Methodology: The Social System of
    Analytic Fieldwork." In *Contemporary Field Research: A Collection of Readings*,
    ed. R. M. Emerson, 127–48. Boston: Little-Brown.

Katz, Jack. 2001. "From How to Why: On Luminous Description and Causal
    Inference in Ethnography (Part I)." *Ethnography* 2(4):443–73.

Keith, Linda Camp, Jennifer S. Holmes, and Banks P. Miller. 2013. "Explaining the
    Divergence in Asylum Grant Rates among Immigration Judges: An Attitudinal
    and Cognitive Approach." *Law & Policy* 35(4):261–89.

Kim, Jaeeun. 2019. "Ethnic Capital, Migration, and Citizenship: A Bourdieusian Perspective." *Ethnic and Racial Studies* 42(3):357–85.

Kobelinsky, Carolina. 2015. "In Search of Truth: How Asylum Applications Are Adjudicated." In *At the Heart of the State: The Moral World of Institutions*, ed. D. Fassin, 67–90. Chicago: Pluto Press.

Koifman, Fábio. 2012. *Imigrante Ideal: O Ministério da Justiça e a entrada de estrangeiros no Brasil (1941–1945)*. Rio de Janeiro: Civilização Brasileira.

Krause, Monika. 2014. *The Good Project: Humanitarian Relief NGOs and the Fragmentation of Reason*. Chicago: University of Chicago Press.

Lawrance, Benjamin N., Iris Berger, Tricia Redeker Hepner, Joanna T. Tague, and Meredith Terretta. 2015. "Introduction: Law, Expertise, and Protean Ideas about African Migrants." In *African Asylum at a Crossroads: Activism, Expert Testimony, and Refugee Rights*, ed. I. Berger, T. R. Hepner, B. N. Lawrance, J. T. Tague, and M. Terretta, 1–37. Athens: Ohio University Press.

Lehmann, David. 2018. *The Prism of Race: The Politics and Ideology of Affirmative Action in Brazil*. Ann Arbor: University of Michigan Press.

Lentin, Alana, and Ronit Lentin. 2006. *Race and State*. Newcastle: Cambridge Scholars Press.

Lesser, Jeffrey. 1991. "Are African-Americans African or American? Brazilian Immigration Policy in the 1920s." *Review of Latin American Studies* 4(1):115–37.

Lesser, Jeffrey. 1994. "Immigration and Shifting Concepts of National Identity in Brazil during the Vargas Era." *Luso-Brazilian Review* 31(2):23–44.

Lesser, Jeffrey. 1996. "(Re)Creating Ethnicity: Middle Eastern Immigration to Brazil." *The Americas* 53(1):45–65.

Lesser, Jeffrey. 1999. *Negotiating National Identity: Immigrants, Minorities, and the Struggle for Ethnicity in Brazil*. Durham, NC: Duke University Press.

Lesser, Jeffrey. 2013. *Immigration, Ethnicity, and National Identity in Brazil, 1808 to the Present*. New York: Cambridge University Press.

Levy, Maria Stella Ferreira. 1974. "O papel da migração internacional na evolução da população brasileira (1872 a 1972)." *Revista Saúde Pública* 8(supl.):49–90.

Light, Michael T., Michael Massoglia, and Ryan D. King. 2014. "Citizenship and Punishment: The Salience of National Membership in U.S. Criminal Courts." *American Sociological Review* 79(5):825–47.

Lipsky, Michael. 1980. *Street-Level Bureaucracy: Dilemmas of the Individual in Public Services*. New York: Russell Sage Foundation.

Loveman, Mara. 2005. "The Modern State and the Primitive Accumulation of Symbolic Power." *American Journal of Sociology* 110(6):1651–83.

Loveman, Mara. 2014. *National Colors: Racial Classification and the State in Latin America*. Oxford: Oxford University Press.

Lowe, Lisa. 1996. *Immigrant Acts: On Asian American Cultural Politics*. Durham, NC: Duke University Press.

Lukes, Steven. 1974. *Power: A Radical View*. New York: Palgrave.

Magalhães, Bruno. 2014. "Enacting Refugees: An Ethnography of Asylum Decisions." PhD diss., The Open University.

Magalhães, Bruno. 2016. "The Politics of Credibility: Assembling Decisions on Asylum Applications in Brazil." *International Political Sociology* 10(2):133–49.

Maghbouleh, Neda. 2017. *The Limits of Whiteness: Iranian Americans and the Everyday Politics of Race*. Stanford, CA: Stanford University Press.

Maghbouleh, Neda. 2020. "From White to What? MENA and Iranian American Non-White Reflected Race." *Ethnic and Racial Studies* 43(4):613–31.

Malkki, Liisa H. 1995. *Purity and Exile: Violence, Memory, and National Cosmology among Hutu Refugees in Tanzania*. Chicago: University of Chicago Press.

Malloch, Margaret S., and Elizabeth Stanley. 2005. "The Detention of Asylum Seekers in the UK: Representing Risk, Managing the Dangerous." *Punishment & Society* 7(1):53–71.

Mantovani, Flávia. 2021a. "Haitianos obtêm direito de vir ao Brasil sem visto após denunciarem irregularidades para obter documento." *Folha de São Paulo*. July 30. https://www1.folha.uol.com.br/mundo/2021/07/haitianos-obtem-direito-de-vir-ao-brasil-sem-visto-apos-denunciarem-irregularidades-para-obter-documento.shtml.

Mantovani, Flávia. 2021b. "Número de imigrantes no Brasil dobra em 1 década, com menos brancos e mais mulheres." *Folha de São Paulo*. December 7. https://www1.folha.uol.com.br/mundo/2021/12/numero-de-imigrantes-dobra-em-1-decada-com-menos-brancos-e-mais-mulheres.shtml.

Mantovani, Flávia. 2022. "Imigrantes negros na Ucrânia dizem ser alvo de racismo e barrados em trens ao tentar fugir." *Folha de São Paulo*. February 28. https://www1.folha.uol.com.br/mundo/2022/02/pessoas-negras-na-ucrania-dizem-ser-alvo-de-racismo-e-barradas-em-trens-ao-tentar-fugir.shtml.

Martínez, Susana Martínez, and Delia Dutra. 2018. "Experiencias de racismo desde la inmigración haitiana y africana en Brasil." *REMHU: Revista Interdisciplinar Da Mobilidade Humana* 26(53):99–113.

Martuscelli, Patrícia Nabuco. 2021. "Fighting for Family Reunification: The Congolese Experience in São Paulo, Brazil." *Journal of Refugee Studies* 34(3):3399–422.

Massey, Douglas S. 1999. "International Migration at the Dawn of the Twenty-First Century: The Role of the State." *Population and Development Review* 25(2):303–22.

Mauss, Marcel. 1925. *The Gift: Forms and Functions of Exchange in Archaic Societies*. London: Cohen and West Ltd.

Mayblin, Lucy. 2017. *Asylum after Empire: Colonial Legacies in the Politics of Asylum Seeking*. Illustrated ed. New York: Rowman & Littlefield Publishers.

Mayblin, Lucy. 2020. *Impoverishment and Asylum: Social Policy as Slow Violence*. New York: Routledge.

Mbembe, Achille. 2003. "Necropolitics." *Public Culture* 15(1):11–40.

McKinnon, Sara L. 2016. *Gendered Asylum: Race and Violence in U.S. Law and Politics*. Urbana: University of Illinois Press.

Mello, Káthia. 2016. "Congoleses driblam dificuldades e se destacam como vendedores no Rio." *O Globo*. January 27. http://g1.globo.com/rio-de-janeiro/

noticia/2016/01/congoleses-driblam-dificuldades-e-se-destacam-como
-vendedores-no-rio.html.

Menezes, Thais Silva, and Stylianos Kostas. 2017. "The Future of the Brazilian
Resettlement Programme." *Forced Migration Review* (56):51–52.

Menjívar, Cecilia. 2006. "Liminal Legality: Salvadoran and Guatemalan Immigrants' Lives in the United States." *American Journal of Sociology*
111(4):999–1037.

Menjívar, Cecilia, and Leisy J. Abrego. 2012. "Legal Violence: Immigration Law
and the Lives of Central American Immigrants." *American Journal of Sociology*
117(5):1380–421.

Menjívar, Cecilia, and Daniel Kanstroom, eds. 2014. *Constructing Immigrant
"Illegality": Critiques, Experiences, and Responses.* Cambridge: Cambridge
University Press.

Menjívar, Cecilia, and Sarah M. Lakhani. 2016. "Transformative Effects of Immigration Law: Immigrants' Personal and Social Metamorphoses through
Regularization." *American Journal of Sociology* 121(6):1818–55.

Mezzadra, Sandro, and Brett Neilson. 2013. *Border as Method, or, the Multiplica-
tion of Labor.* Durham, NC: Duke University Press.

Miles, Robert, and Malcolm Brown. 2003. *Racism.* New York: Routledge.

Mills, C. Wright. 1940. "Situated Actions and Vocabularies of Motive." *American
Sociological Review* 5(6):904.

Mills, Charles W. 1997. *The Racial Contract.* Ithaca, NY: Cornell University Press.

Ministry of Foreign Relations. 2021. "Portaria No. 24, de 3 setembro de 2021."
https://www.in.gov.br/en/web/dou/-/portaria-n-24-de-3-de-setembro-de
-2021-343022178.

Ministry of Justice. 2015. "CONARE renova medida que facilita emissão de vistos
a pessoas afetadas pelo conflito na Síria." September 21. http://www.justica
.gov.br/noticias/conare-renova-medida-que-facilita-emissao-de-vistos-a
-pessoas-afetadas-pelo-conflito-na-siria.

Miraglia, Paula. 2016. *Drugs and Drug Trafficking in Brazil: Trends and Policies.*
Brookings. https://www.brookings.edu/wp-content/uploads/2016/07/
miraglia-brazil-final.pdf.

Molina, Natalia. 2014. *How Race Is Made in America: Immigration, Citizenship,
and the Historical Power of Racial Scripts.* Berkeley: University of California
Press.

Monk, Ellis P. 2016. "The Consequences of 'Race and Color' in Brazil." *Social
Problems* 63(3):413–30.

Morgan, Kimberly J., and Ann Shola Orloff, eds. 2017. *The Many Hands of the
State: Theorizing Political Authority and Social Control.* New York: Cambridge
University Press.

Mountz, Alison. 2003. "Human Smuggling, the Transnational Imaginary, and
Everyday Geographies of the Nation-State." *Antipode* 35(3):622–44.

Mountz, Alison. 2004. "Embodying the Nation-State: Canada's Response to Human Smuggling." *Political Geography* 23(3):323–45.

Mountz, Alison. 2010. *Seeking Asylum: Human Smuggling and Bureaucracy at the Border*. Minneapolis: University of Minnesota Press.

Murji, Karim, and John Solomos. 2005. "Introduction: Racialization in Theory and Practice." In *Racialization: Studies in Theory and Practice*, 1–27. New York: Oxford University Press.

Najar, José D. 2012. "The Privileges of Positivist Whiteness: The Syrian-Lebanese of São Paulo, Brazil (1888–1939)." PhD diss., Department of History, Indiana University.

Nascimento, Abdias do. 1979. *Brazil: Mixture or Massacre? Essays in the Genocide of a Black People*. Dover: Majority Press.

Nevins, Joseph. 2002. *Operation Gatekeeper: The Rise of the "Illegal Alien" and the Making of the U.S.-Mexico Boundary*. New York: Routledge.

Ngai, Mae M. 2004. *Impossible Subjects: Illegal Aliens and the Making of Modern America*. Princeton, NJ: Princeton University Press.

Nobles, Melissa. 2000. *Shades of Citizenship: Race and the Census in Modern Politics*. Stanford, CA: Stanford University Press.

Nogueira, Maria Beatriz, and Carla Cristina Marques. 2008. "Brazil: Ten Years of Refugee Protection." *Forced Migration Review* 30(April):57–58.

Nogueira, Oracy, and Maria Laura Viveiros de Castro Cavalcanti. 1998. *Preconceito de marca: As relações raciais em Itapetininga*. São Paulo: EDUSP.

Norman, Steve. 2007. "Assessing the Credibility of Refugee Applicants: A Judicial Perspective." *International Journal of Refugee Law* 19(2):273–92.

Nyers, Peter. 2005. *Rethinking Refugees Beyond States of Emergency*. New York: Routledge.

Oertli, Johannes Balthasar. 2019. "Forensic Age Estimation in Swiss Asylum Procedures: Race in the Production of Age." *Refuge* 35(1):8–17.

Oliveira, Márcio de. 2019a. *Perfil Socioeconômico dos Refugiados no Brasil: Subsídios para a elaboração de políticas*. Brasília: ACNUR/Brazil. https://www.acnur.org/portugues/wp-content/uploads/2019/07/Pesquisa-Perfil-Socioecon%C3%B4mico-Refugiados-ACNUR.pdf.

Oliveira, Márcio de. 2019b. *Perfil Socioeconômico dos Refugiados no Brasil: Subsídios para políticas—Volume II*. Curitiba: ACNUR. https://www.acnur.org/portugues/wp-content/uploads/2019/06/VOL.-II-PERFIL-SOCIOECONOMICO-DOS-REFUGIADOS-final.pdf.

Oliveira, Márcio de. 2019c. *Socio-Economic Profile of Refugees in Brazil: Subsidies for Policy Making—Executive Summary*. Brasília: ACNUR/Brazil. https://www.acnur.org/portugues/wp-content/uploads/2019/08/Executive-Summary-Online.pdf.

Omi, Michael, and Howard Winant. 1994. *Racial Formation in the United States: From the 1960s to the 1990s*. 2nd ed. New York: Routledge.

Ong, Aihwa. 2003. *Buddha Is Hiding: Refugees, Citizenship, the New America*. Berkeley: University of California Press.

Ordóñez, J. Thomas. 2008. "The State of Confusion: Reflections on Central American Asylum Seekers in the Bay Area." *Ethnography* 9(1):35–60.

Pachirat, Timothy. 2011. *Every Twelve Seconds: Industrialized Slaughter and the Politics of Sight.* New Haven, CT: Yale University Press.

Paixão, Marcelo. 2004. "Waiting for the Sun: An Account of the (Precarious) Social Situation of the African Descendant Population in Contemporary Brazil." *Journal of Black Studies* 34(6):743–65.

Paschel, Tianna S. 2016. *Becoming Black Political Subjects: Movements and Ethno-Racial Rights in Colombia and Brazil.* Princeton, NJ: Princeton University Press.

Paschel, Tianna S. 2017. "Disaggregating the Racial State: Activists, Diplomats, and the Partial Shift toward Racial Equality in Brazil." In *The Many Hands of the State*, ed. K. J. Morgan and A. S. Orloff, 203–26. Cambridge: Cambridge University Press.

Pereira, Analúcia Danilevicz. 2014. "Brazil–Africa Relations: The Strategic Importance of the South Atlantic." *Insight on Africa* 6(1):1–13.

Portal Brasil. 2015. "Brasil prorroga por dois anos emissão de vistos especiais para refugiados sírios." *Brasil Governo Federal.* Retrieved August 20, 2017. http://www.brasil.gov.br/cidadania-e-justica/2015/09/brasil-prorroga-por-dois-anos-emissao-de-vistos-especiais-para-refugiados-sirios.

Pota, Vikas. 2017. "Como o ensino é importante para que refugiados tenham chances futuras de reassentamento." *Nova Escola.* July 3. https://novaescola.org.br/conteudo/5060/como-o-ensino-e-importante-para-que-refugiados-tenham-chances-futuras-de-reassentamento.

Prøitz, Lin. 2018. "Visual Social Media and Affectivity: The Impact of the Image of Alan Kurdi and Young People's Response to the Refugee Crisis in Oslo and Sheffield." *Information, Communication & Society* 21(4):548–63.

Puar, Jasbir. 2007. *Terrorist Assemblages: Homonationalism in Queer Times.* Durham, NC: Duke University Press.

Ramji-Nogales, Jaya, Andrew I. Schoenholtz, and Philip G. Schrag. 2007. "Refugee Roulette: Disparities in Asylum Adjudication." *Stanford Law Review* 60(2):295–411.

Ramji-Nogales, Jaya, Andrew Ian Schoenholtz, and Philip G. Schrag. 2009. *Refugee Roulette: Disparities in Asylum Adjudication and Proposals for Reform.* New York: New York University Press.

Ramos, Arthur. 1939. *The Negro in Brazil.* Washington: The Associated Publishers.

Ramsay, Georgina. 2017. "Central African Refugee Women Resettled in Australia: Colonial Legacies and the Civilising Process." *Journal of Intercultural Studies* 38(2):170–88.

Ray, Victor. 2019. "A Theory of Racialized Organizations." *American Sociological Review* 84(1):26–53.

Ray, Victor, Pamela Herd, and Donald Moynihan. 2022. "Racialized Burdens: Applying Racialized Organization Theory to the Administrative State." *Journal of Public Administration Research and Theory*:1–14.

Reid, Megan. 2013. "Social Policy, 'Deservingness,' and Sociotemporal Marginalization: Katrina Survivors and FEMA." *Sociological Forum* 28(4):742–63.

Reuters. 2015. "Boko Haram Claims Responsibility for Kano Suicide Bomb: Reports." November 29. https://www.ndtv.com/world-news/boko-haram -claims-responsibility-for-kano-suicide-bomb-reports-1248785.

Reyes, Victoria. 2019. *Global Borderlands: Fantasy, Violence, and Empire in Subic Bay, Philippines*. Stanford, CA: Stanford University Press.

Reyes, Victoria. 2020. "Ethnographic Toolkit: Strategic Positionality and Researchers' Visible and Invisible Tools in Field Research." *Ethnography* 21(2):220–40.

Ribeiro Corossacz, Valeria. 2018. *White Middle-Class Men in Rio de Janeiro: The Making of a Dominant Subject*. Lanham, MD: Lexington Books.

Rodriguez, Nestor, and Cristian Paredes. 2014. "Coercive Immigration Enforcement and Bureaucratic Ideology." In *Constructing Immigrant "Illegality": Critiques, Experiences, and Responses*, ed. C. Menjívar and D. Kanstroom, 63–83. Cambridge: Cambridge University Press.

Romero, Simon, and Michael S. Schmidt. 2016. "As ISIS Posts in Portuguese, U.S. and Brazil Bolster Olympics Security." *New York Times*. August 2. https:// www.nytimes.com/2016/08/02/world/americas/rio-de-janeiro-olympics -terrorism-brazil.html.

Roth, Wendy D. 2012. *Race Migrations: Latinos and the Cultural Transformation of Race*. Stanford, CA: Stanford University Press.

Roth-Gordon, Jennifer. 2017. *Race and the Brazilian Body: Blackness, Whiteness, and Everyday Language in Rio de Janeiro*. Oakland: University of California Press.

Rotter, Rebecca. 2016. "Waiting in the Asylum Determination Process: Just an Empty Interlude?" *Time & Society* 25(1):80–101.

Said, Edward. 1978. *Orientalism*. New York: Vintage Books.

Sanches, Mariana. 2014. "São Paulo tem romaria de empresários para contratar imigrantes." *O Globo*. August 17. https://oglobo.globo.com/politica/sao-paulo -tem-romaria-de-empresarios-para-contratar-imigrantes-13633389.

Scheper-Hughes, Nancy. 1993. *Death without Weeping: The Violence of Everyday Life in Brazil*. Berkeley: University of California Press.

Scheurich, James Joseph, and Michelle D. Young. 1997. "Coloring Epistemologies: Are Our Research Epistemologies Racially Biased?" *Educational Researcher* 26(4):4–16.

Schiocchet, Leonardo. 2019. "Outcasts among Undesirables: Palestinian Refugees in Brazil between Humanitarianism and Nationalism." *Latin American Perspectives* 46(3):84–101.

Schoenholtz, Andrew I., Philip G. Schrag, and Jaya Ramji-Nogales. 2014. *Lives in the Balance: Asylum Adjudication by the Department of Homeland Security*. New York: New York University Press.

Schuster, Liza. 1998. "Why Do States Grant Asylum?" *Politics* 18(1):11–16.

Schuster, Liza. 2003. "Common Sense or Racism? The Treatment of Asylum-Seekers in Europe." *Patterns of Prejudice* 37(3):233–56.

Schuster, Liza. 2011. "Turning Refugees into 'Illegal Migrants': Afghan Asylum Seekers in Europe." *Ethnic and Racial Studies* 34(8):1392–407.

Schwarcz, Lilia Moritz. 1998. "Nem preto nem branco, muito pelo contrário: Cor e raça na intimidade." In *História da vida privada no Brasil: Contrastes da intimidade contemporânea*, ed. F. A. Novais and L. M. Schwarcz, 173–244. São Paulo: Companhia das Letras.

Schwarcz, Lilia Moritz. 2012. *Nem preto nem branco, muito pelo contrário: Cor e raça na sociabilidade brasileira.* São Paulo: Claro Enigma.

Schwartz, Barry. 1974. "Waiting, Exchange, and Power: The Distribution of Time in Social Systems." *American Journal of Sociology* 79(4):841–70.

Schwartz, Barry. 1975. *Queuing and Waiting: Studies in the Social Organization of Access and Delay.* Chicago: University of Chicago Press.

Schwartzman, Luisa Farah. 2009. "Seeing Like Citizens: Unofficial Understandings of Official Racial Categories in a Brazilian University." *Journal of Latin American Studies* 41(2):221–50.

Schwartzman, Luisa Farah. 2022. "How Haitian Migrants Are Treated Shows the Ties between Racism and Refugee Policy." *The Conversation.* June 8. https://theconversation.com/how-haitian-migrants-are-treated-shows-the-ties-between-racism-and-refugee-policy-183892.

Scott, James C. 1998. *Seeing Like a State: How Certain Schemes to Improve the Human Condition Have Failed.* New Haven, CT: Yale University Press.

Serricella, Giulianna Silva. 2016. "Refugiados congoleses na cidade do Rio de Janeiro: dificuldades e expectativas." *GeoPUC—Revista da Pós-Graduação em Geografia da PUC-Rio* 9(16):46–63.

Sheriff, Robin E. 2001. *Dreaming Equality: Color, Race, and Racism in Urban Brazil.* New Brunswick, NJ: Rutgers University Press.

Shiff, Talia. 2021. "A Sociology of Discordance: Negotiating Schemas of Worth and Codified Law in US Asylum Status Determinations." *American Journal of Sociology* 127(2):337–75.

Shiff, Talia. 2022. "Regulating Organizational Ambiguity: Unsettled Screening Categories and the Making of US Asylum Policy." *Journal of Ethnic and Migration Studies* 48(7):1802–20.

Shohat, Ella, and Robert Stam. 2014. "Tropical Orientalism: Brazil's Race Debates and the Sephardi-Moorish Atlantic." In *The Middle East and Brazil*, ed. P. Amar, 119–61. Bloomington: Indiana University Press.

Silva, Graziella Moraes. 2016. "After Racial Democracy: Contemporary Puzzles in Race Relations in Brazil, Latin America and Beyond from a Boundaries Perspective." *Current Sociology* 64(5):794–812.

Silva, Graziella Moraes, Luciana Souza Leão, and Barbara Grillo. 2020. "Seeing Whites: Views of Black Brazilians in Rio de Janeiro." *Ethnic and Racial Studies* 43(4):632–51.

Silva, Graziella Moraes, and Marcelo Paixão. 2014. "Mixed and Unequal: New Perspectives on Brazilian Ethnoracial Relations." In *Pigmentocracies*, ed. E. Telles, 172–217. Chapel Hill: University of North Carolina Press.

Silva, Gustavo Junger da, Leonardo Cavalcanti, Antônio Tadeu Ribeiro de Oliveira, Luiz Fernando Lima Costa, and Marília F. R. de Macêdo. 2021. *Refúgio em Números, 6a Edição.* Observatório das Migrações Internacionais; Ministério da Justiça e Segurança Pública/Comitê Nacional para os Refugiados. Brasília: OBMigra.

Sjoberg, Gideon, and Paula Jean Miller. 1973. "Social Research on Bureaucracy: Limitations and Opportunities." *Social Problems* 21(1):129–43.

Skidmore, Thomas E. 1974. *Black into White: Race and Nationality in Brazilian Thought.* New York: Oxford University Press.

Skidmore, Thomas E. 1999. *Brazil: Five Centuries of Change.* New York: Oxford University Press.

Slovic, Paul, Daniel Västfjäll, Arvid Erlandsson, and Robin Gregory. 2017. "Iconic Photographs and the Ebb and Flow of Empathic Response to Humanitarian Disasters." *Proceedings of the National Academy of Sciences* 114(4):640–44.

Smith, Christen A. 2016. *Afro-Paradise: Blackness, Violence, and Performance in Brazil.* Urbana: University of Illinois Press.

Soguk, Nevzat. 1999. *States and Strangers: Refugees and Displacements of State-craft.* Minneapolis: University of Minnesota Press.

Sohlberg, Jacob, Peter Esaiasson, and Johan Martinsson. 2019. "The Changing Political Impact of Compassion-Evoking Pictures: The Case of the Drowned Toddler Alan Kurdi." *Journal of Ethnic and Migration Studies* 45(13):2275–88.

Soss, Joe. 1999. "Lessons of Welfare: Policy Design, Political Learning, and Political Action." *American Political Science Review* 93(2):363–80.

Sousa Arruda, Eloisa de. 2012. "Os sírios estão chegando." *Folha de São Paulo.* August 20. https://m.folha.uol.com.br/opiniao/2012/08/1140061 -tendenciasdebates-os-sirios-estao-chegando.shtml.

Souter, James. 2016. "'Bogus' Asylum Seekers? The Ethics of Truth-Telling in the Asylum System." *Open Democracy.* October 26. https://www.opendemocracy .net/en/5050/bogus-asylum-seekers-ethics-of-truth-telling-in-asylum -system/.

Stam, Robert, and Ella Shohat. 2012. *Race in Translation: Culture Wars around the Postcolonial Atlantic.* New York: New York University Press.

Stuart, Forrest. 2016. *Down, Out, and Under Arrest: Policing and Everyday Life in Skid Row.* Chicago: University of Chicago Press.

Stuenkel, Oliver. 2015. "The Refugee Crisis Presents a Chance for Emerging Countries Like Brazil to Be Players." *New York Times.* September 15. https:// www.nytimes.com/roomfordebate/2015/09/15/what-can-countries-do-to -help-refugees-fleeing-to-europe/the-refugee-crisis-presents-a-chance-for -emerging-countries-like-brazil-to-be-players.

Sullivan, Esther. 2018. *Manufactured Insecurity: Mobile Home Parks and Americans' Tenuous Right to Place.* Oakland: University of California Press.

Tang, Eric. 2015. *Unsettled: Cambodian Refugees in the New York City Hyperghetto.* Philadelphia: Temple University Press.

Taussig, Michael T. 1997. *The Magic of the State.* New York: Routledge.

Taylor, Adam. 2015. "Is It Time to Ditch the Word 'Migrant'?" *Washington Post.*

August 24. https://www.washingtonpost.com/news/worldviews/wp/2015/
08/24/is-it-time-to-ditch-the-word-migrant/.

Taylor, Keeanga-Yamahtta. 2019. *Race for Profit: How Banks and the Real Estate Industry Undermined Black Homeownership*. Chapel Hill: University of North Carolina Press.

Telles, Edward. 2003. "US Foundations and Racial Reasoning in Brazil." *Theory, Culture & Society* 20(4):31–47.

Telles, Edward. 2004. *Race in Another America: The Significance of Skin Color in Brazil*. Princeton, NJ: Princeton University Press.

Telles, Edward. 2012. "The Overlapping Concepts of Race and Colour in Latin America." *Ethnic and Racial Studies* 35(7):1163–68.

Telles, Edward, ed. 2014. *Pigmentocracies: Ethnicity, Race, and Color in Latin America*. Chapel Hill: University of North Carolina Press.

Telles, Edward, and Stanley Bailey. 2013. "Understanding Latin American Beliefs about Racial Inequality." *American Journal of Sociology* 118(6):1559–95.

Telles, Edward, and René Flores. 2013. "Not Just Color: Whiteness, Nation, and Status in Latin America." *Hispanic American Historical Review* 93(3):411–49.

Thomaz, Diana. 2018. "What's in a Category? The Politics of Not Being a Refugee." *Social & Legal Studies* 27(2):200–218.

Thomson, Marnie Jane. 2012. "Black Boxes of Bureaucracy: Transparency and Opacity in the Resettlement Process of Congolese Refugees." *PoLAR: Political and Legal Anthropology Review* 35(2):186–205.

Ticktin, Miriam. 2011. "From Redundancy to Recognition: Transnational Humanitarianism and the Production of Nonmoderns." In *Forces of Compassion: Humanitarianism between Ethics and Politics*, ed. E. Bornstein and P. Redfield, 175–98. Santa Fe: School for Advanced Research Press.

Tilly, Charles. 1998. "The Trouble with Stories." In *The Social Worlds of Higher Education*, ed. B. A. Pescosolido and R. Aminzade, 256–70. Thousand Oaks, CA: Pine Forge Press.

Twine, France Winddance. 1998. *Racism in a Racial Democracy: The Maintenance of White Supremacy in Brazil*. New Brunswick, NJ: Rutgers University Press.

Uebel, Roberto Rodolfo Georg. 2018. "Immigration in Brazil: A Statistical Challenge in the 21st Century." Presented at the International Forum on Migration Statistics, OECD Conference Center, Paris. https://www.oecd.org/migration/forum-migration-statistics/3.Roberto-Rodolfo.pdf.

UNHCR. 2012. "Refworld: The Leader in Refugee Decision Support." www.refworld.org.

UNHCR. 2014. *Global Trends 2013: War's Human Cost*. https://www.unhcr.org/en-us/statistics/country/5399a14f9/unhcr-global-trends-2013.html.

UNHCR. 2019a. *Global Trends: Forced Displacement in 2018*. https://www.unhcr.org/5d08d7ee7.pdf.

UNHCR. 2019b. "UNHCR Welcomes Brazil's Decision to Recognize Thousands of Venezuelans as Refugees." December 9. https://www.unhcr.org/

en-us/news/briefing/2019/12/5dea19f34/unhcr-welcomes-brazils-decision
-recognize-thousands-venezuelans-refugees.html.

UNHCR. 2022a. *Global Trends: Forced Displacement in 2021*. UNHCR.

UNHCR. 2022b. "Refugee Population Statistics Database." https://www.unhcr
.org/refugee-statistics/.

UNHCR. 2022c. "Global Forced Displacement." https://www.unhcr.org/
globaltrends.

United Kingdom Home Office. 2015. *Country Information and Guidance—Nigeria:
Fear of Boko Haram*. United Kingdom Home Office.

United Nations. 1960. *United Nations Treaty Series Volume 377*.

Valentino, Lauren. 2021. "Cultural Logics: Toward Theory and Measurement."
Poetics 88:1–13.

Valverde, Mariana. 2012. *Everyday Law on the Street: City Governance in an Age of
Diversity*. Chicago: University of Chicago Press.

Vargas, João H. Costa. 2004. "Hyperconsciousness of Race and Its Negation: The
Dialectic of White Supremacy in Brazil." *Identities* 11(4):443–70.

Vargas, João H. Costa. 2008. *Never Meant to Survive: Genocide and Utopias in
Black Diaspora Communities*. Lanham, MD: Rowman & Littlefield.

Vargas, João H. Costa, and Jaime Amparo Alves. 2010. "Geographies of Death:
An Intersectional Analysis of Police Lethality and the Racialized Regimes of
Citizenship in São Paulo." *Ethnic and Racial Studies* 33(4):611–36.

Vis, Farida, and Olga Goriunova, eds. 2015. *The Iconic Image on Social Media: A
Rapid Research Response to the Death of Aylan Kurdi*. Visual Social Media Lab.

Vogler, Stefan. 2021. *Sorting Sexualities: Expertise and the Politics of Legal Classification*. Chicago: University of Chicago Press.

Wacquant, Loïc. 2003. "Ethnografeast: A Progress Report on the Practice and
Promise of Ethnography." *Ethnography* 4(1):5–14.

Walker, Michael L. 2016. "Race Making in a Penal Institution." *American Journal
of Sociology* 121(4):1051–78.

Watkins-Hayes, Celeste. 2009. *The New Welfare Bureaucrats: Entanglements of
Race, Class, and Policy Reform*. Chicago: University of Chicago Press.

Weinstein, Barbara. 2015. *The Color of Modernity: São Paulo and the Making of
Race and Nation in Brazil*. Durham, NC: Duke University Press.

Weiss, Robert Stuart. 1995. *Learning from Strangers: The Art and Method of Qualitative Interview Studies*. New York: Free Press.

Wejsa, Shari, and Jeffrey Lesser. 2018. "Migration in Brazil: The Making of a
Multicultural Society." *Migration Policy Institute*. March 29. https://www
.migrationpolicy.org/article/migration-brazil-making-multicultural-society.

White, Ana Guglielmelli. 2012. "A Pillar of Protection: Solidarity Resettlement
for Refugees in Latin America." *UNHCR: Policy Development and Evaluation
Service*. https://www.unhcr.org/en-us/research/working/4fd5d9c79/pillar
-protection-solidarity-resettlement-refugees-latin-america-ana-guglielmelli
.html.

WHO. 2014. "WHO Ghana Ebola Viral Disease (EVD) Preparedness and Re-

sponse Activities." May 30. https://www.afro.who.int/news/who-ghana-ebola
-viral-disease-evd-preparedness-and-response-activities.

Winant, Howard. 2001. *The World Is a Ghetto: Race and Democracy since World War II*. New York: Basic Books.

Wright, Erik Olin. 2015. *Understanding Class*. New York: Verso.

Yang, Shu-Yuan. 2005. "Imagining the State: An Ethnographic Study." *Ethnography* 6(4):487–516.

Zatz, Marjorie S., and Nancy Rodriguez. 2014. "The Limits of Discretion: Challenges and Dilemmas of Prosecutorial Discretion in Immigration Enforcement." *Law & Social Inquiry* 39(3):666–89.

Zolberg, Aristide. 1999. "Matters of State: Theorizing Immigration Policy." In *The Handbook of International Migration: The American Experience*, ed. C. Hirschman, P. Kasinitz, and J. DeWind, 71–93. New York: Russell Sage Foundation.

Zolberg, Aristide. 2008. *A Nation by Design: Immigration Policy in the Fashioning of America*. Cambridge, MA: Harvard University Press.

Zolberg, Aristide, Astri Suhrke, and Sergio Aguayo. 1992. *Escape from Violence: Conflict and the Refugee Crisis in the Developing World*. New York: Oxford University Press.

Zuberi, Tukufu, and Eduardo Bonilla-Silva, eds. 2008. *White Logic, White Methods: Racism and Methodology*. Lanham, MD: Rowman & Littlefield.

Index